A Selection from John Dryden

LONGMAN ENGLISH SERIES

This series includes both period anthologies and selections from the work of individual authors. The introductions and notes have been based upon the most up-to-date criticism and scholarship and the editors have been chosen for their special knowledge of the material.

General Editor Maurice Hussey

*Poetry 1900 to 1965 *Edited by George MacBeth*
(Published jointly with Faber and Faber)
*Poetry of the First World War *Edited by Maurice Hussey*
Poetry of the 1920s *Edited by Sydney Bolt*
Poetry of the 1930s *Edited by Allan Rodway*
*Poetry of the 1940s *Edited by Howard Sergeant*
*A Selection from Henry Vaughan *Edited by Christopher Dixon*
*A Selection from George Crabbe *Edited by John Lucas*
*A Selection from Arthur Hugh Clough *Edited by John Purkis*
*Poetry of the Augustan Age *Edited by Angus Ross*
*Elizabethan Prose *Edited by D. J. Harris*
*Ten Elizabethan Poets *Edited by Philip Hobsbaum*
*Seventeenth Century Prose *Edited by Brian Vickers*
*The Byronic Byron *Edited by Gilbert Phelps*
*Victorian Poetry *Edited by Patrick Scott*
*A Selection from John Dryden *Edited by Donald Thomas*
*Gulliver's Travels *Edited by Angus Ross*

*Available in paperback

A Selection
from John Dryden

*edited with an introduction
and notes by*

Donald Thomas

Longman

LONGMAN GROUP LIMITED

London

Associated companies, branches and
representatives throughout the world

First published 1972

ISBN 0 582 34180 9

Printed in Hong Kong by
Peninsula Press Ltd.

To my mother-in-law

NOTE ON THE EDITOR

Dr Donald Thomas is a Lecturer in the University of Wales. He received
the Eric Gregory Award for his collection of poems, *Points of Contact* (1963)
and is the author of *A Long Time Burning: The History of Literary Censorship
in England* (1969). He has most recently completed a forthcoming edition
of *State Trials*, and is writing a biography of Lord Cardigan, the Victorian
soldier.

Preface

The texts of the poems printed here are, in general, taken from the earliest editions. Where Dryden added passages in second or subsequent editions, I have incorporated these and pointed them out in my notes. In order to produce an edition with the minimum of impediments for the modern reader, I have modernised spelling and punctuation so far as is necessary.

As a general rule, I have described the outlines of the historical background to Dryden's poems in my introduction and given any further information on individuals and incidents at the appropriate point in the notes to the poems. The *Historical Note* to the *Aeneid,* book VI, on p. 216, is intended to serve as a brief background for Dryden's references to Roman history as a whole.

I am grateful to Maurice Hussey, General Editor of this series, for his helpful reading of the manuscript.

Contents

List of Illustrations

Introduction

The Age of Dryden

John Dryden came of age as a writer during the political struggles which followed the death of Oliver Cromwell in 1658 and culminated in the Restoration of Charles II in 1660. He had been born of a Puritan family in Northamptonshire in 1631, two years after Charles I had embarked on that period of 'personal rule' which became the prelude to constitutional deadlock and civil war. As Dryden entered Westminster School with the status of a King's Scholar, the Royalist army went down in its final defeat before Cromwellian power at Naseby in 1645. In 1649, Charles I died on the scaffold in Whitehall, a short distance from where Dryden and his schoolfellows committed to memory the works of Homer, Virgil, or Horace, under the disciplinarian Dr Busby. From Westminster, in 1650, Dryden went as a scholar to Trinity College, Cambridge, and from Trinity, in 1654, he seems to have gone to London as clerk to his cousin, Sir Gilbert Pickering, who was Cromwell's Lord Chamberlain.

Despite his *Heroic Stanzas* on Cromwell's death, Dryden, like most of his contemporaries, concluded that there was no more satisfactory way of replacing the great Protector than by restoring the exiled Charles II. In 1660, after praising Cromwell in 1659, he published *Astraea Redux*, 'A Poem on the Happy Restoration and Return of his Sacred Majesty Charles the Second'. If this conduct seems odd or hypocritical to us, it was nonetheless an oddity or hypocrisy shared by most of his contemporaries. This period of European history, characterized by growing nationalism, stimulated the search for men who could be invested with the mystique of leadership.

For the most part, Dryden's England was an age measured by the uneasy truce of King and Parliament under Charles II; the growing mood of revolution under James II; the bloodless overthrow of the restored monarchy in 1689, and its replacement by William and Mary, who ruled as constitutional monarchs at Parliament's invitation. In religion, Charles II ruled as a believer in the Church of England publicly, and in Catholicism privately, whereas James II ruled openly as a Catholic. With William and Mary the Protestant Succession to the English throne was established by law. In foreign affairs England was bound in an imperial struggle with France and Holland, in America, in Africa, and in the East. Periods of war and uneasy peace, shifting alliances and secret treaties, determined European policy. At sea, England faced the challenge of a powerful Dutch fleet. On the European mainland stood the empire of France under Louis XIV, strong in diplomacy, confident in war, and splendid in the flowering of a great civilisation.

The nature of English society and the texture of life as Dryden experienced it is less easily summarised. Two decades of political crisis, civil war, and republican government had effectively destroyed some, but not all, of the continuity of English life. In looking at the society of the later seventeenth century, certain aspects of it seem surprisingly modern, while others appear to have changed little since the Middle Ages. Traitors were still hanged, drawn, and quartered; Charles II might still dismiss Parliament and rule alone, as Charles I had done; harmless old women were executed as witches; men continued to regard natural disasters as signs of God's anger with a wicked nation. On the other hand, the Royal Society in the 1660s was already carrying out experiments to determine atmospheric pressure and the pressure of steam; Abraham Darby's iron works had opened at Coalbrookdale; the laws of physics and chemistry were being formulated by Sir Isaac Newton and by Robert Boyle; murder cases were decided on medical evidence. The development of banking and finance led to the foundation of the Bank of England before the end of the century, and to the buying and selling of stock. In overseas trade, seventeenth century England had its balance of payments problems, which it tried to solve by imposing import duties. The government raised money not by forced levies but by loans from bankers, whose confidence it was obliged to retain. In politics, the two-party system of Whigs and Tories grew from the crisis of 1679–81, though not even the most extreme Whig would have given the vote to a man who owned little or no property. Finally, just as there were two nations in matters of religion, Puritan and Anglican, so in standards of morality the later seventeenth century was a time of royal mistresses and bawdy innuendoes on the stage, but also the period which saw the Society for the Reformation of Manners established, and the first obscenity prosecutions brought against publishers who issued translations of French erotic dialogues or the poems of the Earl of Rochester.

The most obvious physical change occurred in London, where about a tenth of the country's $5\frac{1}{2}$ million people lived. The fire of 1666 virtually destroyed the medieval city, which was still separate from the city of Westminster or, south of the Thames, the borough of Southwark. Under the guidance of men like Sir Christopher Wren, the new London was built. In its architecture and its way of life it seemed a more leisured and sophisticated city than it had been before the Civil War. The coffee houses, literary salons, playhouses, and pleasure gardens of the eighteenth century had their origins in the age of Dryden and became the focuses of much literary work.

In 1655 Dryden married Lady Elizabeth Howard, daughter of the Earl of Berkshire, though his enemies alleged that he also had a number of mistresses. The pair quarrelled to such an extent that in his poetry Dryden often describes marriage as a state to be avoided, but their quarrels were said to be the result of his wife's bad temper. She once wished, rather waspishly, that she was a book, so that she might enjoy more of his company. 'Be an almanac then, my dear,' said Dryden, 'that I may change you once a year.'

In the 1660s, in order to gain a living, Dryden committed himself to the poetry of public life and political argument, which involved him until his death in the attacks and counter-attacks of slander and innuendo. From 1660 onwards Dryden was for the King, whether that King happened to be Charles II, James II, or, with some reservations, even William III. Like many of his contemporaries, he feared most of all the overthrow of law and order, the outbreak of new civil wars, the anarchy of strife between rival factions in politics and religion. The established order might have its shortcomings, but as he argued in *Absalom and Achitophel*, lines 759–810, any form of 'innovation' would make matters far worse. He stood with the King, the Court, the Tory party, against Whigs, dissenters, and rebels.

Dryden's first great public poem, *Annus Mirabilis: The Year of Wonders, 1666* appeared at the beginning of 1667, and like

3

all his public verse at this stage it was a poetic celebration. There seemed little enough to celebrate: London had been scourged by the Plague of 1665 and nearly destroyed by the Fire of 1666. England had drifted into a colonial and naval war with Holland, which was to culminate in 1667 in the Dutch sailing up the Thames, burning four warships at Chatham and towing away a fifth. Yet Dryden describes the rather indecisive naval battles of 1666 as resounding British victories, won against all odds, and he turns the fire of London into a personal challenge to Charles II, which the King overcomes with God's approval and by His assistance. The poem is political as well as heroic. It was written to vindicate the King and government from attacks and rumours on the part of Puritans and anti-royalists. In 1661 a seditious pamphlet had appeared, *Mirabilis Annus: The Year of Prodigies*, followed by two more, both called *Mirabilis Annus Secundus*, in 1662. They predicted God's vengeance on a nation which tolerated a sinful monarch and a wicked government. Indeed, when the plague and the fire came, even the royalist John Tillotson, later Archbishop of Canterbury, held that these were divine judgments on a godless nation. So Dryden was careful to defend the King by showing his prayer answered by an approving God, as well as Charles's practical measures to ease his subjects' suffering. In 1670 Dryden was made Poet Laureate and Historiographer with an annual salary of £200 and a barrel of sack, though he later complained of delays in payment and often pleaded his poverty.

What may be poverty to one man is wealth to another. It seems unlikely that Dryden's income was much less than £400 a year, which was equivalent to that of a successful merchant or a country gentleman. To supplement his earnings, he began a successful career as a dramatist in 1663 with *The Wild Gallant*, and for almost twenty years he produced a succession of plays, of which *The Conquest of Granada* (1670–71); *Marriage à la Mode* (1672); *All for Love* (1677); and *The Spanish Friar* (1680) are among the best known. In 1667, in collaboration with Sir William Davenant, he produced *The Tempest*, an updated version of Shakespeare, and in 1677 he published *The State of Innocence*, a rhyming play based on Milton's *Paradise Lost*. In 1668, after a few years' theatrical experience, he published his *Essay of Dramatic Poesie*, in which the laws and techniques of verse drama were discussed by four participants.

4

No branch of art or literature was so fraught with rivalry and jealousy in the 1670s as the theatre, and Dryden soon found the enmity of other dramatists turned against him. He was ridiculed as 'Mr Bayes' in the Duke of Buckingham's play *The Rehearsal* (1672), and the nickname stuck to him for life. Elkanah Settle and Thomas Shadwell accused him of stealing lines or plots from other men's works. When Dryden reported the accusation to Charles II, the King 'only desired that they who accuse me of thefts would steal him plays like mine'. But the attacks persisted, and in 1678 the Earl of Rochester published an open attack on Dryden:

> Well, sir, 'tis granted I said Dryden's rhymes
> Were stolen, unequal, nay dull many times;
> What foolish patron is there found of his
> So blindly partial to deny me this?

As for Dryden's attempts to write high comedy:

> Dryden in vain tried this nice way of wit;
> For he to be a tearing blade thought fit
> To give the ladies a dry bawdy bob;[1]
> And thus he got the name of *Poet Squob*.

'Poet Squob', like 'Bayes', was a nickname which followed Dryden for the rest of his life, but Rochester rounds off the attack by considering the great quantity of material on which Dryden's reputation rests:

> Five hundred verses every morning writ,
> Prove him no more a poet than a wit.

In the following year, the Earl of Mulgrave, Dryden's patron, published a verse *Essay upon Satire*, including some lines on Rochester generally thought to be Dryden's own work:

> False are his words, affected is his wit,
> So often does he aim, so seldom hit.
> To every face he cringes, while he speaks,
> But when the back is turned, the head he breaks.
> Mean in each action, lewd in every limb,
> Manners themselves are mischievous in him.

[1] A bob, is a joke, or a jibe.

Whether or not Dryden wrote these lines, Rochester believed them his and announced that he would 'leave the repartee to black Will with a cudgel'. The result was recorded by Anthony à Wood in his journal for December 1679. 'John Dryden, the poet, being at Will's coffee house in Covent Garden, was about 8 at night soundly cudgell'd by 3 men. The reason, as 'tis supposed, because he had reflected on certain persons in his *Essay on Satire.*'

The Popish Plot

The literary squabbles of 1679 were already being overshadowed by the greatest political crisis of the reign. Charles II and Parliament had treated each other with suspicion and unease for most of the nineteen years since the Restoration. Lord Clarendon, the first of the King's advisers, fell from power in 1667 and was replaced in due course by the Cabal, so named after the initials of its five members. When the Cabal collapsed in 1673–74, the King turned to the Earl of Danby. But one member of the Cabal, Anthony Ashley Cooper, Earl of Shaftesbury, went into opposition and, as Whig leader, became one of the King's greatest political enemies. Shaftesbury was a Protestant and sharply critical of the number of Catholics or Catholic sympathisers surrounding Charles II. Moreover, since the King had no legitimate children, the crown would pass, according to law, to his brother James, Duke of York, a Catholic. When Shaftesbury resigned the office of Lord Chancellor and went into opposition, he remarked ominously, 'It is only laying down my gown and putting on my sword'.

In such circumstances, the story of the so-called 'Popish Plot' began to circulate in 1678, and for three more years England seemed to be on the brink of a Whig revolution or, perhaps, a new civil war.

Titus Oates, a former Catholic, and Israel Tonge deposed before Sir Edmund Berry Godfrey, a Westminster magistrate, that the Jesuits were plotting to assassinate Charles II and put his Catholic brother James on the throne in his place. The story was pure fiction, designed to stimulate anti-Catholic feeling, but Oates repeated it to the Privy Council. Soon afterwards, the body of Sir Edmund Berry Godfrey was found in a ditch. The precise cause of death was unknown but Oates assured the authorities that it was the work of the conspirators. There followed a state of national panic and an eagerness for revenge. Catholics were hunted out, interrogated, tried, and condemned for crimes they had never committed. Lord Chief Justice Scroggs himself sentenced no less than twenty-one 'plotters' to die. In the next four years, between thirty and forty Catholics were executed, including the Archbishop of Armagh, of whom Charles II said, 'I cannot pardon him because I dare not'.

The Whigs, under Lord Shaftesbury, joined in the anti-Catholic hunt. They introduced three Exclusion Bills in Parliament to exclude the Duke of York from succession to the throne. As an alternative monarch, some Whigs favoured the Duke of Monmouth, illegitimate son of Charles II and a staunch Protestant.

In the general alarm, the Commons discovered that Danby had been secretly negotiating subsidies to be paid by Louis XIV to Charles II. Proceedings of impeachment were brought against Danby, and Charles dissolved Parliament. The election of 1679, however, returned a Parliament more hostile than ever to the King and his brother. James left London for Flanders, and, as the crisis deepened, Charles banished the Duke of Monmouth from England. However, Monmouth returned and made a triumphal progress through the west of England, with Whig encouragement. In 1681 Parliament met at Oxford, chosen as being free of the political turmoil of London. Charles II addressed its members for the last time, asserting his royal authority. After that he dissolved Parliament and ruled without another for the rest of his reign. When Shaftesbury made a last attempt to persuade the King to name Monmouth as his heir, Charles refused, saying, 'I have law and reason and all right-thinking men on my side'. Shortly afterwards, Shaftesbury was arrested and charged with treason but the Whig jury found that there was no case for him to answer. The Duke of York was awarded £100,000 damages against Titus Oates who had called him a traitor. Oates was later convicted of perjury, for which he was sentenced to be fined, imprisoned for life, pilloried, and flogged in two stages from Aldgate to Tyburn.

During the whole political crisis Dryden remained loyal to Charles II. He was, in any case, the King's Poet Laureate, with little sympathy for the Whig cause, and since almost all his literary enemies chose the Whig side, loyalty must have been a pleasure for Dryden as well as a duty. Long before the crisis was over both sides were engaged in an intense propaganda war but the one piece of propaganda to reach the level of a literary masterpiece was Dryden's political satire, *Absalom and Achitophel*, which appeared in November 1681, just before the trial of Lord Shaftesbury.

At first glance, *Absalom and Achitophel* seems to have nothing to do with the Popish Plot or even seventeenth-century England. It is based on the Old Testament story, in 2 Samuel 14–18, of the rebellion of Absalom (urged on by the wily politician Achitophel) against King David. Dryden describes the development of the treason, the leaders of the two sides, and the way in which David ultimately addresses his court from the throne, imposing his royal authority and the rule of law on his subjects. What this represents is the campaign of Monmouth, encouraged by Shaftesbury, against the authority of Charles II; the portraits of Tories and Whigs, and the King's speech to the Oxford Parliament in 1681, asserting his regal power.

Dryden's choice of the story of Absalom and Achitophel for the basis of his poem makes more sense when we realize that this was a well-known parallel for political writers in the seventeenth century. The name 'Achitophel' was proverbial for a cunning politician, and Nathaniel Carpenter had written *Achitophel: or, The Wicked Politician* as early as 1627. *David's Troubles Remembered* (1638) with its description of Absalom,

> In all the kingdoms of the east not one
> Was found, for beauty, like to Absalom,

comes very close in structure to Dryden's lines,

> Of all this Numerous Progeny was none
> So Beautiful, so brave as *Absalom*.

In 1645, Samuel Gibson used the same parallel in *The Ruin of Authors and Fomentors of Civil Wars*, as did the writer of *Absalom's Conspiracy: or, The Tragedy of Treason* (1680).

When Dryden took up the theme of Absalom's rebellion and Achitophel's treason it was already a useful parallel: when he had finished with it, that parallel was transformed into a series of astute portraits, political logic, and well-wrought maxims on human society. It was far above the level of a mere lampoon, and his victims found themselves immortalised, as

8

if by the historian's pen of Burnet or Clarendon, except that Dryden had immortalised them by his ridicule. For future generations, Shaftesbury was to many people Dryden's Achitophel:

> For close Designs, and crooked Counsels fit;
> Sagacious, Bold, and Turbulent of Wit:

while Buckingham lived on as Zimri:

> Stiff in Opinions, always in the wrong;
> Was Every thing by starts, and nothing long:
> But, in the course of one revolving Moon,
> Was Chemist, Fiddler, Statesman, and Buffoon.

None of Dryden's contemporaries was his equal in the art of political or personal insult, since unlike the authors of angry burlesques or sneering lampoons, he analysed the weaknesses of his enemies with a cool and unflinching accuracy. Naturally, the first result of *Absalom and Achitophel* was a series of attacks on its author by Whig satirists, which Dryden had anticipated in his preface, when he said, 'he who draws his Pen for one Party must expect to make Enemies of the other'. Elkanah Settle replied to Dryden in *Absalom Senior: or, Achitophel Transpros'd*, as did Samuel Pordage in *Azariah and Hushai*. Indeed, Pordage was one of those who chose to attack the sexual, as well as literary, morality of Dryden.

> Tell me, Apollo, for I can't divine
> Why wives he cursed, and praised the concubine;
> Unless it were that he had led his life
> With a teeming matron, ere she was a wife;
> Or that it best with his dear muse did suit,
> Who was for hire a very prostitute.

In the meantime, Shaftesbury had been acquitted and the Whigs had had a medal struck to commemorate this triumph. Prompted by the Whig celebration, Dryden published *The Medal: A Satire Against Sedition* in March 1682, making much of the way in which Shaftesbury had changed sides in the political struggles of the last forty years, even supporting Cromwellian Puritanism when it was profitable to do so.

> Bart'ring his venal wit for sums of gold
> He cast himself into the Saint-like mould;
> Groan'd, sigh'd, and pray'd, while Godliness was gain,
> The loudest Bagpipe of the squeaking Train.

This provoked Thomas Shadwell, the dramatist, to take up the nickname given to Dryden in *The Rehearsal* and to write *The Medal of John Bayes*. What is generally remembered, however, is not *The Medal of John Bayes* but Dryden's devastation of Shadwell in his finest satire of all, *Mac Flecknoe*, published in October 1682. Like Shaftesbury or Buckingham, Shadwell was preserved in literary history, embalmed in Dryden's ridicule. A month later, in November 1682, came the second part of *Absalom and Achitophel*, written mainly by Nahum Tate but with a long passage of Dryden's own describing Doeg and Og, his two arch-enemies, Settle and Shadwell.

Later Poems

Dryden's involvement in the Popish Plot controversy was followed by his participation in disputes over religious beliefs and allegiances which lasted for the remainder of his life. Before 1682 Dryden was not conspicuous as a champion of Christian doctrine, but in that year there appeared Henry Dickinson's translation of Father Simon's *Histoire Critique du Vieux Testament*, an account of the textual obscurity of parts of the Old Testament, on which Protestant theology relied. From this weakness he deduced that the unbroken Catholic tradition was also necessary for the complete maintenance of Christian truth. In November 1682 Dryden published *Religio Laici*, a poem answering Father Simon's work, and pointing out that if written texts can err so can oral tradition. Such errors are only to be corrected by God's revelation:

> *Reveal'd Religion* first inform'd thy Sight,
> And *Reason* saw not till *Faith* sprung the Light.

Dryden himself defends the middle path of the Church of England, yet his disagreement with Catholic theology is significantly milder than his attacks on dissenters in 1681–82. However, his support for the established order is always clear in religion, as in politics:

> For points obscure are of small use to learn,
> But *Common Quiet* is *Mankind's concern*.

With the death of Charles II in 1685 his brother, the Catholic Duke of York, became King, despite all the efforts of the Whigs. In the following year, Dryden announced his own conversion to Catholicism and, in 1687, published *The Hind and the Panther*, defending the Catholic Church against the Church of England. To many of his contemporaries this convenient conversion was too blatant a piece of opportunism to be excused. Thomas Heyrick described him derisively in *The New Atlantis* (1687) as,

> A Proselyte, whose servile Pen can write
> For fear, reward, for mischief or for spite.

Anthony à Wood records in his journal a rhyme about Dryden and, incidentally, his wife, which was circulating in 1686:

> On all religions present, and on past,
> Long hast thou rail'd,–and chose the worst at last.
> 'Tis like thyself; 'tis what thou didst before;
> Rail'd against all women,–and then married a whore.

It was easy enough to mock Dryden for having changed his religion at a convenient moment. Yet there are two points to be made in his favour. *Religio Laici* is the earliest indication that Dryden had speculated seriously on the philosophical basis of Christianity and there is little in the poem to suggest that he was committed to the Church of England except as an intellectual exercise. It is not impossible to imagine the author of *Religio Laici* as having taken the first, unwitting, step along the road to Rome. In the second place, when James II was deposed and Catholics were once more a persecuted minority, Dryden remained loyal to his new faith, even though he lost his official position and salary in consequence, and became an object of scorn. By a peculiar irony, it was Shadwell who replaced him as Poet Laureate.

The last decade of his life, 1690–1700, was the decade of Dryden the translator. After the public poems of the 1660s; the plays of the late 1660s and 1670s; the satires of 1681–82, and the poetry of religious debate, he turned in old age to the literature of Europe, ancient, medieval, and Renaissance.

1693 saw the publication of the satires of Juvenal and Persius, which he had translated with the assistance of others, and which he prefaced with his *Discourse Concerning the Original and Progress of Satire*. In 1697 he published his translation of the works of Virgil, which he had completed in three years, and which is one of the few masterpieces of translation in the whole of English literature. In 1700, the year of his death, he published *Fables Ancient and Modern*, translations into contemporary English from Ovid, Chaucer, and Boccaccio. Throughout his life, his major poems, plays, and critical essays were interspersed with odes, verse letters, addresses, prologues to his own and to other men's plays. Poems *To the Memory of Mr Oldham* or *To the Pious Memory of Mrs Anne Killigrew* and odes like *Alexander's Feast* were among the best shorter poems of the later seventeenth century. He began, but never completed, a translation of Homer's *Iliad*. He contemplated, but never began, a great epic poem from British history, which would celebrate the greatness of Britain as Virgil had celebrated the greatness of ancient Rome.

Dryden in adversity, like Dryden triumphant, remained the target of abuse. A rival epic poet, Sir Richard Blackmore, published a *Satire on Wit* at the time of Dryden's death, remarking,

> Vanine, that looked on all the danger past,
> Because he 'scaped so long, is seized at last;
> By pox, by hunger, and by Dryden bit,
> He grins and snarls, and in his dogged fit,
> Froths at the mouth, a certain sign of wit.

To this sort of insult Dryden was accustomed. He had spent too long in the thick of political invective and personal abuse to be dismayed by the sneers of his enemies, as he himself admitted:

> As for *knave*, and *sycophant*, and *rascal*, and *impudent*, and *devil*, and *old serpent*, and a thousand such good-morrows, I take them to be only names of parties; and could return *murderer*, and *cheat*, and *whig-napper*, and *sodomite*; and in short the goodly number of the seven deadly sins, with all their kindred and relations.

In 1700, Dryden suffered an inflammation in one leg, which became gangrenous. His doctor advised him that only amputation of the leg would save his life. According to Edward Ward in the *London Spy*, the sixty-nine-year-old poet replied 'that he was an old man, and had not long to live by course of nature, and therefore did not care to part with one limb, at such an age, to preserve an uncomfortable life on the rest'. He died on 1 May 1700 and was buried in Westminster Abbey. Looking back on his life, in one of his last recorded conversations at Will's Coffee House, and considering his epic hopes and satiric achievements, he concluded, 'If anything of mine is good, 'tis my *MacFlecknoe*; and I shall value myself the more on it, because it is the first piece of ridicule written in heroics.'

The New Poetry of the Restoration

When Samuel Johnson summed up Dryden's poetic achievement, he chose a brevity of phrase and aptness of image worthy of the best of Dryden's own literary criticism. 'What was said of Rome, adorned by Augustus, may be applied by an easy metaphor to English poetry embellished by Dryden, "Lateritiam invenit, marmoream reliquit" (He found it brick and he left it marble).' Despite its impressive finality of tone, the remark needs explanation. In English poetry, what was 'brick' and what was 'marble', and how were the two distinguished? What made Dryden so different from poets who preceded him?

The early seventeenth century is conveniently classified in the history of English literature as a period dominated by the poetry of John Donne and his contemporaries, who chose for the poetry of love or religion a style that was dramatic, startling in many of its rhythms, farfetched in its images or metaphors, ingenious in its conceits or metaphorical comparisons. As a group, these poets later acquired the description 'metaphysical', but when it was applied to them by Dryden or Johnson it was not complimentary but disparaging.

Like all other styles, that of comparing two lovers to a pair of compasses, describing the body of one's mistress as America unexplored, or haranguing God in sharp, dramatic phrases, became unfashionable. By the middle of the seventeenth century, poets and critics had tired of such novelties and looked instead for plainer language and smoother rhythms. In 1650 the philosopher Thomas Hobbes attacked the practice of philosophising in poetry:

To this palpable darkness I may also add the ambitious

13

obscurity of expressing more than is perfectly conceived, or perfect conception in fewer words than it requires. Which expressions, though they have had the honour to be called strong lines, are indeed no better than riddles, and, not only to the reader but also after a little time to the writer himself, dark and troublesome.

In 1662 the Royal Society, of which Dryden was a member, received its charter. As well as its concern with pure science, it encouraged the development of plain language. Thomas Sprat in his *History of the Royal Society* (1667) attacked the use of ingenious images and figures of speech, demanding, 'Who can behold without indignation how many mists and uncertainties these specious *Tropes* and *Figures* have brought on our knowledge?'

In due course, Dryden joined in the debate on the metaphysical poets, though he was not so obtuse as to be unaware of some of their merits. He comments on Donne's 'numbers' or metre in *A Discourse concerning the Original and Progress of Satire*, asking, 'Would not Donne's *Satires*, which abound with so much wit, appear more charming, if he had taken care of his words, and of his numbers?' As for the ingenious metaphors or conceits of Donne's poems, these are a sign that 'he affects the metaphysics, not only in his satires, but in his amorous verses, where nature only should reign; and perplexes the minds of the fair sex with nice speculations of philosophy, when he should engage their hearts, and entertain them with the softnesses of love'. The reference to nature is significant, since critics by Dryden's time were insistent that poetry must not violate the rules of nature, which the conceits of the metaphysical poets often did. Of course, Dryden does not deny Donne's energy or striking wit, but he concludes, 'if we are not so great wits as Donne, yet, certainly, we are better poets'.

Couplet and triplet

If English poetry was 'brick', unpolished in rhythm, forced in imagery, when practised by the metaphysical poets, what means might be used to transform it into 'marble'? Two poets whose work was taken as an example to be followed were Sir John Denham (1615–69) and Edmund Waller (1606–87). Denham is little known except for his poem *Cooper's Hill*, but both he and Waller avoided the extravagant imagery and broken rhythms of metaphysical poetry, in favour of clarity of expression and smoothness of metre, often in *rhymed couplets*. The ambitions of those poets who followed the new form of versification might have been summed up in the often-quoted lines in *Cooper's Hill*, addressed to the Thames:

> O could I flow like thee, and make thy stream
> My great example, as it is my theme!
> Though deep, yet clear; though gentle, yet not dull;
> Strong without rage, without o'erflowing full.

Dryden was heir to this style of verse, pioneered by Denham and Waller, but he was more than a mere heir, as Pope later pointed out:

> Waller was smooth; but Dryden taught to join
> The varying verse, the full-resounding line,
> The long majestic March, and Energy divine.

The style of Dryden's couplets, the use he made of the verse form which Denham and Waller had introduced is best described by Pope's reference to 'The varying verse'. Of course, the couplet in itself was no more 'natural' than any other verse form and, indeed, a succession of couplets following monotonously one from the other might seem a great deal less natural than either blank verse or the broken rhythms of metaphysical poetry. Dryden showed that, in a way Denham or Waller would hardly have suspected, the rhymed couplet served equally well for panegyric, satire, political argument, religious debate, or straightforward narrative. It may have the solemn formality of a funeral oration or the idiomatic tone of a conversational aside. The couplet was not in itself natural: Dryden, by his mastery of the verse form, made it sound natural.

At one extreme, it is easy enough to recognise the very formal style of couplet, which would have been the most familiar to his predecessors. It is on the whole characteristic of his panegyric or memorial poetry, where the rhythm has a solemn regularity and the sound of a letter, word, or syllable is reflected along the length of a line,

> Farewell, too little and too lately known,

or even from one line to another:

> Discord like that of Music's various parts,
> Discord that makes the harmony of Hearts,

where the repeated word 'Discord', the repeated sound of the rhyme and slighter repetitions, such as that of the letter 'm', reflect the sounds throughout the couplet, almost as light may be reflected along polished marble. This formal reflection occurs in the rhythmic structure of the couplet as well as in its sound. One line of the couplet may reflect the structure of the other, as the two halves of each individual line echo one another:

> Some cried a *Venus*, some a *Thetis* pass'd:
> But this was not so fair, nor that so chaste.

In Dryden's satire, there is a great deal of latitude in the use of the couplet. When he chooses to drive home the point of his argument, as in his summary of Buckingham's character, there is the same reflection of sound and antithetical structure as in some of his panegyric verse. The difference is in the tone of voice:

> Thus, wicked but in will, of Means bereft,
> He left not Faction, but of that was left.

The emphasis which naturally falls on words like 'wicked', 'Will', 'Means' and 'bereft' overrides the regular beat of a iambic line. Again, Dryden finds his own freedom within the rules of the verse form, what might have sounded artificial becomes more 'natural'. At the other extreme to panegyric formality, he uses lines in his satire which have the informal ease of a conversational throw-away:

> They Got a Villain, and we lost a Fool.

Dryden adapts the couplet to serve for the vehicle of political or religious discussion as well as for praise or insult. The strict barriers of the couplet are then broken down and the structure of sentences, as well as the sense of the argument spreads over several lines. The end of a line, or even of a couplet, may no longer mark the most important break or pause in a sentence:

> What shall we think! Can People give away,
> Both for themselves and Sons, their Native sway?
> Then they are left Defenceless to the Sword

> Of each unbounded, Arbitrary Lord;
> And Laws are vain . . .

As Dryden's style develops, this freedom of rhythm within the couplet form becomes increasingly marked, as for instance in the translation of Virgil:

> Receive my Counsel. In the Neighb'ring Grove
> There stands a Tree; the Queen of *Stygian Jove*
> Claims it her own; thick Woods, and gloomy Night,
> Conceal the happy Plant from Human sight.

Only once in the four lines is there a significant halt at the end of a line.

Dryden's use of *the triplet* is an indication of the way in which his verse spreads beyond the confines of the couplet. In *Absalom and Achitophel* he uses the device eight times, but sixteen years later in the sixth book of the *Aeneid*, which is 1,247 lines, compared to 1,031 in *Absalom and Achitophel*, he uses the triplet more than fifty times. In argument and narrative, and in satire it is the means of a looser, more conversational style:

> When two or three were gather'd to declaim
> Against the Monarch of *Jerusalem*,
> *Shimei* was always in the midst of them.

If Dryden can allow his verse to become prosaic without at the same time being flat, it is because he was one of the great prose stylists of his time. The freshness and clarity of Dryden's prose at its best, the apt imagery and aphoristic judgments, fix it in the reader's mind as easily as the maxims of some of his verse.

> We are naturally displeas'd with an unknown Critic, as the Ladies are with a Lampooner, because we are bitten in the dark, and know not where to fasten our Revenge.

> [The French] Language is not strung with Sinews like the English. It has the nimbleness of a Greyhound, but not the bulk and body of a Mastiff.

> We cannot read a verse of Cleveland's without making a face at it, as if every word were a Pill to swallow: he gives us many times a hard Nut to break our Teeth, without a Kernel for our pains.

The natural order
In his criticism and in his own poetry Dryden appears to be in
complete agreement with a critic like John Dennis, who wrote,
in *The Grounds and Criticism of Poetry* (1704), 'there are proper
means for the attaining of every end, and those proper means
in poetry we call the rules'. To the Romantic poets of the
nineteenth century, the erection of such a barrier of rules around
poetry seemed totally unnatural, but in the later seventeenth
century it seemed natural, in the sense that it conformed with
nature. (Dryden argues in his *Essay of Dramatic Poesie* that
couplets are not more unnatural than blank verse, which is
itself only metrical prose.) To the poet, as to the scientist, of
the 1660s nature was no longer the corrupt, unregenerate force
which it appeared even in Milton's *Ode on the Morning of Christ's
Nativity*, for as Pope remarked,

> Nature and Nature's laws lay hid in night:
> God said, *Let Newton be!* and all was light!

Of course, there were still reservations about human nature.
Thomas Hobbes in *Leviathan* (1651) described the natural state
of man as one of war between individuals, only to be prevented
by the rule of a monarch, or his equivalent, a view which
influences Dryden's political thought in *Absalom and Achitophel*,
and elsewhere. However, where non-human nature is con-
cerned, Dryden shares the scientific view of his contemporaries.
In this view, the laws of nature formulated by Sir Isaac Newton
in physics, or Robert Boyle in chemistry, made the old-
fashioned idea of nature as a dark, hostile force quite untenable.
Yet the new laws of natural science, far from destroying the
basis of Christian philosophy, showed God's wisdom in the
creation of the universe to be even more wonderful than pre-
Baconian philosophers had believed. The power of nature was
the power not of darkness but of light. In 1663, in his poem
To My Honour'd Friend Dr Charleton, Dryden paid tribute to
scientists like Boyle, and Harvey who traced the circulation
of the blood, and to the general laws of natural science.

Yet nature imposed laws on poetry, as well as on chemistry
or physics. Dryden believed that in poetry 'the knowledge of
Nature was the original rule', and that 'those things, which
delight all ages, must have been an imitation of Nature'.
Nature, in this view, justifies the verbal clarity and metrical

smoothness which rhymed couplets afford. To achieve this fluency, however, they should be couplets of ten-syllable lines, rather than the hurried eight-syllable jog-trot of Samuel Butler's long poem attacking Puritanism, *Hudibras*:

> For his religion it was fit
> To match his learning and his wit;
> 'Twas Presbyterian true blue
> For he was of that stubborn crew
> Of errant saints whom all men grant
> To be the true church militant.

According to Dryden, this shorter line 'loses many Beauties without gaining one advantage'. Rhyming couplets are like 'a Tennis-Court, when the Strokes of greater force are given, when we strike out and play at length'.

If nature approved the rhymed couplet in the later seventeenth century view, it disapproved of the forced conceits and imagery of metaphysical poetry. Poets who indulged in such conceits had allowed their fancy or imagination to get the better of their judgment. Dryden and his contemporaries believed that exuberance of imagination had to be tempered by soberness of judgment to produce true wit rather than unnatural or false art. 'Fancy, without help of judgment, is not commended as a virtue', wrote Hobbes in the eighth chapter of *Leviathan*, while Dryden echoed the opinion in a memorable prose image. 'Imagination is a faculty so wild and lawless, that like a high-ranging spaniel, it must have clogs tied to it, lest it outrun the judgment.'

The advance of scientific thought had outmoded the notion of wild and lawless nature, as the new classicism had dismissed the extravagances of metaphysical poetry. Nature had given new laws to literature and science alike, laws which were eagerly formulated by poets and dramatists, anticipating the advice of Pope's *Essay on Criticism*:

> First follow Nature, and your judgment frame
> By her just standard, which is still the same.

Heroic and mock-heroic
If the later seventeenth century could justify the naturalness of a certain style of versification, its critics could as easily offer

a justification of the purpose to which that style should be put. Dryden was no less dogmatic than the rest. 'A Heroic Poem, truly such, is undoubtedly the greatest Work which the Soul of Man is capable to perform.' By the seventeenth century it seemed that the Renaissance desire to imitate the epic achievements of Homer and Virgil in modern terms, might at length be fulfilled in England. Nor was it merely to be a literary achievement for its own sake: the seventeenth century epic would celebrate the truths of Christianity or the power of Christendom, and, at a more secular level, it would voice the nationalism of a European state in the seventeenth century. Dryden's ambition was to celebrate the greatness of Britain under Charles II, as Virgil had celebrated that of Rome under Augustus.

The Italian Renaissance was, in part, created by a new awareness of Greek and Roman culture, and produced such epics as Ludovico Ariosto's *Orlando Furioso* (1532) and Torquato Tasso's *Gerusalemme Liberata* or *Jerusalem Delivered* (1576–93). The two poems were soon translated into English, and both in England and in France men began to devote themselves to the theory and practice of the epic or heroic poem. This genre was represented in England by Sir William Davenant's unfinished *Gondibert* (1651), a tale of chivalry; Abraham Cowley's *Davideis* (1656), a poem on the biblical history of King David, though Cowley wrote only four of the twelve projected books; and Milton's *Paradise Lost* (1667), which adapted the epic or heroic style to the biblical story of the Fall of Man.

While Milton and Cowley wrote their heroic poems, critics in England and France expounded the rules of such writing, which were based largely on their own interpretations of the theory of the epic in Aristotle's *Poetics*, and its practice by Homer in the *Iliad* or Virgil in the *Aeneid*. Of these critics, the most influential was René Le Bossu, whose *Traité du Poème Epique* (1693) appeared in English in 1695. Le Bossu, like most critics, recognised three fundamental rules of the heroic poem, apart from the grandeur of its tone.

1. Its purpose is to teach morality by example.
2. The action chosen for this must be free of digressions.
3. The poem must have a single moral theme as its basis, to which the story and characters are then added. In the case of the *Iliad*, this theme or 'fable' is that disunion among princes

is ruinous to the state. This is then illustrated by the quarrel of Achilles and Agamemnon.

Dryden himself describes the theory of the epic in terms of this third rule in the introduction to his translation of Du Fresnoy's *Art of Painting* (1695):

> For the moral (as Bossu observes), is the first business of the poet, as being the groundwork of his instruction. This being formed, he contrives such a design, or fable, as may be most suitable to the moral; after this he begins to think of the persons whom he is to employ in carrying on his design; and gives them the manners which are most proper to their several characters. The thoughts and words are the last parts, which give beauty and colouring to the piece.

However 'heroic' the incidents or characters of a poem may be, it is not to be classed as an epic unless it has the necessary moral fable and unity of action. To describe a series of historical events in a grand manner is not the same as writing an epic. Dryden admits that *Annus Mirabilis* is 'tied too severely to the Laws of History', and adds, 'I have call'd my Poem *Historical*, not *Epic*, though both the Actions and Actors are as much Heroic as any Poem can contain'. In other words, *Annus Mirabilis* is heroic in tone, but not epic in form, since it presents loosely linked incidents rather than a strict moral fable. The use of Virgilian similes, divine intervention, and the presentation of men and events as larger or grander than they really are, remind the reader of heroic pretensions even in a poem which is merely historical. A pair of burning ships locked in combat assumes the proportions of volcanoes as 'Two grappling *Etnas*', while in the tradition of Homer or Virgil, immortals as well as mortals are involved in the action:

> To see this Fleet upon the Ocean move
> Angels drew wide the Curtains of the skies:
> And Heav'n, as if there wanted Lights above,
> For Tapers made two glaring Comets rise.

In poems like *Annus Mirabilis* Dryden adapted the heroic tone to occasions of national celebration or personal panegyric, but his great British epic poem remained unwritten.

Yet that was not the end of the matter. Aristotle in his *Poetics* had laid down that just as comedy on the stage was the obverse of tragedy, so there was a type of poetry which was the obverse of epic. A lost poem of Homer's, the *Margites*, corresponded to the *Iliad* as stage comedy did to stage tragedy. As there was heroic poetry, so there was mock-heroic poetry, with no reason why one poet should not write both kinds. It is a commonplace of neoclassical criticism in the seventeenth and eighteenth centuries that on one side of nature or reality lies the grandeur of epic or tragedy, while on the other lies the art of mockery or burlesque. The Author's Preface to Fielding's *Joseph Andrews* discusses this admirably, as does Dryden throughout his literary criticism. Both styles appear in painting or drawing, as in literature: on the one hand, the noble or heroic presentation of great men, as in Antonio Verrio's *Sea Triumph of Charles II* (opposite p. 111), on the other, the caricatures of the late seventeenth and eighteenth centuries. Dryden compares the two in terms of visual art, remarking of the grand manner,

> Such descriptions or images, well wrought . . . are, as I have said, the adequate delight of heroic Poesie, for they beget admiration, which is its proper object; as the images of the Burlesque, which is contrary to this, by the same reason beget laughter; for the one shows Nature beautified, as in the picture of a fair Woman, which we all admire; the other shows her deformed as in that of a Lazar, or of a fool with distorted face and antic gestures, at which we cannot forbear to laugh because it is a deviation from Nature.

In *Annus Mirabilis* or the *Prologue to the Duchess on her Return from Scotland*; in the translations of Virgil and much of his panegyric poetry, Dryden shows 'Nature beautified'. He describes the sea-nymphs holding back the Duchess of York's ship in order to admire her, as Verrio's painting shows Charles II surrounded by a cloud of mythological beings, bearing him above the waves.

Yet, as Dryden says, if the images of heroic poetry beget admiration, those of mock-heroic poetry beget laughter. Not all mock-heroic poetry is satire but in the late seventeenth century it became one of the commonest vehicles for satire. What better than to present one's enemy so much larger than

22

life as to make him appear totally ridiculous? Dryden uses this technique from time to time in satires which are not mock-heroic throughout, but in his treatment of Thomas Shadwell in *Mac Flecknoe* he achieves the complete mock-heroic poem. The imagery of a coronation procession and ceremony, the similes of royal and biblical succession are painstakingly applied to a man who is, in Dryden's view, a paragon of dullness and stupidity. Shadwell's dullness is treated as though it were an heroic virtue, when the ageing Flecknoe addresses him in a speech which deliberately echoes a genuine epic speech from Cowley's *Davideis*:

> *Shadwell* alone my perfect image bears,
> Mature in dullness from his tender years;
> *Shadwell* alone of all my Sons is he
> Who stands confirm'd in full stupidity.
> The rest to some faint meaning make pretence,
> But *Shadwell* never deviates into sense.

In keeping with this treatment, Shadwell's throne is set up among the brothels and theatrical 'nurseries' of the Barbican. The new 'prince' is enthroned, holding 'a mighty Mug of potent Ale' instead of an orb. After a final speech, the old bard Flecknoe disappears through a stage trapdoor, leaving Shadwell undisputed ruler of the realms of Nonsense.

In *Mac Flecknoe*, Dryden evidently felt that he had succeeded more completely than in any other poem of any kind, 'and I shall value myself the more on it, because it is the first piece of ridicule written in heroics'. Dryden was never to write the great British epic, the complete heroic poem of a new scientific age, but in mock-heroic writing he achieved something more in keeping with his time and more enduring in its appeal than that epic might have been. Moreover, his mock-heroic achievement was, in contemporary terms, a demonstration of the validity of the heroic ideal on which it was based.

The art of the satirist
Satire, in Dryden's view, was primarily the means of punishing and reforming men's social or political vices, but it was not necessarily intended to make its readers laugh. In Roman literature, Dryden regarded the satires of Horace as those

23

which attempted to laugh men out of their follies, while those of Juvenal expressed a bitter indignation with the vices of the time. '*Horace* is always on the Amble, *Juvenal* on the Gallop. . . . The Meat of *Horace* is more nourishing; but the Cookery of *Juvenal* more exquisite.'

It is necessary to make this distinction, since a great deal of Dryden's satire in poems like *Absalom and Achitophel* does not raise a smile, let alone a belly-laugh. Nonetheless, it may be satire, imitating the indignation of Juvenal rather than the mockery of Horace. Even in satire the poet should not entirely forsake truth to nature, so in dealing with the Duke of Monmouth as Absalom, or Shaftesbury as Achitophel, Dryden employs the sharp edge of political criticism rather than the blunt impact of a crude personal lampoon. Compare, for instance, these three descriptions of Shaftesbury:

1.   'Mongst these there was a politician,
        With more heads than a beast in vision,[1]
        And more intrigues in every one
        Than all the whores of Babylon;
        So politic, as if one eye
        Upon the other were a spy . . .
        And in his dark pragmatic way,
        As busy as a child at play.
        He had seen three governments run down,
        And had a hand in every one;
        Was for 'em and against 'em all,
        But barb'rous when they came to fall.
                                Samuel Butler, *Hudibras* (1678), canto iii.

2.   Of these the false *Achitophel* was first
     A name to all succeeding Ages curs'd.
     For close Designs, and crooked Counsels fit;
     Sagacious, Bold, and Turbulent of wit:
     Restless, unfix'd in Principles and Place;
     In Power unpleas'd, impatient of Disgrace.
     A fiery Soul, which working out its way,
     Fretted the Pigmy Body to decay:
     And o'er informed the Tenement of Clay.

[1] In the vision of St John the Divine, cf. Revelation 13: 1–3.

A daring Pilot in extremity;
Pleas'd with the Danger, when the Waves went high
He sought the Storms; but for a Calm unfit,
Would Steer too nigh the Sands, to boast his Wit.
Great Wits are sure to Madness near allied;
And thin Partitions do their Bounds divide:
Else, why should he, with Wealth and Honour bless'd,
Refuse his Age the needful hours of Rest?
Punish a Body which he could not please;
Bankrupt of Life, yet Prodigal of Ease?
And all to leave, what with his Toil he won,
To that unfeather'd, two-legged thing, a Son.

John Dryden, *Absalom and Achitophel*

3.   His strength lay in the knowledge of *England*, and of all
     the considerable men in it. He understood well the size of
     their understandings, and their tempers: and he knew
     how to apply himself to them so dextrously, that, though
     by his changing sides so often it was very visible how little
     he was to be depended on, yet he was to the last much
     trusted by all the discontented party. He was not ashamed
     to reckon up the many turns he had made: and he valued
     himself on the doing it at the properest season, and in the
     best manner. This he did with so much vanity, and so
     little discretion, that he lost many by it. And his reputation
     was at last run so low, that he could not have held much
     longer, had he not died in good time, either for his family
     or for his party. The former would have been ruined, if he
     had not saved it by betraying the latter.

Gilbert Burnet, *The History of his Own Times* (1724–34)

In these three descriptions, one might expect those of Butler
and Dryden, as poets, to have more in common in their style
than either would have with a historian like Burnet. Yet, in
many respects, it is Dryden and Burnet who share an attitude
towards Shaftesbury, highlighting his deformities of character,
yet not unaware of his capabilities. Butler's style is closer to
that of the lampoon, or 'burlesque', as Dryden called it. It
offers a vivid caricature of the devious, squinting politician,
deftly changing his loyalties so that he always emerges on the
winning side. Shaftesbury's reputation is demolished by the

blows of the short, eight-syllable lines. It is a splendid display of verbal fireworks, but like all such displays, it may fade quickly from the eye and from the mind.

Dryden's satire in *Absalom and Achitophel* is not of this kind. Much as he may detest Shaftesbury, he draws the man's portrait in a way which many political historians might envy. It is a hostile, satiric portrait, but not unflattering in every detail. Many politicians might feel almost complimented by a line like 'Sagacious, Bold, and Turbulent of wit'. Dryden, like Burnet, presents Shaftesbury's inconstancy, but there are moments when we may wonder if they intend us to admire him in spite of it, though such a doubt would be impossible in Butler's poem. Dryden and Burnet show the same penetrating, epigrammatic judgments of character. Dryden describes

> A daring Pilot in extremity;
> Pleas'd with the Danger, when the Waves went high
> He sought the Storms; but for a Calm unfit,
> Would Steer too nigh the Sands, to boast his Wit.

To Burnet, Shaftesbury is a man of family and of political party, but 'The former would have been ruined, if he had not saved it by betraying the latter.' The sentiment is one which Dryden might well have used in a couplet of his own.

At times, Dryden may seem more of a political or historical poet than a thoroughgoing satirist. *Absalom and Achitophel* has splendid political portraits in it, but it also has panegyric, and even the discussion of political theory. That is to say, it often recalls the political and social criticism of Juvenal, rather than the laughter of Horace.

Dryden was much concerned in his criticism with the morality of satire, remarking in his *Original and Progress of Satire*, 'We have no Moral right on the Reputation of other Men'. He deplored the use of lampoons against individuals as contrary to the Christian doctrine of forgiving one's enemies. However, there were two occasions on which personal satire was justified. The first of these was when the other man had begun the attack and the satire was merely an answer to him, the second occasion was when the man had become a 'Public Nuisance', for, as Dryden remarks, ''Tis an Action of Virtue to make Examples of vicious Men'. On both counts, Dryden would have regarded himself as justified, for instance, in his attack on Shadwell in *MacFlecknoe*, where for over 200 lines Shadwell and Shadwell alone is ridiculed. His plays, his physical appearance, his personal habits, are exposed to withering invective, which still provokes a smile after 300 years and must have produced something closer to a belly-laugh in 1682.

Dryden holds that satire is further justified when it is not mere lampoon but reaches the level of 'fineness of Raillery', where satire is a delicate art. 'Neither is it true that this fineness of Raillery is offensive. A witty Man is tickled while he is hurt in this manner; a Fool feels it not.' In satire as an art, 'there is still a vast difference between the slovenly Butchering of a Man and the fineness of a stroke that separates the Head from the Body and leaves it standing in its place'.

Clearly there is a delicacy in the treatment of Shadwell which lampooners rarely used in attacking Dryden, but it is a delicacy which sharpens the wit. Throughout Flecknoe's speech in lines 13–30 of the poem, Shadwell is raised higher and higher, the ridicule growing progressively gentler, until by the line, 'Thoughtless as Monarch Oaks that shade the plain,' satire has almost been forgotten in an image from pastoral or landscape poetry. (Certainly, when Dryden compares the Duke of Albemarle to an oak tree in lines 243–244 of *Annus Mirabilis*, the intention is flattery, not insult.) The next couplet seems at first only to raise the rare and precious quality of Shadwell to a new height: '*Heywood* and *Shirley* were but Types of thee,' and then in the second line of the couplet the scorn explodes, bringing down in ruins the image of Shadwell's eminence: 'Thou last great Prophet of Tautology.'

If Dryden is more effective in his ridicule than the writers of lampoons, and even, in this respect, than a stronger poet like Pope, it is because he does not try to make each couplet a self-contained insult. Each couplet develops the victim's character a little further, expanding his personality as though there were a narrative theme underlying the pattern of insults. To stop reading Flecknoe's speech after four or six lines is to miss the quality as well as the quantity of it, since Dryden is prepared to delay the final blow until the victim's reputation has been suitably prepared. Individual couplets may be memorable but in Dryden's style they form part of a continuous development of the attack.

Imagery and metaphor

Samuel Johnson remarked, in his life of Dryden, 'His works abound with knowledge and sparkle with illustrations. There is scarcely any science or faculty that does not supply him with occasional images and lucky similitudes; every page discovers a mind very widely acquainted both with art and nature, and in full possession of great stores of intellectual wealth.'

There is abundant evidence of the way in which Dryden deliberately decorated a poem like *Annus Mirabilis* with images, or, more precisely, similes in the manner of Virgil. Indeed, they were often copied from Virgil's poems. Imagery, in this sense, was ornamentation added to the narrative theme or argument of a poem, like carvings on a building, as an embellishment or additional attraction. The structure of the poem, like that of the building, could stand without them, but neo-classical criticism laid down that they should be added as the final touch of elegance.

With a few exceptions, Dryden kept to the sensible, straightforward imagery approved by such criticism, rarely being tempted into the use of those metaphysical conceits, which Hobbes and others deplored. True, in his first poem, *Upon the death of the Lord Hastings*, published when he was only eighteen, Dryden employed the bizarre conceit of comparing the secretion of smallpox pimples to tears of lamentation:

> Each little Pimple had a Tear in it,
> To wail the fault its rising did commit,

but this was attributable to the continuing influence of the metaphysical style in 1649. There are some deliberately grotesque images in Dryden's mature poetry but they usually relate directly to the event described, as in *Annus Mirabilis*, when an English shot explodes among a Dutch cargo of porcelain and spice:

> Some preciously by shatter'd Porcelain fall,
> And some by Aromatic splinters die.

The grim humour of men shot to death by the fragments of a precious cargo is not out of place in the battle scene. On the other hand there is something unnatural, almost disfiguring, in an image from Dryden's poem *To the Duchess of Ormond*:

> Whose Face is Paradise, but fenc'd from Sin:
> For God in either Eye has plac'd a Cherubin.

Yet if Dryden was generally less adventurous than the metaphysical poets in his imagery, he nonetheless combined classical, biblical, and scientific allusion in a manner worthy of a member of the Royal Society. *Annus Mirabilis* shows quite clearly the Virgilian simile, the most celebrated style of classical image. The main action of the poem stops and for one or two stanzas a comparison is introduced from the animal world, or from hunting. Such formal, emphasised imagery is easy enough to pick out:

> So *Libyan* Huntsmen, on some sandy plain . . .

> As in a drought the thirsty creatures cry . . .

> So the false Spider when her Nets are spread . . .

Less easily identified are the allusive classical images, which now require some explanation to relate them to their literary or historical origin. In *Annus Mirabilis*, for instance, the Dutch are in awe of Albemarle's courage, and Dryden adds,

> With such respect in enter'd *Rome* they gaz'd,
> Who on high Chairs the God-like Fathers saw.

Whereas the Virgilian animal imagery is self-explanatory, an allusion of this sort may mean little without the information that it refers to the sack of Rome by the Gauls in 390 B.C. When the invaders entered the city, instead of terror and chaos, they were overawed to find the senators and public officials in their places, calmly discharging their civic duty.

It is a commonplace to write of the imagery, classical in style or reference, used by English poets at this time. In Dryden's case, however, there is a far more significant source of imagery and metaphor: the Bible. Not every reader of Dryden's poetry had the benefits of his classical education, but there must have been few who could not identify King David, Absalom, or Achitophel. The common heritage of biblical knowledge and, often, evangelical theology, is drawn on by poets like Isaac Watts at the turn of the century and, of course, by the hymns of John and Charles Wesley in the eighteenth century. The difference between Dryden's poetry and such poems of Watts as 'Jesus shall reign where'er the sun', or 'When I survey the wondrous Cross' is that Watts uses biblical imagery for devotional purposes, whereas Dryden often uses it for political argument or for satire. For example, in *MacFlecknoe* there is an allusion in lines 31–4 which compares Flecknoe to St John the Baptist, and the poem ends with an image of Flecknoe's mantle falling on Shadwell, as that of Elijah fell on Elisha in 2 Kings 2: 11–14.

In the heroic tradition, the classical or biblical cosmographies of human and supernatural states are mingled in Dryden's imagery. Angels 'drew wide the Curtains of the skies' to watch the sea battles of 1666, like spectators in a private box at the theatre. Sea-nymphs delayed the ship carrying the Duchess of York, in order to admire her. God is shown putting out the fire of London with an 'Extinguisher' which consists of a 'hollow crystal Pyramid', filled with 'firmamental Waters'. It is much easier to sympathise with Dryden's visual description of such ideas if one bears in mind the tradition of political-allegorical paintings, which appeared in England in the seventeenth and eighteenth centuries. I have already referred to Antonio Verrio's *Sea Triumph of Charles II* but no less remarkable is Thornhill's *Glorification of the Protestant Succession*, part of the ceiling of the Painted Hall at Greenwich (opposite p. 110). Mortals and immortals, naked or discreetly draped, rise to heaven in a baroque design of interwoven bodies, bearing up the emblems of British sea-power and of the new sciences in the age of the Royal Society. If Dryden's use of supernatural or mythological dimensions in his poetry seems an empty device to the twentieth century, it is in part because we have lost the habit of relating the printed words to the wider experience of art and tradition available to Dryden's contemporaries. Nothing could seem more vapid than a reference to some personified action, such as Time unveiling Truth. Yet, for instance, Tiepolo painted a picture of this subject in which Time appeared as a spry old man and Truth as a well-developed young lady, whose unveiling has obvious erotic as well as mythological significance.

Dryden was both a traditionalist and an innovator in imagery. Indeed, Johnson criticized him for using 'appropriated terms of art', that is to say images relating to trades or crafts. The number of images relating to science and its practical applications is remarkable in a poem like *Annus Mirabilis*. We begin in lines 5–6 with Harvey's discovery of the circulation of the blood:

> Trade, which like blood should circularly flow,
> Stopp'd in their Channels, found its freedom lost.

Within the first 100 lines, weights, poises, counter-balances, and limbecs or distillation flasks are introduced. A reference to the projection of images on glass (lines 211–12),

> Their valour works like bodies on a glass,
> And does its Image on their men project,

reminds us that this was the age of the telescope, microscope, and *camera obscura*, as well as of classical education and familiarity with Old Testament history. At the level of literal narrative, Dryden even describes the use of the caulking-iron and of cere-cloth in ship-repairing, 'terms of art' which Johnson found unpoetic.

It is possible to collect a wide range of individual images from Dryden's poetry and to show the way in which he drew on traditional and novel sources. Yet there is a further development which is more significant still, the use of metaphor to contain an entire poem. In *MacFlecknoe*, the stage coronation of Shadwell is an image or metaphor which embraces the whole poem. The constant reference and allusion to the theatre, right up to the final moment when Flecknoe disappears through the stage trapdoor, reminds us that this is only a theatrical representation of a coronation. The symbols have no true regal value, any more than Shadwell himself: the man and the symbols are bogus in their pretensions. Similarly, in *Absalom and Achitophel*, the story of the Popish Plot and the disloyalty of the Whigs is presented totally in the metaphor of the Old Testament story told in 2 Samuel 14–18. Of course, no one in 1681 would have found it hard to see how the story applied to contemporary politics, though Dryden had little reason to fear this so long as the authorities were on his side. Yet just as the coronation of Shadwell, by its mock-theatricality, becomes a parallel for all bogus claimants to artistic eminence, so *Absalom and Achitophel*, by its reference to the biblical story, becomes more than a poem about the Popish Plot and takes on the significance of a general political parable for the Judaeo-Christian world.

Dryden's life is so much a part of the political and religious controversies of his age that it is hard to imagine any true appreciation of his work which failed to take account of these. Yet, as in his use of metaphor, there is a universality of appeal in much of his writing: the truth of his maxims,

> Great Wits are sure to Madness near allied;
> And thin Partitions do their Bounds divide:

the unanswerable quality of some of his insults,

> I will not rake the Dunghill of thy Crimes,
> For who would read thy Life that reads thy Rhymes?

ring as clearly in the twentieth century as in the seventeenth. Indeed it was the Victorian age, notably Matthew Arnold, who dismissed Dryden and Pope as being only the poets of an age of prose and regarded them as lacking the finer poetic sensibility. It was left to T. S. Eliot in the twentieth century to reassert that 'Dryden's unique merit consists in his ability to make the small into the great, the prosaic into the poetic, the trivial into the magnificent.'

Annus Mirabilis: The Year of Wonders, 1666
An Historical Poem

from   An Account of the ensuing Poem
in a Letter to the Honourable,
Sir Robert Howard

For I have chosen the most heroic Subject which any Poet
could desire. I have taken upon me to describe the motives, the
beginning, progress and successes of a most just and necessary
War; in it, the care, management and prudence of our King;
the conduct and valour of a Royal Admiral, and of two in-
comparable Generals; the invincible courage of our Captains
and Seamen, and three glorious Victories, the result of all.
After this I have, in the Fire, the most deplorable, but withall
the greatest Argument that can be imagin'd: the destruction
10 being so swift, so sudden, so vast and miserable, as nothing can
parallel in Story. The former part of this Poem, relating to the
War, is but a due expiation for my not serving my King and
Country in it. All Gentlemen are almost oblig'd to it: and I
know no reason we should give that advantage to the Com-
monalty of *England* to be foremost in brave actions, which the
Noblesse of *France* would never suffer in their Peasants. I should
not have written this but to a Person, who has been ever forward
to appear in all employments, whither his Honour and Gener-
osity have call'd him. The latter part of my Poem, which
20 describes the Fire, I owe first to the Piety and Fatherly Affection
of our Monarch to his suffering Subjects; and, in the second
place, to the courage, loyalty and magnanimity of the City:
both which were so conspicuous, that I have wanted words to
celebrate them as they deserve. I have call'd my Poem *Historical*,
not *Epic*, though both the Actions and Actors are as much
Heroic, as any Poem can contain. But since the Action is not

33

properly one, nor that accomplish'd in the last successes, I have judg'd it too bold a Title for a few *Stanzas*, which are little more in number than a single *Iliad*, or the longest of the *Aeneids*.
30 For this reason (I mean not of length, but broken action, tied too severely to the Laws of History), I am apt to agree with those who rank *Lucan* rather among Historians in Verse, than Epic Poets: in whose room, if I am not deceiv'd, *Silius Italicus*, though a worse Writer, may more justly be admitted. I have chosen to write my Poem in *Quatrains* or *Stanzas* of four in alternate rhyme, because I have ever judg'd them more noble, and of greater dignity, both for the sound and number, than any other Verse in use amongst us; in which I am sure I have your approbation. The learned Languages have, certainly, a
40 great advantage of us, in not being tied to the slavery of any Rhyme; and were less constrain'd in the quantity of every syllable, which they might vary with *Spondees* or *Dactyls*, besides so many other helps of Grammatical Figures, for the lengthening or abbreviation of them, than the Modern are in the close of that one Syllable, which often confines, and more often corrupts the sense of all the rest. But in this necessity of our Rhymes, I have always found the couplet Verse most easy, (though not so proper for this occasion) for there the work is sooner at an end, every two lines concluding the labour of the
50 Poet: but in Quatrains he is to carry it farther on; and not only so, but to bear along in his head the troublesome sense of four lines together. For those who write correctly in this kind must needs acknowledge, that the last line of the Stanza is to be consider'd in the composition of the first. Neither can we give ourselves the liberty of making any part of a verse for the sake of Rhyme, or concluding with a word which is not current *English*, or using the variety of Female Rhymes, all which our Fathers practis'd.

*

For my own part, if I had little knowledge of the Sea, yet I
60 have thought it no shame to learn: and if I have made some few mistakes, 'tis only, as you can bear me witness, because I have wanted opportunity to correct them, the whole Poem being first written, and now sent you from a place, where I have not so much as the converse of any Seaman. Yet, though the trouble I had in writing it was great, it was more than recompens'd by the pleasure, I found myself so warm in celebrating

34

the praises of military men, two such especially as the *Prince*
and *General*, that it is no wonder if they inspir'd me with
thoughts above my ordinary level. And I am well satisfied,
70 that as they are incomparably the best subject I have ever had,
excepting only the *Royal Family*; so also, that this I have written
of them is much better than what I have perform'd on any
other. I have been forc'd to help out other Arguments, but this
has been bountiful to me; they have been low and barren of
praise, and I have exalted them, and made them fruitful. But
here – *Omnia sponte sue reddit justissima tellus*. I have had a large,
a fair and a pleasant field, so fertile, that, without my cultivating,
it has given me two Harvests in a Summer, and in both oppress'd
the Reaper. All other greatness in subjects is only counterfeit,
80 it will not endure the test of danger; the greatness of Arms is
only real. Other greatness burdens a Nation with its weight,
this supports it with its strength. And as it is the happiness of
the Age, so is it the peculiar goodness of the best of Kings,
that we may praise his Subjects without offending him. Doubt-
less it proceeds from a just confidence of his own virtue, which
the lustre of no other can be so great as to darken in him. For
the Good or the Valiant are never safely prais'd under a bad or a
degenerate Prince. But to return from this digression to a
farther account of my Poem, I must crave leave to tell you,
90 that as I have endeavour'd to adorn it with noble thoughts,
so much more to express those thoughts with elocution. The
composition of all Poems is or ought to be of wit, and wit in
the Poet, or wit writing (if you will give me leave to use a
School distinction), is no other than the faculty of imagination
in the writer, which, like a nimble Spaniel, beats over and
ranges through the field of Memory, till it springs the Quarry
it hunted after; or, without metaphor, which searches over all
the memory for the species or Ideas of those things which it
designs to represent. Wit written, is that which is well defin'd,
100 the happy result of thought, or product of that imagination.
But to proceed from wit in the general notion of it, to the
proper wit of an Heroic or Historical Poem, I judge it chiefly to
consist in the delightful imaging of persons, actions, passions,
or things. 'Tis not the jerk or sting of an Epigram, nor the
seeming contradiction of a poor Antithesis (the delight of an
ill judging Audience in a Play of Rhyme), nor the jingle of a
more poor *Paranomasia*: neither is it so much the morality of

35

a grave sentence, affected by *Lucan*, but more sparingly used by *Virgil*; but it is some lively and apt description, dress'd in such colours of speech, that it sets before your eyes the absent object, as perfectly and more delightfully than nature. So then, the first happiness of the Poet's imagination is properly Invention, or finding of the thought; the second is Fancy, or the variation, deriving or moulding of that thought, as the judgment represents it proper to the subject; the third is Elocution, or the Art of clothing and adorning that thought so found and varied, in apt, significant and sounding words. The quickness of the Imagination is seen in the Invention, the fertility in the Fancy, and the accuracy in the Expression. For the two first of these *Ovid* is famous amongst the Poets, for the latter *Virgil*.

*

Yet before I leave *Virgil*, I must own the vanity to tell you, and by you the world, that he has been my Master in this Poem. I have followed him everywhere, I know not with what success, but I am sure with diligence enough. My Images are many of them copied from him, and the rest are imitations of him. My expressions also are as near as the Idioms of the two Languages would admit of in translation. And this, Sir, I have done with that boldness, for which I will stand accountable to any of our little Critics, who, perhaps, are not better acquainted with him than I am. . . . In some places, where either the fancy, or the words, were his, or any others, I have noted it . . . that I might not seem a Plagiary. In others I have neglected it, to avoid as well the tediousness, as the affectation of doing it too often. Such descriptions or images, well wrought, which I promise not for mine, are, as I have said, the adequate delight of heroic Poesie, for they beget admiration, which is its proper object; as the images of the Burlesque, which is contrary to this, by the same reason beget laughter; for the one shows Nature beautified, as in the picture of a fair Woman, which we all admire; the other shows her deformed, as in that of a Lazar, or of a fool with distorted face and antic gestures, at which we cannot forbear to laugh, because it is a deviation from Nature.

1

In thriving Arts long time had *Holland* grown
    Crouching at home, and cruel when abroad:
Scarce leaving us the means to claim our own.
    Our King they courted, and our Merchants aw'd.

2

Trade, which like blood should circularly flow,
    Stopp'd in their Channels, found its freedom lost:
Thither the wealth of all the world did go,
    And seem'd but shipwreck'd on so base a Coast.

3

For them alone the Heav'ns had kindly heat,
10   In Eastern Quarries ripening precious Dew:
For them the *Idumaean* Balm did sweat,
    And in hot *Ceylon* Spicy Forests grew.

4

The Sun but seem'd the lab'rer of their Year;
    Each waxing Moon supplied her wat'ry store,
To swell those Tides, which from the Line did bear
    Their brim-full Vessels to the *Belgian* shore.

5

Thus mighty in her Ships stood *Carthage* long,
    And swept the riches of the world from far;
Yet stoop'd to *Rome*, less wealthy, but more strong:
20   And this may prove our second Punic War.

6

What peace can be where both to one pretend?
    (But they more diligent, and we more strong)
Or if a peace, it soon must have an end
    For they would grow too powerful were it long.

7

Behold two Nations then, engag'd so far,
    That each seven years the fit must shake each Land:
Where *France* will side to weaken us by War,
    Who only can his vast designs withstand.

8

See how he feeds th' *Iberian* with delays,
30   To render us his timely friendship vain;
And, while his secret Soul on *Flanders* preys,
    He rocks the Cradle of the Babe of *Spain*.

9

Such deep designs of Empire does he lay
    O'er them whose cause he seems to take in hand:
And, prudently, would make them Lords at Sea,
    To whom with ease he can give Laws by Land.

10

This saw our King; and long within his breast
    His pensive counsels balanc'd to and fro;
He griev'd the Land he freed should be oppress'd,
40   And he less for it than Usurpers do.

11

His gen'rous mind the fair Ideas drew
    Of Fame and Honour which in dangers lay;
Where wealth, like fruit on precipices, grew,
    Not to be gather'd but by Birds of prey.

12

The loss and gain each fatally were great;
    And still his Subjects call'd aloud for war:
But peaceful Kings o'er martial people set,
    Each other's poise and counter-balance are.

13

He, first, survey'd the charge with careful eyes,
50   Which none but mighty Monarchs could maintain;
Yet judg'd, like vapours that from Limbecs rise,
    It would in richer showers descend again.

14

At length resolv'd t' assert the wat'ry Ball,
    He in himself did whole Armadas bring:
Him, aged Seamen might their Master call,
    And choose for General were he not their King.

15

It seems as every Ship their Sovereign knows,
    His awful summons they so soon obey;
So hear the scaly Herd when *Proteus* blows,
60   And so to pasture follow through the Sea.

16

To see this Fleet upon the Ocean move
    Angels drew wide the Curtains of the skies:
And Heav'n, as if there wanted Lights above,
    For Tapers made two glaring Comets rise.

17

Whether they unctuous Exhalations are,
    Fir'd by the Sun, or seeming so alone,
Or each some more remote and slippery Star,
    Which loses footing when to Mortals shown.

18

Or one that bright companion of the Sun,
70   Whose glorious aspect seal'd our new-born King;
And now a round of greater years begun,
    New influence from his walks of light did bring.

Victorious *York* did, first, with fam'd success,
　To his known valour make the *Dutch* give place:
Thus Heav'n our Monarch's fortune did confess,
　Beginning conquest from his Royal Race.

20

But since it was decreed, Auspicious King,
　In *Britain*'s right that thou should'st wed the Main,
Heav'n, as a gage, would cast some precious thing
80　And therefore doom'd that *Lawson* should be slain.

21

Lawson amongst the foremost met his fate,
　Whom Sea-green *Sirens* from the Rocks lament:
Thus as an off'ring for the *Grecian* State
　He first was kill'd who first to Battle went.

22

Their Chief blown up, in air, not waves expir'd,
　To which his pride presum'd to give the Law:
The *Dutch* confess'd Heav'n present, and retir'd,
　And all was *Britain* the wide Ocean saw.

23

To nearest Ports their shatter'd Ships repair,
90　Where by our dreadful Cannon they lay aw'd:
So reverently men quit the open air
　When thunder speaks the angry Gods abroad.

24

And now approach'd their Fleet from *India*, fraught
　With all the riches of the rising Sun:
And precious Sand from Southern Climates brought,
　(The fatal Regions where the War begun.)

Like hunted *Castors*, conscious of their store,
    Their waylaid wealth to *Norway*'s coasts they bring:
There first the North's cold bosom Spices bore,
100   And Winter brooded on the Eastern Spring.

26

By the rich scent we found our perfum'd prey,
    Which flank'd with Rocks did close in covert lie:
And round about their murdering Cannon lay,
    At once to threaten and invite the eye.

27

Fiercer than Cannon, and than Rocks more hard,
    The *English* undertake th' unequal War:
Seven Ships alone, by which the Port is barr'd,
    Besiege the *Indies*, and all *Denmark* dare.

28

These fight like Husbands, but like Lovers those:
110   These fain would keep, and those more fain enjoy:
And to such height their frantic passion grows,
    That what both love, both hazard to destroy.

29

Amidst whole heaps of Spices lights a Ball,
    And now their Odours arm'd against them fly:
Some preciously by shatter'd Porc'lain fall,
    And some by Aromatic splinters die.

30

And though by Tempests of the prize bereft,
    In Heaven's inclemency some ease we find:
Our foes we vanquish'd by our valour left,
120   And only yielded to the Seas and Wind.

Nor wholly lost we so deserv'd a prey;
    For storms, repenting, part of it restor'd:
Which, as a tribute from the *Baltic* Sea,
    The *British* Ocean sent her mighty Lord.

32

Go, Mortals, now, and vex yourselves in vain
    For wealth, which so uncertainly must come:
When what was brought so far, and with such pain,
    Was only kept to lose it nearer home.

33

The Son, who, twice three months on th' Ocean toss'd,
130   Prepar'd to tell what he had pass'd before,
Now sees, in *English* Ships the *Holland* Coast,
    And Parents' arms in vain stretch'd from the shore.

34

This careful Husband had been long away,
    Whom his chaste wife and little children mourn:
Who on their fingers learn'd to tell the day
    On which their Father promis'd to return.

35

Such are the proud designs of human kind,
    And so we suffer Shipwreck everywhere!
Alas, what Port can such a Pilot find,
140   Who in the night of Fate must blindly steer!

36

The undistinguish'd seeds of good and ill
    Heav'n, in his bosom, from our knowledge hides;
And draws them in contempt of human skill,
    Which oft, for friends, mistaken foes provides.

Let *Munster*'s Prelate ever be accurs'd,
    In whom we seek the *German* faith in vain:
Alas, that he should teach the *English* first
    That fraud and avarice in the Church could reign!

38

Happy who never trust a Stranger's will,
150   Whose friendship's in his interest understood!
Since money giv'n but tempts him to be ill
    When power is too remote to make him good.

39

Till now, alone the Mighty Nations strove:
    The rest, at gaze, without the Lists did stand:
And threat'ning *France*, plac'd like a painted *Jove*,
    Kept idle thunder in his lifted hand.

40

That Eunuch Guardian of rich *Holland*'s trade,
    Who envies us what he wants power t' enjoy!
Whose noiseful valour does no foe invade,
160   And weak assistance will his friends destroy.

41

Offended that we fought without his leave,
    He takes this time his secret hate to show:
Which *Charles* does with a mind so calm receive
    As one that neither seeks nor shuns his foe.

42

With *France*, to aid the *Dutch*, the *Danes* unite:
    France as their Tyrant, *Denmark* as their Slave.
But when with one three Nations join to fight,
    They silently confess that one more brave.

Lewis had chas'd the *English* from his shore;
170   But *Charles* the *French* as Subjects does invite.
Would Heav'n for each some *Solomon* restore,
    Who, by their mercy, may decide their right.

44

Were Subjects so but only by their choice,
    And not from Birth did forc'd Dominion take,
Our Prince alone would have the public voice;
    And all his Neighbours' Realms would deserts make.

45

He without fear a dangerous War pursues,
    Which without rashness he began before.
As Honour made him first the danger choose,
180   So still he makes it good on virtue's score.

46

The doubled charge his Subjects' love supplies,
    Who, in that bounty, to themselves are kind:
So glad *Egyptians* see their *Nilus* rise,
    And in his plenty their abundance find.

47

With equal power he does two Chiefs create,
    Two such, as each seem'd worthiest when alone:
Each able to sustain a Nation's fate,
    Since both had found a greater in their own.

48

Both great in courage, Conduct and in Fame,
190   Yet neither envious of the other's praise;
Their duty, faith, and int'rest too the same,
    Like mighty Partners equally they raise.

The Prince long time had courted Fortune's love,
    But once possess'd did absolutely reign;
Thus with their *Amazons* the *Heroes* strove,
    And conquer'd first those Beauties they would gain.

50

The Duke beheld, like *Scipio*, with disdain
    That *Carthage*, which he ruin'd, rise once more:
And shook aloft the Fasces of the Main,
    To fright those Slaves with what they felt before.

200

51

Together to the wat'ry Camp they haste,
    Whom Matrons passing, to their children show:
Infants' first vows for them to Heav'n are cast,
    And future people bless them as they go.

52

With them no riotous pomp, nor *Asian* train,
    T' infect a Navy with their gaudy fears:
To make slow fights, and victories but vain;
    But war, severely, like itself, appears.

53

Diffusive of themselves, where'er they pass,
    They make that warmth in others they expect:
Their valour works like bodies on a glass,
    And does its Image on their men project.

210

54

Our Fleet divides, and straight the *Dutch* appear,
    In number, and a fam'd Commander, bold:
The Narrow Seas can scarce their Navy bear,
    Or crowded Vessels can their Soldiers hold.

The Duke, less numerous, but in courage more,
    On wings of all the winds to combat flies:
His murdering Guns a loud defiance roar,
220   And bloody Crosses on his Flagstaffs rise.

56

Both furl their sails, and strip them for the fight,
    Their folded sheets dismiss the useless air:
Th' *Elean* Plains could boast no nobler sight,
    When struggling Champions did their bodies bare.

57

Borne each by other in a distant Line,
    The Sea-built Forts in dreadful order move:
So vast the noise, as if not Fleets did join,
    But Lands unfix'd, and floating Nations, strove.

58

Now pass'd, on either side they nimbly tack,
230   Both strive to intercept and guide the wind:
And, in its eye, more closely they come back
    To finish all the deaths they left behind.

59

On high-rais'd Decks the haughty *Belgians* ride,
    Beneath whose shade our humble Frigates go:
Such port the *Elephant* bears, and so defied
    By the *Rhinoceros* her unequal foe.

60

And as the build, so different is the fight;
    Their mounting shot is on our sails design'd;
Deep in their hulls our deadly bullets light,
240   And through the yielding planks a passage find.

Our dreaded Admiral from far they threat,
    Whose batter'd rigging their whole war receives.
All bare, like some old Oak which tempests beat,
    He stands, and sees below his scatter'd leaves.

62

Heroes of old, when wounded, shelter sought,
    But he, who meets all danger with disdain,
Ev'n in their face his ship to Anchor brought,
    And Steeple high stood propp'd upon the Main.

63

At this excess of courage, all amaz'd,
250   The foremost of his foes a while withdraw.
With such respect in enter'd *Rome* they gaz'd,
    Who on high Chairs the Godlike Fathers saw.

64

And now, as where *Patroclus'* body lay,
    Here *Trojan* Chiefs advanc'd, and there the *Greek*:
Ours o'er the Duke their pious wings display,
    And theirs the noblest spoils of *Britain* seek.

65

Meantime, his busy Mariners he hastes,
    His shatter'd sails with rigging to restore:
And willing Pines ascend his broken Masts,
260   Whose lofty heads rise higher than before.

66

Straight to the *Dutch* he turns his dreadful prow,
    More fierce th' important quarrel to decide.
Like Swans, in long array his Vessels show,
    Whose crests, advancing, do the waves divide.

They charge, re-charge, and all along the Sea
  They drive, and squander the huge *Belgian* Fleet.
Berkeley alone, who nearest Danger lay,
  Did a like fate with lost *Creüsa* meet.

The night comes on, we, eager to pursue
270 The Combat still, and they asham'd to leave:
Till the last streaks of dying day withdrew,
  And doubtful Moonlight did our rage deceive.

In th' *English* Fleet each ship resounds with joy,
  And loud applause of their great Leader's fame.
In fiery dreams the *Dutch* they still destroy,
  And, slumb'ring, smile at the imagin'd flame.

Not so the *Holland* Fleet, who tir'd and done,
  Stretch'd on their decks like weary Oxen lie:
Faint sweats all down their mighty members run,
280 (Vast bulks which little souls but ill supply.)

In dreams they fearful precipices tread,
  Or, shipwreck'd, labour to some distant shore:
Or in dark Churches walk among the dead:
  They wake with horror, and dare sleep no more.

The morn they look on with unwilling eyes,
  Till, from their Maintop, joyful news they hear
Of ships, which by their mould bring new supplies,
  And in their colours *Belgian* Lions bear.

Our watchful General had discern'd, from far,
290   This mighty succour which made glad the foe.
He sigh'd, but, like a Father of the War,
     His face spoke hope, while deep his sorrows flow.

74

His wounded men he first sends off to shore:
     (Never, till now, unwilling to obey.)
They, not their wounds but want of strength deplore,
     And think them happy who with him can stay.

75

Then, to the rest, 'Rejoice,' (said he) 'today
     In you the fortune of *Great Britain* lies:
Among so brave a people you are they
300   Whom Heav'n has chose to fight for such a Prize.

76

'If number *English* courages could quell,
     We should at first have shunn'd, not met our foes;
Whose numerous sails the fearful only tell:
     Courage from hearts, and not from numbers grows.'

77

He said; nor needed more to say: with haste
     To their known stations cheerfully they go:
And all at once, disdaining to be last,
     Solicit every gale to meet the foe.

78

Nor did th' encourag'd *Belgians* long delay,
310   But, bold in others, not themselves, they stood:
So thick, our Navy scarce could sheer their way,
     But seem'd to wander in a moving wood.

Our little Fleet was now engag'd so far,
    That, like the Swordfish in the Whale, they fought.
The Combat only seem'd a Civil War,
    Till through their bowels we our passage wrought.

80

Never had valour, no not ours before,
    Done ought like this upon the Land or Main:
Where not to be o'ercome was to do more
320   Than all the Conquests former Kings did gain.

81

The mighty Ghosts of our great *Harries* rose,
    And armed *Edwards* look'd with anxious eyes,
To see this Fleet among unequal foes,
    By which fate promis'd them their *Charles* should rise.

82

Meantime the *Belgians* tack upon our Rear,
    And raking Chase-guns through our sterns they send:
Close by, their Fire-ships, like *Jackals*, appear,
    Who on their Lions for the prey attend.

83

Silent in smoke of Cannons they come on:
330   (Such vapours once did fiery *Cacus* hide.)
In these the height of pleas'd revenge is shown,
    Who burn contented by another's side.

84

Sometimes, from fighting Squadrons of each Fleet,
    (Deceiv'd themselves, or to preserve some friend)
Two grappling *Etnas* on the Ocean meet,
    And *English* fires with *Belgian* flames contend.

Now, at each Tack, our little Fleet grows less;
   And, like maim'd fowl, swim lagging on the Main.
Their greater loss their numbers scarce confess
340   While they lose cheaper than the *English* gain.

86

Have you not seen when, whistled from the fist,
   Some Falcon stoops at what her eye design'd,
And, with her eagerness, the quarry miss'd,
   Straight flies at check, and clips it down the wind,

87

The dastard Crow, that to the wood made wing,
   And sees the Groves no shelter can afford,
With her loud Caws her Craven kind does bring,
   Who, safe in numbers cuff the noble Bird?

88

Among the *Dutch* thus *Albemarle* did fare:
350   He could not conquer, and disdain'd to fly.
Past hope of safety, 'twas his latest care,
   Like falling *Caesar*, decently to die.

89

Yet pity did his manly spirit move
   To see those perish who so well had fought:
And, generously, with his despair he strove,
   Resolv'd to live till he their safety wrought.

90

Let other Muses write his prosp'rous fate,
   Of conquer'd Nations tell, and Kings restor'd:
But mine shall sing of his eclips'd estate,
360   Which, like the Sun's, more wonders does afford.

He drew his mighty Frigates all before,
   On which the foe his fruitless force employs:
His weak ones deep into his Rear he bore,
   Remote from Guns as sick men are from noise.

92

His fiery Cannon did their passage guide,
   And foll'wing smoke obscur'd them from the foe.
Thus *Israel* safe from the *Egyptian*'s pride,
   By flaming pillars, and by clouds did go.

93

Elsewhere the *Belgian* force we did defeat,
370   But here our courages did theirs subdue:
So *Xenophon* once led that fam'd retreat,
   Which first the *Asian* Empire overthrew.

94

The foe approach'd: and one, for his bold sin,
   Was sunk (as he that touch'd the Ark was slain);
The wild waves master'd him, and suck'd him in,
   And smiling Eddies dimpled on the Main.

95

This seen, the rest at awful distance stood;
   As if they had been there as servants set,
To stay, or to go on, as he thought good,
380   And not pursue, but wait on his retreat.

96

So *Libyan* Huntsmen, on some sandy plain,
   From shady coverts rous'd, the Lion chase:
The Kingly beast roars out with loud disdain,
   And slowly moves, unknowing to give place.

97

But if someone approach to dare his force,
  He swings his tail, and swiftly turns him round:
With one paw seizes on his trembling Horse,
  And with the other tears him to the ground.

98

Amidst these toils succeeds the balmy night,
  Now hissing waters the quench'd guns restore;
And weary waves, withdrawing from the fight,
  Lie lull'd and panting on the silent shore.

99

The Moon shone clear on the becalmed flood,
  Where, while her beams like glittering silver play,
Upon the Deck our careful General stood,
  And deeply mus'd on the succeeding day.

100

'That happy Sun,' said he, 'will rise again,
  Who twice victorious did our Navy see:
And I alone must view him rise in vain,
  Without one ray of all his Star for me.

101

'Yet, like an *English* Gen'ral will I die,
  And all the Ocean make my spacious grave.
Women and Cowards on the Land may lie,
  The Sea's a Tomb that's proper for the brave.'

102

Restless he pass'd the remnants of the night,
  Till the fresh air proclaim'd the morning nigh,
And burning ships, the Martyrs of the fight,
  With paler fires beheld the Eastern sky.

But now, his Stores of Ammunition spent,
410   His naked valour is his only guard:
Rare thunders are from his dumb Cannon sent,
    And solitary Guns are scarcely heard.

104

Thus far had Fortune power, here forc'd to stay,
    Nor longer durst with virtue be at strife:
This, as a Ransom, *Albemarle* did pay
    For all the glories of so great a life.

105

For now brave *Rupert* from afar appears,
    Whose waving Streamers the glad General knows:
With full spread Sails his eager Navy steers,
420   And every Ship in swift proportion grows.

106

The anxious Prince had heard the Cannon long,
    And from that length of time dire *Omens* drew
Of *English* overmatch'd, and *Dutch* too strong,
    Who never fought three days but to pursue.

107

Then, as an Eagle (who, with pious care,
    Was beating widely on the wing for prey),
To her now silent Eyrie does repair,
    And finds her callow Infants forc'd away;

108

Stung with her love she stoops upon the plain,
430   The broken air loud whistling as she flies:
She stops, and listens, and shoots forth again,
    And guides her pinions by her young ones' cries:

With such kind passion hastes the Prince to fight,
    And spreads his flying canvas to the sound:
Him, whom no danger, were he there, could fright,
    Now, absent, every little noise can wound.

110

As, in a drought, the thirsty creatures cry,
    And gape upon the gather'd clouds for rain,
And first the Martlet meets it in the sky,
440   And with wet wings, joys all the feather'd train,

111

With such glad hearts did our despairing men
    Salute th' appearance of the Prince's Fleet:
And each ambitiously would claim the Ken
    That with first eyes did distant safety meet.

112

The *Dutch*, who came like greedy Hinds before,
    To reap the harvest their ripe ears did yield,
Now look like those, when rolling thunders roar,
    And sheets of Lightning blast the standing field.

113

Full in the Prince's passage, hills of sand
450   And dang'rous flats in secret ambush lay,
Where the false tides skim o'er the cover'd Land,
    And Seamen with dissembled depths betray:

114

The wily *Dutch*, who, like fall'n Angels, fear'd
    This new *Messiah*'s coming, there did wait,
And round the verge their braving Vessels steer'd,
    To tempt his courage with so fair a bait.

But he, unmov'd, contemns their idle threat,
　　Secure of fame whene'er he please to fight:
His cold experience tempers all his heat,
460　　And inbred worth does boasting valour slight.

116

Heroic virtue did his actions guide,
　　And he the substance not th'appearance chose:
To rescue one such friend he took more pride
　　Than to destroy whole thousands of such foes.

117

But, when approach'd, in strict embraces bound,
　　Rupert and *Albemarle* together grow:
He joys to have his friend in safety found,
　　Which he to none but to that friend would owe.

118

The cheerful Soldiers, with new stores supplied,
470　　Now long to execute their spleenful will;
And, in revenge for those three days they tried,
　　Wish one, like *Joshua*'s, when the Sun stood still.

119

Thus reinforc'd, against the adverse Fleet
　　Still doubling ours, brave *Rupert* leads the way.
With the first blushes of the Morn they meet,
　　And bring night back upon the new-born day.

120

His presence soon blows up the kindling fight,
　　And his loud Guns speak thick like angry men:
It seem'd as slaughter had been breath'd all night,
480　　And death new pointed his dull dart again.

The *Dutch*, too well his mighty Conduct knew,
   And matchless Courage since the former fight:
Whose Navy like a stiff stretch'd cord did show
   Till he bore in, and bent them into flight.

122

The wind he shares while half their Fleet offends
   His open side, and high above him shows,
Upon the rest at pleasure he descends,
   And, doubly harm'd, he double harms bestows.

123

Behind, the Gen'ral mends his weary pace,
490   And sullenly to his revenge he sails:
So glides some trodden Serpent on the grass,
   And long behind his wounded volume trails.

124

Th' increasing sound is borne to either shore,
   And for their stakes the throwing Nations fear.
Their passions double with the Cannons' roar,
   And with warm wishes each man combats there.

125

Plied thick and close as when the fight begun,
   Their huge unwieldy Navy wastes away:
So sicken waning Moons too near the Sun,
500   And blunt their crescents on the edge of day.

126

And now reduc'd on equal terms to fight,
   Their Ships like wasted Patrimonies show:
Where the thin scatt'ring Trees admit the light,
   And shun each others' shadows as they grow.

The warlike Prince had sever'd from the rest
    Two giant ships, the pride of all the Main;
Which, with his one, so vigorously he press'd,
    And flew so home they could not rise again.

128

Already batter'd, by his Lee they lay,
510   In vain upon the passing winds they call:
The passing winds through their torn canvas play,
    And flagging sails on heartless Sailors fall.

129

Their open'd sides receive a gloomy light,
    Dreadful as day let in to shades below:
Without, grim death rides bare-fac'd in their sight,
    And urges ent'ring billows as they flow.

130

When one dire shot, the last they could supply,
    Close by the board the Prince's Mainmast bore:
All three now, helpless, by each other lie,
520   And this offends not, and those fear no more.

131

So have I seen some fearful Hare maintain
    A course, till tired before the Dog she lay:
Who stretch'd behind her, pants upon the plain,
    Past power to kill as she to get away.

132

With his loll'd tongue he faintly licks his prey,
    His warm breath blows her flix up as she lies:
She, trembling, creeps upon the ground away,
    And looks back to him with beseeching eyes.

530

The Prince unjustly does his Stars accuse,
    Which hinder'd him to push his fortune on:
For what they to his courage did refuse,
    By mortal valour never must be done.

134

This lucky hour the wise *Batavian* takes,
    And warns his tatter'd Fleet to follow home:
Proud to have so got off with equal stakes,
    Where 'twas a triumph not to be o'ercome.

135

The General's force, as kept alive by fight,
    Now, not oppos'd, no longer can pursue:
Lasting till Heav'n had done his courage right,
540   When he had conquer'd he his weakness knew.

136

He casts a frown on the departing foe,
    And sighs to see him quit the wat'ry field:
His stern fix'd eyes no satisfaction show,
    For all the glories which the Fight did yield.

137

Though, as when Fiends did Miracles avow,
    He stands confess'd ev'n by the boastful *Dutch*,
He only does his conquest disavow,
    And thinks too little what they found too much.

138

Return'd, he with the Fleet resolv'd to stay,
550   No tender thoughts of home his heart divide:
Domestic joys and cares he puts away,
    For Realms are households which the Great must guide.

As those who unripe veins in Mines explore,
   On the rich bed again the warm turf lay,
Till time digests the yet imperfect Ore,
   And know it will be Gold another day:

140

So looks our Monarch on this early fight,
   Th' essay, and rudiments of great success,
Which all–maturing time must bring to light,
560   While he, like Heav'n, does each day's labour bless.

141

Heav'n ended not the first or second day,
   Yet each was perfect to the work design'd:
God and Kings work, when they their work survey,
   And passive aptness in all subjects find.

142

In burden'd Vessels, first, with speedy care,
   His plenteous Stores do season'd timber send:
Thither the brawny Carpenters repair,
   And as the Surgeons of maim'd ships attend.

143

With Cord and Canvas from rich *Hamburg* sent,
570   His Navies' moulted wings he imps once more:
Tall *Norway* Fir, their Masts in Battle spent,
   And *English* Oak sprung leaks and planks restore.

144

All hands employ'd, the Royal work grows warm,
   Like labouring Bees on a long Summer's day,
Some sound the Trumpet for the rest to swarm,
   And some on bells of tasted Lilies play:

With gluey wax some new foundation lay
    Of Virgin combs, which from the roof are hung:
Some arm'd within doors, upon duty stay,
580   Or tend the sick, or educate the young.

146

So here, some pick out bullets from the sides,
    Some drive old Oakum through each seam and rift:
Their left hand does the Caulking-iron guide,
    The rattling Mallet with the right they lift.

147

With boiling Pitch another near at hand
    (From friendly *Sweden* brought) the seams instops:
Which well paid o'er the salt Sea waves withstand,
    And shakes them from the rising beak in drops.

148

Some the gall'd ropes with dauby Marling bind,
590   Or cere-cloth Masts with strong Tarpaulin coats:
To try new shrouds one mounts into the wind,
    And one, below, their ease or stiffness notes.

149

Our careful Monarch stands in Person by,
    His new-cast Cannons' firmness to explore:
The strength of big-corn'd powder loves to try,
    And Ball and Cartridge sorts for every bore.

150

Each day brings fresh supplies of Arms and Men,
    And Ships which all last Winter were abroad:
And such as fitted since the Fight had been,
600   Or new from Stocks were fall'n into the Road.

151

The goodly *London* in her gallant trim,
   (The *Phoenix* daughter of the vanish'd old):
Like a rich Bride does to the Ocean swim,
   And on her shadow rides in floating gold.

152

Her Flag aloft spread ruffling to the wind,
   And sanguine Streamers seem the flood to fire:
The Weaver charm'd with what his Loom design'd,
   Goes on to Sea, and knows not to retire.

153

With roomy decks, her Guns of mighty strength,
610   (Whose low-laid mouths each mounting billow laves):
Deep in her draught, and warlike in her length,
   She seems a Sea-wasp flying on the waves.

154

This martial Present, piously design'd,
   The Loyal City give their best-lov'd King:
And with a bounty ample as the wind,
   Built, fitted and maintain'd to aid him bring.

155

By viewing Nature, Nature's Handmaid, Art,
   Makes mighty things from small beginnings grow:
Thus fishes first to shipping did impart
620   Their tail the Rudder, and their head the Prow.

156

Some Log, perhaps, upon the waters swam
   An useless drift, which, rudely cut within,
And hollow'd, first a floating trough became,
   And cross some Riv'let passage did begin.

In shipping such as this the *Irish Kern*,
    And untaught *Indian*, on the stream did glide:
Ere sharp-keel'd Boats to stem the flood did learn,
    Or fin-like Oars did spread from either side.

158

Add but a Sail, and *Saturn* so appear'd,
    When, from lost Empire, he to Exile went,
And with the Golden age to *Tiber* steer'd,
    Where Coin and first Commerce he did invent.

630

159

Rude as their Ships was Navigation, then;
    No useful Compass or Meridian known:
Coasting, they kept the Land within their ken,
    And knew no North but when the Pole star shone.

160

Of all who since have us'd the open Sea,
    Than the bold *English* none more fame have won:
Beyond the Year, and out of Heav'n's highway,
    They make discoveries where they see no Sun.

640

161

But what so long in vain, and yet unknown,
    By poor mankind's benighted wit is sought,
Shall in this Age to *Britain* first be shown,
    And hence be to admiring Nations taught.

162

The Ebbs of Tides, and their mysterious flow,
    We, as Art's Elements shall understand:
And as by Line upon the Ocean go,
    Whose paths shall be familiar as the Land.

Instructed ships shall sail to quick Commerce;
650 By which remotest Regions are allied:
Which makes one City of the Universe,
    Where some may gain, and all may be supplied.

164

Then, we upon our Globe's last verge shall go,
    And view the Ocean leaning on the sky:
From thence our rolling Neighbours we shall know,
    And on the Lunar world securely pry.

165

This I foretell, from your auspicious care,
    Who great in search of God and Nature grow:
Who best your wise Creator's praise declare,
660   Since best to praise his works is best to know.

166

O truly Royal! who behold the Law,
    And rule of beings in your Maker's mind,
And thence, like Limbecs, rich Ideas draw,
    To fit the levell'd use of human kind.

167

But first the toils of war we must endure,
    And, from th' Injurious *Dutch* redeem the Seas.
War makes the valiant of his right secure,
    And gives up fraud to be chastis'd with ease.

168

Already were the *Belgians* on our coast,
670   Whose Fleet more mighty every day became,
By late success, which they did falsely boast,
    And now, by first appearing seem'd to claim.

Designing, subtle, diligent, and close,
    They knew to manage War with wise delay:
Yet all those arts their vanity did cross,
    And, by their pride, their prudence did betray.

170

Nor stayed the English long: but, well supplied,
    Appear as numerous as th' insulting foe.
The Combat now by courage must be tried,
680   And the success the braver Nation show.

171

There was the *Plymouth* Squadron new come in,
    Which in the *Straits* last Winter was abroad:
Which twice on *Biscay*'s working Bay had been,
    And on the Mid-land Sea the *French* had aw'd.

172

Old expert *Allin*, loyal all along,
    Fam'd for his action on the *Smyrna* Fleet,
And *Holmes*, whose name shall live in Epic Song,
    While Music Numbers, or while Verse has Feet.

173

Holmes, the *Achates* of the Gen'rals' fight,
690   Who first bewitch'd our eyes with *Guinea* Gold:
As once old *Cato* in the *Roman*'s sight
    The tempting fruits of *Afric* did unfold.

174

With him went *Spragge*, as bountiful as brave,
    Whom his high courage to command had brought:
Harman, who did the twice fir'd *Harry* save,
    And in his burning ship undaunted fought.

Young *Hollis*, on a *Muse* by *Mars* begot
    Born, *Caesar*-like, to write and act great deeds:
Impatient to revenge his fatal shot,
700   His right hand doubly to his left succeeds.

176

Thousands were there in darker fame that dwell,
    Whose deeds some nobler Poem shall adorn:
And, though to me unknown, they, sure, fought well,
    Whom *Rupert* led, and who were British born.

177

Of every size an hundred fighting Sail,
    So vast the Navy now at Anchor rides,
That underneath it the press'd waters fail,
    And, with its weight, it shoulders off the Tides.

178

Now Anchors weigh'd, the Seamen shout so shrill,
710   That Heav'n and Earth and the wide Ocean rings:
A breeze from Westward waits their sails to fill,
    And rests, in those high beds, his downy wings.

179

The wary *Dutch* this gathering storm foresaw,
    And durst not bide it on the *English* coast:
Behind their treach'rous shallows they withdraw,
    And there lay snares to catch the *British* Host.

180

So the false Spider, when her Nets are spread,
    Deep ambush'd in her silent den does lie:
And feels, far off, the trembling of her thread,
720   Whose filmy cord should bind the struggling Fly.

Then, if at last, she find him fast beset,
   She issues forth, and runs along her Loom:
She joys to touch the Captive in her Net,
   And drags the little wretch in triumph home.

The *Belgians* hop'd that, with disorder'd haste,
   Our deep-cut keels upon the sands might run:
Or, if with caution leisurely were past,
   Their numerous gross might charge us one by one.

But, with a fore-wind pushing them above,
730   And swelling tide that heav'd them from below,
O'er the blind flats our warlike Squadrons move,
   And, with spread sails, to welcome Battle go.

It seem'd as there the *British Neptune* stood,
   With all his host of waters at command,
Beneath them to submit th' officious flood:
   And, with his Trident, shov'd them off the sand.

To the pale foes they suddenly draw near,
   And summon them to unexpected fight:
They start like Murderers when Ghosts appear,
740   And draw their Curtains in the dead of night.

Now Van to Van the foremost Squadrons meet,
   The midmost Battles hasting up behind,
Who view, far off, the storm of falling Sleet,
   And hear their thunder rattling in the wind.

At length the adverse Admirals appear;
   (The two bold Champions of each Country's right)
Their eyes describe the lists as they come near,
   And draw the lines of death before they fight.

The distance judg'd for shot of every size,
750   The Linstocks touch, the pond'rous ball expires:
The vig'rous Seaman every porthole plies,
   And adds his heart to every Gun he fires.

Fierce was the fight on the proud *Belgians'* side,
   For honour, which they seldom sought before:
But now they by their own vain boasts were tied,
   And forc'd, at least in show, to prize it more.

But sharp remembrance on the *English* part,
   And shame of being match'd by such a foe,
Rouse conscious virtue up in every heart,
760   And seeming to be stronger makes them so.

Nor long the *Belgians* could that Fleet sustain,
   Which did two Gen'rals' fates and *Caesar's* bear.
Each several Ship a victory did gain,
   As *Rupert* or as *Albemarle* were there.

Their batter'd Admiral too soon withdrew,
   Unthank'd by ours for his unfinish'd fight:
But he the minds of his *Dutch* Masters knew,
   Who call'd that providence which we call'd flight.

Never did men more joyfully obey,
770   Or sooner understood the sign to fly:
With such alacrity they bore away,
   As if to praise them all the States stood by.

194

O famous Leader of the *Belgian* Fleet,
   Thy Monument inscrib'd such praise shall wear
As *Varro*, timely flying, once did meet,
   Because he did not of his *Rome* despair.

195

Behold that Navy which a while before
   Provok'd the tardy *English* to the fight,
Now draw their beaten vessels close to shore,
780   As Larks lie dar'd to shun the Hobby's flight.

196

Whoe'er would *English* Monuments survey,
   In other records may our courage know:
But let them hide the story of this day,
   Whose fame was blemish'd by too base a foe.

197

Or if too busily they will inquire
   Into a victory which we disdain:
Then let them know, the *Belgians* did retire
   Before the Patron Saint of injur'd *Spain*.

198

Repenting *England* this revengeful day
790   To *Philip*'s Manes did an off'ring bring:
England, which first, by leading them astray,
   Hatch'd up Rebellion to destroy her King.

Our Fathers bent their baneful industry
　　To check a Monarchy that slowly grew:
But did not *France* or *Holland*'s fate foresee,
　　Whose rising power to swift Dominion flew.

200

In fortune's Empire blindly thus we go,
　　And wander after pathless destiny:
Whose dark resorts since prudence cannot know
800　　In vain it would provide for what shall be.

201

But whate'er *English* to the bless'd shall go,
　　And the fourth *Harry* or first *Orange* meet:
Find him disowning of a *Bourbon* foe,
　　And him detesting a *Batavian* Fleet.

202

Now on their coasts our conquering Navy rides,
　　Waylays their Merchants, and their Land besets:
Each day new wealth without their care provides,
　　They lie asleep with prizes in their nets.

203

So, close behind some Promontory lie
810　　The huge Leviathans t' attend their prey:
And give no chase, but swallow in the fry,
　　Which through their gaping jaws mistake the way.

204

Nor was this all: in Ports and Roads remote,
　　Destructive Fires among whole Fleets we send:
Triumphant flames upon the water float,
　　And out-bound ships at home their voyage end.

Those various Squadrons, variously design'd,
　　Each vessel freighted with a several load:
Each squadron waiting for a several wind,
820　　All find but one, to burn them in the Road.

206

Some bound for *Guinea*, golden sand to find,
　　Bore all the gauds the simple Natives wear:
Some for the pride of *Turkish* Courts design'd,
　　For folded *Turbans* finest *Holland* bear.

207

Some *English* Wool, vex'd in a *Belgian* Loom,
　　And into Cloth of spongy softness made:
Did into *France* or colder *Denmark* doom,
　　To ruin with worse ware our staple Trade.

208

Our greedy Seamen rummage every hold,
830　　Smile on the booty of each wealthier Chest:
And, as the Priests who with their gods make bold,
　　Take what they like, and sacrifice the rest.

209

But ah! how unsincere are all our joys!
　　Which, sent from Heav'n, like Lightning make no stay:
Their palling taste the journey's length destroys,
　　Or grief, sent post, o'ertakes them on the way.

210

Swell'd with our late successes on the Foe,
　　Which *France* and *Holland* wanted power to cross:
We urge an unseen Fate to lay us low,
840　　And feed their envious eyes with *English* loss.

Each Element his dread command obeys,
 Who makes or ruins with a smile or frown;
Who as by one he did our Nation raise,
 So now he with another pulls us down.

Yet, *London*, Empress of the Northern Clime,
 By an high fate thou greatly didst expire;
Great as the world's, which at the death of time
 Must fall, and rise a nobler frame by fire.

As when some dire Usurper Heav'n provides,
850 To scourge his Country with a lawless sway:
His birth, perhaps, some petty Village hides,
 And sets his Cradle out of Fortune's way:

Till fully ripe his swelling fate breaks out,
 And hurries him to mighty mischiefs on:
His Prince surpris'd at first, no ill could doubt,
 And wants the power to meet it when 'tis known:

Such was the rise of this prodigious fire,
 Which in mean buildings first obscurely bred,
From thence did soon to open streets aspire,
860 And straight to Palaces and Temples spread.

The diligence of Trades and noiseful gain,
 And luxury, more late, asleep were laid:
All was the night's, and in her silent reign,
 No sound the rest of Nature did invade.

In this deep quiet, from what source unknown,
  Those seeds of fire their fatal birth disclose:
And first, few scatt'ring sparks about were blown,
  Big with the flames that to our ruin rose.

Then, in some close-pent room it crept along,
870   And, smould'ring as it went, in silence fed:
Till th' infant monster, with devouring strong,
  Walk'd boldly upright with exalted head.

Now, like some rich or mighty Murderer,
  Too great for prison, which he breaks with gold:
Who fresher for new mischiefs does appear,
  And dares the world to tax him with the old:

So 'scapes th' insulting fire his narrow Jail,
  And makes small outlets into open air:
There the fierce winds his tender force assail,
880   And beat him downward to his first repair.

The winds, like crafty Courtesans, withheld
  His flames from burning, but to blow them more:
And, every fresh attempt, he is repell'd
  With faint denials, weaker than before.

And now, no longer letted of his prey,
  He leaps up at it with enrag'd desire:
O'erlooks the neighbours with a wide survey,
  And nods at every house his threat'ning fire.

890　The Ghosts of Traitors, from the *Bridge* descend,
　　　　With bold Fanatic Spectres to rejoice:
　　　About the fire into a Dance they bend,
　　　　And sing their Sabbath Notes with feeble voice.

224

Our Guardian Angel saw them where he sate
　　Above the Palace of our slumb'ring King,
He sigh'd, abandoning his charge to Fate,
　　And, drooping, oft look'd back upon the wing.

225

At length the crackling noise and dreadful blaze,
　　Call'd up some waking Lover to the sight:
And long it was ere he the rest could raise,
900　　Whose heavy eyelids yet were full of night.

226

The next to danger, hot pursu'd by fate,
　　Half cloth'd, half naked, hastily retire:
And frighted Mothers stike their breasts, too late,
　　For helpless Infants left amidst the fire.

227

Their cries soon waken all the dwellers near:
　　Now murmuring noises rise in every street:
The more remote run stumbling with their fear,
　　And, in the dark, men jostle as they meet.

228

So weary Bees in little Cells repose:
910　　But if night-robbers lift the well-stor'd Hive,
An humming through their waxen City grows,
　　And out upon each others' wings they drive.

Now streets grow throng'd and busy as by day:
    Some run for Buckets to the hallow'd Choir:
Some cut the Pipes, and some the Engines Play,
    And some more bold mount Ladders to the fire.

230

In vain: for, from the East, a *Belgian* wind,
    His hostile breath through the dry rafters sent:
The flames impell'd, soon left their foes behind,
920   And forward, with a wanton fury went.

231

A Quay of fire ran all along the shore,
    And lighten'd all the River with the blaze:
The waken'd Tides began again to roar,
    And wond'ring Fish in shining waters gaze.

232

Old Father *Thames* rais'd up his reverend head,
    But fear'd the fate of *Simois* would return:
Deep in his *Ooze* he sought his sedgy bed,
    And shrunk his waters back into his Urn.

233

The fire, meantime, walks in a broader gross,
930   To either hand his wings he opens wide:
He wades the streets, and straight he reaches cross,
    And plays his longing flames on th' other side.

234

At first they warm, then scorch, and then they take:
    Now with long necks from side to side they feed:
At length, grown strong, their Mother fire forsake,
    And a new Colony of flames succeed.

To every nobler portion of the Town,
　　The curling billows roll their restless Tide:
In parties now they straggle up and down,
　　As Armies, unoppos'd, for prey divide.

940

236

One mighty Squadron, with a side wind sped,
　　Through narrow lanes his cumber'd fire does haste:
By powerful charms of gold and silver led,
　　The *Lombard* Bankers and the *Change* to waste.

237

Another backward to the *Tower* would go,
　　And slowly eats his way against the wind:
But the main body of the marching foe
　　Against th' Imperial Palace is design'd.

238

Now day appears, and with the day the King,
　　Whose early care had robb'd him of his rest:
Far off the cracks of falling houses ring,
　　And shrieks of subjects pierce his tender breast.

950

239

Near as he draws, thick harbingers of smoke,
　　With gloomy pillars, cover all the place:
Whose little intervals of night are broke
　　By sparks that drive against his Sacred Face.

240

More than his Guards his sorrows made him known,
　　And pious tears which down his cheeks did show'r:
The wretched in his grief forgot their own:
　　(So much the pity of a King has power.)

960

He wept the flames of what he lov'd so well,
    And what so well had merited his love.
For never Prince in grace did more excel,
    Or Royal City more in duty strove.

Nor with an idle care did he behold:
    (Subjects may grieve, but Monarchs must redress.)
He cheers the fearful, and commends the bold,
    And makes despairers hope for good success.

Himself directs what first is to be done,
970   And orders all the succours which they bring.
The helpful and the good about him run,
    And form an army worthy such a King.

He sees the dire contagion spread so fast,
    That where it seizes, all relief is vain:
And therefore must unwillingly lay waste
    That Country which would, else, the foe maintain.

The powder blows up all before the fire:
    Th' amazed flames stand gather'd on a heap;
And from the precipice's brink retire,
980   Afraid to venture on so large a leap.

Thus fighting fires awhile themselves consume,
    But straight, like *Turks*, forc'd on to win or die,
They first lay tender bridges of their fume,
    And o'er the breach in unctuous vapours fly.

Part stays for passage till a gust of wind
   Ships o'er their forces in a shining sheet:
Part, creeping under ground, their journey blind,
   And, climbing from below, their fellows meet.

248

Thus, to some desert plain, or old wood side,
990   Dire night-hags come from far to dance their round:
And o'er broad Rivers on their fiends they ride,
   Or sweep in clouds above the blasted ground.

249

No help avails: for, *Hydra*-like, the fire,
   Lifts up his hundred heads to aim his way.
And scarce the wealthy can one half retire,
   Before he rushes in to share the prey.

250

The rich grow suppliant, and the poor grow proud:
   Those offer mighty gain, and these ask more.
So void of pity is th' ignoble crowd,
1000   When others' ruin may increase their store.

251

As those who live by shores with joy behold
   Some wealthy vessel split or stranded nigh;
And, from the Rocks, leap down for shipwreck'd Gold,
   And seek the Tempest which the others fly:

252

So these but wait the Owners' last despair,
   And what's permitted to the flames invade:
Ev'n from their jaws they hungry morsels tear,
   And, on their backs, the spoils of *Vulcan* lade.

The days were all in this lost labour spent;
    And when the weary King gave place to night,
His Beams he to his Royal Brother lent,
    And so shone still in his reflective light.

1010

254

Night came, but without darkness or repose,
    A dismal picture of the gen'ral doom:
Where Souls distracted when the Trumpet blows,
    And half unready with their bodies come.

255

Those who have homes, when home they do repair
    To a last lodging call their wand'ring friends.
Their short uneasy sleeps are broke with care,
    To look how near their own destruction tends.

1020

256

Those who have none sit round where once it was,
    And with full eyes each wonted room require:
Haunting the yet warm ashes of the place,
    As murder'd men walk where they did expire.

257

Some stir up coals and watch the Vestal fire,
    Others in vain from sight of ruin run:
And, while through burning Lab'rinths they retire,
    With loathing eyes repeat what they would shun.

258

The most, in fields, like herded beasts lie down;
    To dews obnoxious on the grassy floor:
And while their Babes in sleep their sorrows drown,
    Sad Parents watch the remnants of their store.

1030

While by the motion of the flames they guess
    What streets are burning now, and what are near:
An Infant, waking, to the paps would press,
    And meets, instead of milk, a falling tear.

260

No thought can ease them but their Sovereign's care,
    Whose praise th'afflicted as their comfort sing:
Ev'n those whom want might drive to just despair,
1040   Think life a blessing under such a King.

261

Meantime he sadly suffers in their grief,
    Outweeps an Hermit, and outprays a Saint:
All the long night he studies their relief,
    How they may be supplied, and he may want.

262

'O God,' said he, 'Thou Patron of my days,
    Guide of my youth in exile and distress!
Who me unfriended, brought'st by wondrous ways
    The Kingdom of my Fathers to possess:

263

'Be thou my Judge, with what unwearied care
1050   I since have labour'd for my People's good:
To bind the bruises of a Civil War,
    And stop the issues of their wasting blood.

264

'Thou, who hast taught me to forgive the ill,
    And recompense, as friends, the good misled;
If mercy be a Precept of thy will,
    Return that mercy on thy Servant's head.

'Or, if my heedless Youth has stepp'd astray,
 Too soon forgetful of thy gracious hand:
On me alone thy just displeasure lay,
1060 But take thy judgments from this mourning Land.

266

'We all have sinn'd, and thou hast laid us low,
 As humble Earth from whence at first we came:
Like flying shades before the Clouds we show,
 And shrink like Parchment in consuming flame.

267

'O let it be enough what thou hast done,
 When spotted deaths ran arm'd through every street,
With poison'd darts, which not the good could shun,
 The speedy could outfly, or valiant meet.

268

'The living few, and frequent funerals then,
1070 Proclaim'd thy wrath on this forsaken place:
And now those few who are return'd again
 Thy searching judgments to their dwellings trace.

269

'O pass not, Lord, an absolute decree,
 Or bind thy sentence unconditional:
But in thy sentence our remorse foresee,
 And, in that foresight, this thy doom recall.

270

'Thy threat'nings, Lord, as thine thou may'st revoke:
 But, if immutable and fix'd they stand,
Continue still thyself to give the stroke,
1080 And let not foreign foes oppress thy Land.'

Th' Eternal heard, and from the Heav'nly Choir,
    Chose out the Cherub with the flaming sword:
And bad him swiftly drive th' approaching fire
    From where our Naval Magazines were stor'd.

The blessed Minister his wings display'd,
    And like a shooting Star he cleft the night:
He charg'd the flames, and those that disobey'd,
    He lash'd to duty with his sword of light.

The fugitive flames, chastis'd, went forth to prey
1090   On pious Structures, by our Fathers rear'd:
By which to Heav'n they did affect the way,
    Ere Faith in Churchmen without Works was heard.

The wanting Orphans saw, with wat'ry eyes,
    Their Founder's charity in dust laid low:
And sent to God their ever-answer'd cries,
    (For he protects the poor who made them so.)

Nor could thy Fabric, *Paul*'s defend thee long,
    Though thou wert Sacred to thy Maker's praise:
Though made immortal by a Poet's Song;
1100   And Poets' Songs the *Theban* walls could raise.

The daring flames peep'd in and saw from far,
    The awful beauties of the Sacred Choir:
But, since it was profan'd by Civil War,
    Heav'n thought it fit to have it purg'd by fire.

Now down the narrow streets it swiftly came,
    And, widely opening, did on both sides prey.
This benefit we sadly owe the flame,
    If only ruin must enlarge our way.

278

And now four days the Sun had seen our woes,
    Four nights the Moon beheld th' incessant fire:
It seem'd as if the Stars more sickly rose,
    And farther from the fev'rish North retire.

279

In th' Empyrean Heaven (the bless'd abode),
    The Thrones and the Dominions prostrate lie,
Not daring to behold their angry God:
    And an hush'd silence damps the tuneful sky.

280

At length th' Almighty cast a pitying eye,
    And mercy softly touch'd his melting breast:
He saw the Town's one half in rubbish lie,
    And eager flames give on to storm the rest.

281

An hollow crystal Pyramid he takes,
    In firmamental waters dipp'd above;
Of it a broad Extinguisher he makes,
    And hoods the flames that to their quarry strove.

282

The vanquish'd fires withdraw from every place,
    Or full with feeding, sink into a sleep:
Each household Genius shows again his face,
    And, from the hearths, the little Lares creep.

1110

1120

Our King this more than natural change beholds;
1130   With sober joy his heart and eyes abound:
To the All-good his lifted hands he folds,
    And thanks him low on his redeemed ground.

284

As when sharp frosts had long constrain'd the earth,
    A kindly thaw unlocks it with mild rain:
And first the tender blade peeps up to birth,
    And straight the green fields laugh with promis'd grain.

285

By such degrees, the spreading gladness grew
    In every heart, which fear had froze before:
The standing streets with so much joy they view,
1140   That with less grief the perish'd they deplore.

286

The Father of the people open'd wide
    His stores, and all the poor with plenty fed:
Thus God's Anointed God's own place supplied,
    And fill'd the empty with his daily bread.

287

This Royal bounty brought its own reward,
    And, in their minds, so deep did print the sense:
That if their ruins sadly they regard,
    'Tis but with fear the sight might drive him thence.

288

But so may he live long, that Town to sway,
1150   Which by his Auspice they will nobler make,
As he will hatch their ashes by his stay,
    And not their humble ruins now forsake.

They have not lost their Loyalty by fire;
    Nor is their courage or their wealth so low,
That from his Wars they poorly would retire,
    Or beg the pity of a vanquish'd foe.

290

Not with more constancy the *Jews* of old,
    By *Cyrus* from rewarded Exile sent:
Their Royal City did in dust behold,
    Or with more vigour to rebuild it went.

1160

291

The utmost malice of their Stars is past,
    And two dire Comets which have scourg'd the Town,
In their own Plague and Fire have breath'd their last,
    Or, dimly, in their sinking sockets frown.

292

Now frequent Trines the happier lights among,
    And high-rais'd *Jove* from his dark prison freed:
(Those weights took off that on his Planet hung)
    Will gloriously the new laid work succeed.

293

Methinks already, from this Chemic flame,
    I see a City of more precious mould:
Rich as the Town which gives the *Indies* name,
    With Silver pav'd, and all divine with Gold.

1170

294

Already, Labouring with a mighty fate,
    She shakes the rubbish from her mounting brow,
And seems to have renew'd her Charter's date,
    Which Heav'n will to the death of time allow.

More great than human, now, and more *August*,
    New deified she from her fires does rise:
Her widening streets on new foundations trust,
1180   And, opening, into larger parts she flies.

296

Before, she like some Shepherdess did show,
    Who sat to bathe her by a River's side:
Not answering to her fame, but rude and low,
    Nor taught the beauteous Arts of Modern pride.

297

Now, like a Maiden Queen, she will behold,
    From her high Turrets, hourly Suitors come:
The East with Incense, and the West with Gold,
    Will stand, like Suppliants, to receive her doom.

298

The silver *Thames*, her own domestic Flood,
1190   Shall bear her Vessels, like a sweeping Train;
And often wind (as of his Mistress proud)
    With longing eyes to meet her face again.

299

The wealthy *Tagus*, and the wealthier *Rhine*,
    The glory of their Towns no more shall boast:
And *Seine*, that would with *Belgian* Rivers join,
    Shall find her lustre stain'd, and Traffic lost.

300

The vent'rous Merchant, who design'd more far,
    And touches on our hospitable shore:
Charm'd with the splendour of this Northern Star,
1200   Shall here unlade him, and depart no more.

Our powerful Navy shall no longer meet,
    The wealth of *France* or *Holland* to invade:
The beauty of this Town, without a Fleet,
    From all the world shall vindicate her Trade.

302

And, while this fam'd Emporium we prepare,
    The *British* Ocean shall such triumphs boast,
That those who now disdain our Trade to share,
    Shall rob like Pirates on our wealthy Coast.

303

Already we have conquer'd half the War,
1210   And the less dang'rous part is left behind:
Our trouble now is but to make them dare,
    And not so great to vanquish as to find.

304

Thus to the Eastern wealth through storms we go;
    But now, the Cape once doubled, fear no more:
A constant Trade wind will securely blow,
    And gently lay us on the Spicy shore.

Absalom and Achitophel
A Poem

−Si Propius stes Te Capiet Magis
TO THE READER

'Tis not my intention to make an Apology for my *Poem*: some will think it needs no Excuse; and others will receive none. The Design, I am sure, is honest: but he who draws his Pen for one Party, must expect to make Enemies of the other. For, *Wit* and *Fool*, are Consequents of *Whig* and *Tory*: and every man is a Knave or an Ass to the contrary side. There's a Treasury of Merits in the *Fanatic Church*, as well as in the *Papist*; and a Pennyworth to be had of Saintship, Honesty, and Poetry, for the Lewd, the Factious, and the Blockheads. But the longest

10 Chapter in *Deuteronomy*, has not Curses enough for an *Anti-Bromingham*. My Comfort is, their manifest Prejudice to my Cause, will render their Judgment of less Authority against me. Yet if a *Poem* have a *Genius*, it will force its own reception in the World. For there's a sweetness in good Verse, which Tickles even while it Hurts: and, no man can be heartily angry with him, who pleases him against his will. The Commendation of Adversaries, is the greatest Triumph of a Writer; because it never comes unless Extorted. But I can be satisfied on more easy terms. If I happen to please the more Moderate sort, I

20 shall be sure of an honest Party; and, in all probability, of the best Judges; for the least Concern'd, are commonly the least Corrupt. And, I confess, I have laid in for those, by rebating the *Satire* (where Justice would allow it), from carrying too sharp an Edge. They, who can Criticize so weakly, as to imagine I have done my Worst, may be Convinc'd, at their own Cost, that I can write Severely, with more ease, than I can Gently. I have but laugh'd at some men's Follies, when I could have declaim'd against their Vices; and, other men's Virtues I have commended, as freely as I have tax'd their Crimes. And now,

30 if you are a Malicious *Reader*, I expect you should return upon

me, that I affect to be thought more Impartial than I am. But, if men are not to be judg'd by their Professions, God forgive you *Commonwealth's-men*, for professing so plausibly for the Government. You cannot be so Unconscionable, as to charge me for not Subscribing of my Name; for that would reflect too grossly upon your own Party, who never dare, though they have the advantage of a Jury to secure them. If you like not my *Poem*, the fault may, possibly, be in my Writing: (though 'tis hard for an Author to judge against himself;) but, more
40 probably, 'tis in your Morals, which cannot bear the truth of it. The Violent, on both sides, will condemn the Character of *Absalom*, as either too favourably, or too hardly drawn. But, they are not the Violent, whom I desire to please. The fault, on the right hand, is to Extenuate, Palliate and Indulge; and, to confess freely, I have endeavour'd to commit it. Besides the respect which I owe his Birth, I have a greater for his Heroic Virtues; and, *David* himself, could not be more tender of the Young Man's Life, than I would be of his Reputation. But, since the most excellent Natures are always the most easy;
50 and, as being such, are the soonest perverted by ill Counsels, especially when baited with Fame and Glory; 'tis no more a wonder that he withstood not the temptations of *Achitophel*, than it was for *Adam*, not to have resisted the two Devils; the Serpent, and the Woman. The conclusion of the Story, I purposely forbore to prosecute; because, I could not obtain from myself, to show *Absalom* Unfortunate. The Frame of it, was cut out, but for a Picture to the Waist; and, if the Draught be so far true, 'tis as much as I design'd.

Were I the Inventor, who am only the Historian, I should
60 certainly conclude the Piece, with the Reconcilement of *Absalom* to *David*. And, who knows but this may come to pass? Things were not brought to an Extremity where I left the Story: there seems, yet, to be room left for a Composure; hereafter, there may only be for pity. I have not, so much as an uncharitable Wish against *Achitophel*; but, am content to be Accus'd of a good natur'd Error; and, to hope with *Origen*, that the Devil himself may, at last, be sav'd. For which reason, in this Poem, he is neither brought to set his House in order, nor to dispose of his Person afterwards, as he in Wisdom
70 shall think fit. God is infinitely merciful; and his Vicegerent is only not so, because he is not Infinite.

The true end of *Satire*, is the amendment of Vices by correction. And he who writes Honestly, is no more an Enemy to the Offender, than the Physician to the Patient, when he prescribes harsh Remedies to an inveterate Disease: for those are only in order to prevent the Surgeon's work of an *Ense rescindendum*, which I wish not to my very Enemies. To conclude all, if the Body Politic have any Analogy to the Natural, in my weak judgment, an Act of *Oblivion* were as necessary in a
80   Hot, Distemper'd State, as an *Opiate* would be in a Raging Fever.

> In pious times, ere Priestcraft did begin,
> Before *Polygamy* was made a sin;
> When man, on many multiply'd his kind,
> Ere one to one was, cursedly, confin'd:
> When Nature prompted, and no law deny'd
> Promiscuous use of Concubine and Bride;
> Then, *Israel*'s Monarch, after Heaven's own heart,
> His vigorous warmth did, variously, impart
> To Wives and Slaves: and, wide as his Command,
10   > Scatter'd his Maker's Image through the Land.
> *Michal*, of Royal blood, the Crown did wear,
> A Soil ungrateful to the Tiller's care:
> Not so the rest; for several Mothers bore
> To Godlike *David*, several Sons before.
> But since like slaves his bed they did ascend,
> No True Succession could their seed attend.
> Of all this Numerous Progeny was none
> So Beautiful, so brave as *Absalom*:
> Whether, inspir'd by some diviner Lust,
20   > His Father got him with a greater Gust;
> Or that his Conscious destiny made way
> By manly beauty to Imperial sway.
> Early in Foreign fields he won Renown,
> With Kings and States allied to *Israel*'s Crown:
> In Peace the thoughts of War he could remove,
> And seem'd as he were only born for love.
> Whate'er he did was done with so much ease,
> In him alone, 'twas Natural to please;

His motions all accompanied with grace,
30 And *Paradise* was open'd in his face
With secret Joy, indulgent *David* view'd
His Youthful Image in his Son renew'd:
To all his wishes Nothing he denied,
And made the Charming *Annabel* his Bride.
What faults he had (for who from faults is free?)
His Father could not, or he would not see.
Some warm excesses, which the Law forbore,
Were constru'd Youth that purg'd by boiling o'er;
And *Amnon*'s Murder, by a specious Name,
40 Was call'd a Just Revenge for injur'd Fame.
Thus Prais'd, and Lov'd, the Noble Youth remain'd,
While *David*, undisturb'd, in *Sion* reign'd.
But Life can never be sincerely blest:
Heaven punishes the bad, and proves the best.
The *Jews*, a Headstrong, Moody, Murmuring race,
As ever tried th' extent and stretch of grace;
God's pamper'd people whom, debauch'd with ease,
No King could govern, nor no God could please;
(Gods they had tried of every shape and size
50 That God-smiths could produce, or Priests devise:)
These *Adam*-wits, too fortunately free,
Began to dream they wanted liberty;
And when no rule, no precedent was found
Of men, by Laws less circumscrib'd and bound,
They led their wild desires to Woods and Caves,
And thought that all but Savages were Slaves.
They who when *Saul* was dead, without a blow,
Made foolish *Ishbosheth* the Crown forgo;
Who banish'd *David* did from *Hebron* bring,
60 And, with a General Shout, proclaim'd him King:
Those very *Jews*, who, at their very best,
Their Humour more than Loyalty express'd,
Now, wonder'd why, so long, they had obey'd
An Idol Monarch which their hands had made:
Thought they might ruin him they could create;
Or melt him to that Golden Calf, a State.

But these were random bolts: no form'd Design,
Nor Interest made the Factious Crowd to join:
The sober part of *Israel*, free from stain,
70   Well knew the value of a peaceful reign:
And, looking backward with a wise affright,
Saw Seams of wounds, dishonest to the sight;
In contemplation of whose ugly Scars,
They Curs'd the memory of Civil Wars.
The moderate sort of Men, thus qualified,
Inclin'd the Balance to the better side:
And *David*'s mildness manag'd it so well,
The Bad found no occasion to Rebel.
But, when to Sin our bias'd Nature leans,
80   The careful Devil is still at hand with means;
And providently Pimps for ill desires:
The Good old Cause reviv'd, a Plot requires.
Plots, true or false, are necessary things,
To raise up Commonwealths, and ruin Kings.
  Th' inhabitants of old *Jerusalem*
Were *Jebusites*: the Town so call'd from them;
And theirs the Native right—
But when the chosen people grew more strong,
The rightful cause at length became the wrong:
90   And every loss the men of *Jebus* bore,
They still were thought God's enemies the more.
Thus, worn and weaken'd, well or ill content,
Submit they must to *David*'s Government:
Impoverish'd and depriv'd of all Command,
Their Taxes doubled as they lost their Land,
And, what was harder yet to flesh and blood,
Their Gods disgrac'd, and burnt like common wood.
This set the Heathen Priesthood in a flame;
For Priests of all Religions are the same:
100   Of whatsoe'er descent their Godhead be,
Stock, Stone, or other homely pedigree,
In his defence his Servants are as bold
As if he had been born of beaten gold.
The *Jewish Rabbins*, though their Enemies,

In this conclude them honest men and wise:
For 'twas their duty, all the Learned think,
T' espouse his Cause by whom they eat and drink.
From hence began that Plot, the Nation's Curse,
Bad in itself, but represented worse.
110 Rais'd in extremes, and in extremes decried;
With Oaths affirm'd, with dying Vows denied.
Not weigh'd, or winnow'd by the Multitude;
But swallow'd in the Mass, unchew'd and Crude.
Some Truth there was, but dash'd and brew'd with Lies;
To please the Fools, and puzzle all the Wise.
Succeeding times did equal folly call,
Believing nothing, or believing all.
Th' *Egyptian* Rites the *Jebusites* embrac'd;
Where Gods were recommended by their Taste.
120 Such savoury Deities must needs be good,
As serv'd at once for Worship and for Food.
By force they could not Introduce these Gods;
For Ten to One, in former days was odds.
So Fraud was us'd (the Sacrificer's trade,)
Fools are more hard to Conquer than Persuade.
Their busy Teachers mingled with the *Jews*;
And rak'd, for Converts, even the Court and Stews:
Which *Hebrew* Priests the more unkindly took,
Because the Fleece accompanies the Flock.
130 Some thought they God's Anointed meant to Slay
By Guns, invented since full many a day:
Our Author swears it not; but who can know
How far the Devil and *Jebusites* may go?
This Plot, which fail'd for want of common Sense,
Had yet a deep and dangerous Consequence:
For, as when raging Fevers boil the Blood,
The standing Lake soon floats into a Flood;
And every hostile Humour, which before
Slept quiet in its Channels, bubbles o'er;
140 So, several Factions from this first Ferment,
Work up to Foam, and threat the Government.
Some by their Friends, more by themselves thought wise,

Oppos'd the Power to which they could not rise.
Some had in Courts been great, and thrown from thence,
Like Fiends, were harden'd in Impenitence.
Some by their Monarch's fatal mercy grown,
From Pardon'd Rebels, Kinsmen to the Throne;
Were rais'd in Power and public Office high:
Strong Bands, if Bands ungrateful men could tie.

150   Of these the false *Achitophel* was first:
A Name to all succeeding Ages Curs'd.
For close Designs, and crooked Counsels fit;
Sagacious, Bold, and Turbulent of wit:
Restless, unfix'd in Principles and Place;
In Power unpleas'd, impatient of Disgrace.
A fiery Soul, which working out its way,
Fretted the Pigmy Body to decay:
And o'er inform'd the Tenement of Clay.
A daring Pilot in extremity;

160 Pleas'd with the Danger, when the Waves went high
He sought the Storms; but for a Calm unfit,
Would Steer too nigh the Sands, to boast his Wit.
Great Wits are sure to Madness near allied;
And thin Partitions do their Bounds divide:
Else, why should he, with Wealth and Honour bless'd,
Refuse his Age the needful hours of Rest?
Punish a Body which he could not please;
Bankrupt of Life, yet Prodigal of Ease?
And all to leave, what with his Toil he won,

170 To that unfeather'd, two Legg'd thing, a Son:
Got, while his Soul did huddled Notions try;
And born a shapeless Lump, like Anarchy.
In Friendship False, Implacable in Hate:
Resolv'd to Ruin or to Rule the State.
To Compass this the Triple Bond he broke;
The Pillars of the public Safety shook.
And fitted *Israel* for a Foreign Yoke.
Then, seiz'd with Fear, yet still affecting Fame,
Usurp'd a Patriot's All-atoning Name.

180 So easy still it proves in Factious Times,

With public Zeal to cancel private Crimes:
How safe is Treason, and how sacred ill,
Where none can sin against the People's Will:
Where Crowds can wink; and no offence be known,
Since in another's guilt they find their own.
Yet, Fame deserv'd, no Enemy can grudge;
The Statesman we abhor, but praise the Judge.
In *Israel*'s Courts ne'er sat an *Abbethdin*
With more discerning Eyes, or Hands more clean:
190   Unbrib'd, unsought, the Wretched to redress;
Swift of Dispatch, and easy of Access.
Oh, had he been content to serve the Crown,
With virtues only proper to the Gown;
Or, had the rankness of the Soil been freed
From Cockle, that oppress'd the Noble seed:
David, for him his tuneful Harp had strung,
And·Heaven had wanted one Immortal song.
But wild Ambition loves to slide, not stand;
And Fortune's Ice prefers to Virtue's Land:
200   *Achitophel*, grown weary to possess
A lawful Fame, and lazy Happiness;
Disdain'd the Golden fruit to gather free,
And lent the Crowd his Arm to shake the Tree.
Now, manifest of Crimes, contriv'd long since,
He stood at bold Defiance with his Prince:
Held up the Buckler of the People's Cause,
Against the Crown; and skulk'd behind the Laws.
The wish'd occasion of the Plot he takes,
Some Circumstances finds, but more he makes.
210   By buzzing Emissaries, fills the ears
Of list'ning Crowds, with Jealousies and Fears
Of Arbitrary Counsels brought to light,
And proves the King himself a *Jebusite*:
Weak Arguments! which yet he knew full well,
Were strong with People easy to Rebel.
For, govern'd by the *Moon*, the giddy *Jews*
Tread the same track when she the Prime renews:
And once in twenty Years, their Scribes Record,

By natural Instinct they change their Lord.
220   *Achitophel* still wants a Chief, and none
Was found so fit as Warlike *Absalom*:
Not, that he wish'd his Greatness to create,
(For Politicians neither love nor hate:)
But, for he knew, his Title not allow'd,
Would keep him still depending on the Crowd:
That Kingly power, thus ebbing out, might be
Drawn to the dregs of a Democracy.
Him he attempts, with studied Arts to please,
And sheds his Venom, in such words as these.

230   'Auspicious Prince! at whose Nativity
Some Royal Planet rul'd the Southern sky;
Thy longing Country's Darling and Desire;
Their cloudy Pillar, and their guardian Fire:
Their second *Moses*, whose extended Wand
Divides the Seas, and shows the promis'd Land:
Whose dawning Day, in every distant age,
Has exercis'd the Sacred Prophets' rage:
The People's Prayer, the glad Diviners' Theme,
The Young Men's Vision, and the Old Men's Dream!
240   Thee, *Saviour*, Thee, the Nation's Vows confess
And, never satisfied with seeing, bless:
Swift, unbespoken Pomps thy steps proclaim,
And stammering Babes are taught to lisp thy Name.
How long wilt thou the general Joy detain,
Starve and defraud the People of thy Reign?
Content ingloriously to pass thy days
Like one of Virtue's Fools that feeds on Praise,
Till thy fresh Glories, which now shine so bright,
Grow Stale and Tarnish with our daily sight.
250   Believe me, Royal Youth, thy Fruit must be
Or gather'd Ripe or rot upon the Tree.
Heav'n has to all allotted, soon or late,
Some lucky Revolution of their Fate;
Whose Motions if we watch and guide with Skill
(For human Good depends on human Will)
Our Fortune rolls as from a smooth Descent,

And from the first Impression takes the Bent;
But, if unseiz'd, she glides away like wind,
And leaves repenting Folly far behind.
Now, now she meets you with a glorious prize,
And spreads her Locks before her as she flies.
Had thus Old *David*, from whose Loins you spring,
Not dar'd, when Fortune call'd him, to be King,
At *Gath* an Exile he might still remain,
And Heaven's Anointing Oil had been in vain.
Let his successful Youth your hopes engage,
But shun th' example of Declining Age:
Behold him setting in his Western Skies,
The Shadows length'ning as the Vapours rise.
He is not now as when on *Jordan*'s Sand
The Joyful People throng'd to see him Land,
Cov'ring the *Beach*, and black'ning all the *Strand*;
But, like the Prince of Angels from his height,
Comes tumbling downward with diminish'd light;
Betray'd by one poor Plot to public Scorn
(Our only blessing since his Curs'd Return);
Those heaps of People which one Sheaf did bind,
Blown off and scatter'd by a puff of Wind.
What strength can he to your Designs oppose,
Naked of Friends, and round beset with Foes?
If *Pharaoh*'s doubtful Succour he should use,
A Foreign Aid would more Incense the *Jews*:
Proud *Egypt* would dissembled Friendship bring,
Foment the War, but not support the King;
Nor would the Royal Party e'er unite
With *Pharaoh*'s Arms t' assist the *Jebusite*;
Or, if they should, their Interest soon would break,
And with such odious Aid make *David* weak.
All sorts of men by my successful Arts,
Abhorring Kings, estrange their alter'd Hearts
From *David*'s Rule: and 'tis the general Cry,
"Religion, Commonwealth, and Liberty."
If you, as Champion of the public Good,
Add to their Arms a Chief of Royal Blood,

What may not *Israel* hope, and what Applause
Might such a General gain by such a Cause?
Not barren Praise alone, that Gaudy Flower
Fair only to the sight, but solid Power;
And Nobler is a limited Command,
300   Giv'n by the Love of all your Native Land,
Than a Successive Title, Long, and Dark,
Drawn from the Mouldy Rolls of *Noah*'s Ark.'
    What cannot Praise effect in Mighty Minds,
When Flattery Sooths, and when Ambition Blinds!
Desire of Power, on Earth a Vicious Weed,
Yet, sprung from High, is of Celestial Seed:
In God 'tis Glory; and when men Aspire
'Tis but a Spark too much of Heav'nly Fire.
Th' Ambitious Youth, too Covetous of Fame,
310   Too full of Angel's Metal in his Frame,
Unwarily was led from Virtue's ways;
Made Drunk with Honour, and Debauch'd with Praise.
Half loath, and half consenting to the Ill
(For Loyal Blood within him struggled still),
He thus replied: 'And what Pretence have I
To take up Arms for Public Liberty?
My Father Governs with unquestion'd Right,
The Faith's Defender, and Mankind's Delight;
Good, Gracious, Just, observant of the Laws;
320   And Heav'n by Wonders has Espous'd his Cause.
Whom has he Wrong'd in all his Peaceful Reign?
Who sues for Justice to his Throne in Vain?
What Millions has he Pardon'd of his Foes,
Whom Just Revenge did to his Wrath expose?
Mild, Easy, Humble, Studious of our Good;
Inclin'd to Mercy, and averse from Blood.
If Mildness Ill with Stubborn *Israel* Suit,
His Crime is God's beloved Attribute.
What could he gain, his People to Betray,
330   Or change his Right for Arbitrary Sway?
Let Haughty *Pharaoh* Curse with such a Reign
His Fruitful *Nile*, and Yoke a Servile Train.

98

If *David*'s Rule *Jerusalem* Displease,
The *Dog-star* heats their Brains to this Disease.
Why then should I, Encouraging the Bad,
Turn Rebel and run Popularly Mad?
Were he a Tyrant who, by Lawless Might,
Oppress'd the *Jews* and Rais'd the *Jebusite*,
Well might I Mourn; but Nature's Holy Bands
340   Would Curb my Spirits and Restrain my Hands:
The People might assert their Liberty,
But what was Right in them were Crime in me.
His Favour leaves me nothing to require;
Prevents my Wishes, and outruns Desire.
What more can I expect while *David* lives?
All but his Kingly Diadem he gives;
And that—'but there he Paus'd; then Sighing, said,
'Is Justly Destin'd for a Worthier Head;
For when my Father from his Toils shall Rest
350   And late Augment the Number of the Bless'd,
His Lawful Issue shall the Throne ascend,
Or the *Collateral* Line, where that shall end.
His Brother, though Oppress'd with Vulgar Spite,
Yet Dauntless and Secure of Native Right,
Of every Royal Virtue stands possess'd;
Still Dear to all the Bravest and the Best.
His Courage Foes, his Friends his Truth Proclaim,
His Loyalty the King, the World his Fame.
His Mercy even th' Offending Crowd will find,
360   For sure he comes of a Forgiving Kind.
Why should I then repine at Heaven's Decree,
Which gives me no Pretence to Royalty?
Yet Oh that Fate, Propitiously Inclin'd,
Had rais'd my Birth, or had debas'd my Mind;
To my large Soul not all her Treasure lent
And then Betray'd it to a mean Descent.
I find, I find my mounting Spirits Bold,
And *David*'s Part disdains my Mother's Mould.
Why am I Scanted by a Niggard Birth?
370   My Soul Disclaims the Kindred of her Earth,

And, made for Empire, Whispers me within.
"Desire of Greatness is a Godlike Sin." '
   Him Staggering so when Hell's dire Agent found,
While fainting Virtue scarce maintain'd her Ground,
He pours fresh Forces in, and thus Replies:
   'Th' Eternal God, Supremely Good and Wise,
Imparts not these Prodigious Gifts in vain:
What Wonders are Reserv'd to bless your Reign?
Against your will your Arguments have shown

380   Such Virtue's only given to guide a Throne.
Not that your Father's Mildness I contemn,
But Manly Force becomes the Diadem.
'Tis true, he grants the People all they crave,
And more perhaps than Subjects ought to have:
For Lavish grants suppose a Monarch tame,
And more his Goodness than his Wit proclaim.
But when should People strive their Bonds to break
If not when Kings are Negligent or Weak?
Let him give on till he can give no more,

390   The Thrifty Sanhedrin shall keep him poor;
And every Shekel which he can receive
Shall cost a Limb of his Prerogative.
To ply him with new Plots shall be my care,
Or plunge him deep in some Expensive War;
Which, when his Treasure can no more Supply,
He must with the Remains of Kingship buy.
His faithful Friends our Jealousies and Fears
Call *Jebusites*, and *Pharaoh*'s Pensioners;
Whom when our Fury from his Aid has torn,

400   He shall be Naked left to public Scorn.
The next Successor, whom I fear and hate,
My Arts have made Obnoxious to the State;
Turn'd all his Virtues to his Overthrow,
And gain'd our Elders to pronounce a Foe.
His Right, for Sums of necessary Gold,
Shall first be Pawn'd, and afterwards be Sold;
Till time shall Ever-wanting *David* draw
To pass your doubtful Title into Law.

If not, the People have a Right Supreme
To make their Kings; for Kings are made for them.
All Empire is no more than Power in Trust,
Which, when resum'd, can be no longer Just.
Succession for the general Good design'd,
In its own wrong a Nation cannot bind:
If altering that, the People can relieve,
Better one Suffer, than a Nation grieve.
The *Jews* well know their power: ere *Saul* they Chose,
God was their King, and God they durst depose.
Urge now your Piety, your Filial Name,
A Father's Right, and fear of future Fame;
The public Good, that Universal Call,
To which even Heav'n Submitted, answers all.
Nor let his Love Enchant your generous Mind;
'Tis Nature's trick to Propagate her Kind.
Our fond Begetters, who would never die,
Love but themselves in their Posterity.
Or let his Kindness by th' Effects be tried,
Or let him lay his vain Pretence aside.
God said he lov'd your Father; could he bring
A better Proof than to Anoint him King?
It surely show'd he lov'd the Shepherd well,
Who gave so fair a Flock as *Israel*.
Would *David* have you thought his Darling Son?
What means he then to Alienate the Crown?
The name of Godly he may blush to bear:
'Tis after God's own heart to Cheat his Heir.
He to his Brother gives Supreme Command;
To you a Legacy of Barren Land:
Perhaps th' old Harp, on which he thrums his Lays,
Or some dull *Hebrew* Ballad in your Praise.
Then the next Heir, a Prince Severe and Wise,
Already looks on you with Jealous Eyes;
Sees through the thin Disguises of your Arts,
And marks your Progress in the People's Hearts.
Though now his mighty Soul its Grief contains,
He meditates Revenge who least Complains.

And like a Lion, Slumb'ring in the way,
Or Sleep-dissembling, while he waits his Prey,
His fearless Foes within his Distance draws;
450   Constrains his Roaring, and Contracts his Paws;
Till at the last, his time for Fury found,
He shoots with sudden Vengeance from the Ground:
The Prostrate Vulgar passes o'er and Spares,
But with a Lordly Rage his Hunters tears.
Your Case no tame Expedients will afford;
Resolve on Death, or Conquest by the Sword,
Which for no less a Stake than Life you Draw;
And Self-defence is Nature's Eldest Law.
Leave the warm People no Considering time;
460   For then Rebellion may be thought a Crime.
Prevail yourself of what Occasion gives,
But try your Title while your Father lives:
And that your Arms may have a fair Pretence,
Proclaim you take them in the King's Defence:
Whose Sacred Life each minute would Expose
To Plots, from seeming Friends, and secret Foes.
And who can sound the depth of *David*'s Soul?
Perhaps his fear his kindness may Control.
He fears his Brother, though he loves his Son,
470   For plighted Vows too late to be undone.
If so, by Force he wishes to be gain'd,
Like women's Lechery, to seem Constrain'd:
Doubt not, but, when he most affects the Frown,
Commit a pleasing Rape upon the Crown.
Secure his Person to secure your Cause:
They who possess the Prince, possess the Laws.'
  He said, and this Advice above the rest,
With *Absalom*'s Mild nature suited best;
Unblam'd of Life (Ambition set aside),
480   Not stain'd with Cruelty, nor puff'd with Pride;
How happy had he been, if Destiny
Had higher plac'd his Birth, or not so high!
His Kingly Virtues might have claim'd a Throne,
And blest all other Countries but his own:

But charming Greatness since so few refuse,
'Tis juster to Lament him than Accuse.
Strong were his hopes a Rival to remove,
With blandishments to gain the public Love;
To Head the Faction while their Zeal was hot,
And Popularly prosecute the Plot.
To further this, *Achitophel* Unites
The Malcontents of all the *Israelites*;
Whose differing Parties he could wisely Join,
For several Ends, to serve the same Design.
The Best, and of the Princes some were such,
Who thought the power of Monarchy too much:
Mistaken Men, and Patriots in their Hearts;
Not Wicked, but Seduc'd by Impious Arts.
By these the Springs of Property were bent,
And wound so high they Crack'd the Government.
The next for Interest sought t' embroil the State,
To sell their Duty at a dearer rate;
And make their *Jewish* Markets of the Throne,
Pretending public Good, to serve their own.
Others thought Kings an useless heavy Load,
Who Cost too much, and did too little Good.
These were for laying Honest *David* by,
On principles of pure good Husbandry.
With them Join'd all th' Haranguers of the Throng,
That thought to get Preferment by the Tongue.
Who follow next a double Danger bring,
Not only hating *David*, but the King,
The *Solymaean* Rout, well Vers'd of old
In Godly Faction, and in Treason bold,
Cow'ring and Quaking at a Conqueror's Sword,
But Lofty to a Lawful Prince Restor'd,
Saw with Disdain an *Ethnic* Plot begun
And Scorn'd by *Jebusites* to be Outdone.
Hot *Levites* Headed these; who, pull'd before
From th' *Ark*, which in the Judges' days they bore,
Resum'd their Cant, and with a Zealous Cry,
Pursu'd their old belov'd Theocracy.

490

500

510

520

Where Sanhedrin and Priest enslav'd the Nation,
And justified their Spoils by Inspiration;
For who so fit for Reign as *Aaron*'s Race,
If once Dominion they could found in Grace?
These led the Pack; though not of surest scent,
Yet deepest mouth'd against the Government.
A numerous Host of dreaming Saints succeed;
530   Of the true old Enthusiastic breed:
'Gainst Form and Order they their Power employ;
Nothing to Build and all things to Destroy.
But far more numerous was the herd of such,
Who think too little, and who talk too much.
These, out of mere instinct, they knew not why,
Ador'd their fathers' God, and Property:
And, by the same blind benefit of Fate,
The Devil and the *Jebusite* did hate:
Born to be sav'd, even in their own despite,
540   Because they could not help believing right.
Such were the tools; but a whole Hydra more
Remains, of sprouting heads too long to score.
    Some of their Chiefs were Princes of the Land:
In the first Rank of these did *Zimri* stand:
A man so various, that he seem'd to be
Not one, but all Mankind's Epitome.
Stiff in Opinions, always in the wrong;
Was everything by starts, and nothing long:
But, in the course of one revolving Moon,
550   Was Chemist, Fiddler, Statesman, and Buffoon:
Then all for Women, Painting, Rhyming, Drinking;
Besides ten thousand freaks that died in thinking.
Bless'd Madman, who could every hour employ,
With something New to wish, or to enjoy!
Railing and praising were his usual Themes;
And both (to show his Judgment) in Extremes:
So over Violent, or over Civil,
That every man, with him, was God or Devil.
In squand'ring Wealth was his peculiar Art:
560   Nothing went unrewarded, but Desert.

Beggar'd by Fools, whom still he found too late;
He had his Jest, and they had his Estate.
He laugh'd himself from Court, then sought Relief
By forming Parties, but could n'er be Chief:
For, spite of him, the weight of Business fell
On *Absalom* and wise *Achitophel*:
Thus, wicked but in will, of means bereft,
He left not Faction, but of that was left.

    Titles and Names 'twere tedious to Rehearse
570   Of Lords, below the Dignity of Verse.
Wits, warriors, Commonwealth's-men, were the best:
Kind Husbands and mere Nobles all the rest.
And, therefore, in the name of Dullness, be
The well-hung *Balaam* and cold *Caleb* free.
And Canting *Nadab* let Oblivion damn,
Who made new porridge for the Paschal Lamb.
Let Friendship's holy band some Names assure:
Some their own Worth, and some let Scorn secure.
Nor shall the Rascal Rabble here have Place,
580   Whom Kings no Titles gave, and God no Grace:
Not Bull-fac'd *Jonas*, who could Statutes draw
To mean Rebellion, and make Treason Law.
But he, though bad, is follow'd by a worse,
The wretch who Heav'n's Anointed dar'd to Curse.
Shimei, whose Youth did early Promise bring
Of Zeal to God and Hatred to his King;
Did wisely from Expensive Sins refrain,
And never broke the Sabbath, but for Gain:
Nor ever was he known an Oath to vent,
590   Or Curse unless against the Government.
Thus, heaping Wealth by the most ready way
Among the *Jews*, which was to Cheat and Pray;
The City, to reward his pious Hate
Against his Master, chose him Magistrate:
His Hand a Vare of Justice did uphold;
His Neck was loaded with a Chain of Gold.
During his Office, Treason was no Crime.
The Sons of *Belial* had a glorious Time:

For *Shimei*, though not prodigal of pelf,
600   Yet lov'd his wicked Neighbour as himself:
When two or three were gather'd to declaim
Against the Monarch of *Jerusalem*,
Shimei was always in the midst of them.
And, if they Curs'd the King when he was by,
Would rather Curse, than break good Company.
If any durst his Factious Friends accuse,
He pack'd a Jury of dissenting *Jews*:
Whose fellow-feeling, in the godly Cause,
Would free the suff'ring Saint from Human Laws.
610   For Laws are only made to Punish those,
Who serve the King, and to protect his Foes.
If any leisure time he had from Power,
(Because 'tis Sin to misemploy an hour;)
His business was, by Writing, to Persuade,
That Kings were Useless, and a Clog to Trade:
And, that his noble Style he might refine,
No *Rechabite* more shunn'd the fumes of Wine.
Chaste were his Cellars, and his Shrieval Board
The Grossness of a City Feast abhorr'd:
620   His Cooks, with long disuse, their Trade forgot;
Cool was his Kitchen, though his Brains were hot.
Such frugal Virtue Malice may accuse,
But sure 'twas necessary to the *Jews*:
For Towns once burnt, such Magistrats require
As dare not tempt God's Providence by fire.
With Spiritual food he fed his Servants well,
But free from flesh, that made the *Jews* Rebel:
And *Moses*'s Laws he held in more account,
For forty days of Fasting in the Mount.
630   To speak the rest, who better are forgot,
Would tire a well-breath'd Witness of the Plot:
Yet, *Corah*, thou shalt from Oblivion pass;
Erect thyself, thou Monumental Brass:
High as the Serpent of thy metal made,
While Nations stand secure beneath thy shade.
What though his Birth were base, yet Comets rise

From Earthy Vapours ere they shine in Skies.
Prodigious Actions may as well be done
By Weaver's issue, as by Prince's Son.
640　This Arch-Attestor for the Public Good,
By that one Deed Ennobles all his Blood.
Who ever ask'd the Witnesses' high race,
Whose Oath with Martyrdom did *Stephen* grace?
Ours was a *Levite*, and as times went then,
His Tribe were God Almighty's Gentlemen.
Sunk were his Eyes, his Voice was harsh and loud,
Sure signs he neither Choleric was, nor Proud:
His long Chin prov'd his Wit; his Saintlike Grace
A Church Vermilion, and a *Moses*'s Face;
650　His Memory, miraculously great,
Could Plots, exceeding man's belief, repeat;
Which therefore cannot be accounted Lies,
For human Wit could never such devise.
Some future Truths are mingled in his Book;
But where the witness fail'd the Prophet Spoke:
Some things like Visionary flights appear;
The Spirit caught him up, the Lord knows where:
And gave him his *Rabbinical* degree
Unknown to Foreign University.
660　His Judgment yet his Memory did excel;
Which piec'd his wondrous Evidence so well,
And suited to the temper of the times;
Then groaning under *Jebusitic* Crimes.
Let *Israel*'s foes suspect his heav'nly call,
And rashly judge his Writ Apocryphal;
Our Laws for such affronts have forfeits made:
He takes his life, who takes away his trade.
Were I myself in witness *Corah*'s place,
The wretch who did me such a dire disgrace,
670　Should whet my memory, though once forgot,
To make him an Appendix of my Plot.
His Zeal to heav'n, made him his Prince despise,
And load his person with indignities:
But Zeal peculiar privilege affords;

107

Indulging latitude to deeds and words.
And *Corah* might for *Agag*'s murder call,
In terms as coarse as *Samuel* used to *Saul*.
What others in his Evidence did Join,
(The best that could be had for love or coin,)
680   In *Corah*'s own predicament will fall:
For *witness* is a Common Name to all.
    Surrounded thus with Friends of every sort,
Deluded *Absalom* forsakes the Court:
Impatient of high hopes, urg'd with renown,
And Fir'd with near possession of a Crown:
Th' admiring Crowd are dazzled with surprise,
And on his goodly person feed their eyes:
His joy conceal'd, he sets himself to show;
On each side bowing popularly low:
690   His looks, his gestures, and his words he frames,
And with familiar ease repeats their Names.
Thus, form'd by Nature, furnish'd out with Arts,
He glides unfelt into their secret hearts:
Then with a kind compassionating look,
And sighs, bespeaking pity ere he spoke,
Few words he said; but easy those and fit:
More slow than Hybla drops, and far more sweet.
    'I mourn, my Countrymen, your lost Estate;
Though far unable to prevent your fate:
700   Behold a Banished man, for your dear cause
Expos'd a prey to Arbitrary laws!
Yet oh! that I alone could be undone,
Cut off from Empire, and no more a Son!
Now all your Liberties a spoil are made;
Egypt and *Tyrus* intercept your Trade,
And *Jebusites* your Sacred Rites invade.
My Father, whom with reverence yet I name,
Charm'd into Ease, is careless of his Fame:
And, brib'd with petty sums of Foreign Gold,
710   Is grown in *Bathsheba*'s Embraces old:
Exalts his Enemies, his Friends destroys:
And all his power against himself employs.

108

He gives, and let him give my right away:
But why should he his own, and yours betray?
He only, he can make the Nation bleed,
And he alone from my revenge is freed.
Take then my tears (with that he wip'd his Eyes)
'Tis all the Aid my present power supplies:
No Court Informer can these Arms accuse,
720   These Arms may Sons against their Fathers use,
And 'tis my wish the next Successor's Reign
May make no other *Israelite* complain.'
    Youth, Beauty, Graceful Action, seldom fail:
But Common Interest always will prevail:
And pity never Ceases to be shown
To him, who makes the people's wrongs his own.
The Crowd (that still believe their Kings oppress)
With lifted hands their young *Messiah* bless:
Who now begins his Progress to ordain;
730   With Chariots, Horsemen, and a numerous train:
From East to West his Glories he displays:
And, like the Sun, the promis'd land surveys.
Fame runs before him, as the morning Star;
And shouts of Joy salute him from afar:
Each house receives him as a Guardian God;
And Consecrates the Place of his abode:
But hospitable treats did most Commend
Wise *Issachar*, his wealthy western friend.
This moving Court, that caught the people's Eyes,
740   And seem'd but Pomp, did other ends disguise:
Achitophel had form'd it, with intent
To sound the depths, and fathom where it went,
The People's hearts; distinguish Friends from Foes;
And try their strength, before they came to blows:
Yet all was colour'd with a smooth pretence
Of specious love, and duty to their Prince.
Religion, and Redress of Grievances,
Two names, that always cheat and always please,
Are often urg'd; and good King *David*'s life
750   Endanger'd by a Brother and a Wife.

Thus, in a Pageant Show, a Plot is made;
And Peace itself is War in Masquerade.
Oh foolish *Israel*! never warn'd by ill,
Still the same bait, and circumvented still!
Did ever men forsake their present ease,
In midst of health Imagine a disease;
Take pains Contingent mischiefs to foresee,
Make Heirs for Monarchs, and for God decree?
What shall we think! can People give away
760 Both for themselves and Sons, their Native sway?
Then they are left Defenceless, to the Sword
Of each unbounded Arbitrary Lord:
And Laws are vain, by which we Right enjoy,
If Kings unquestion'd can those laws destroy.
Yet, if the Crowd be Judge of fit and Just,
And Kings are only Officers in trust,
Then this resuming Cov'nant was declar'd
When Kings were made, or is for ever barr'd:
If those who gave the Sceptre, could not tie
770 By their own deed their own Posterity,
How then could *Adam* bind his future Race?
How could his forfeit on mankind take place?
Or how could heavenly Justice damn us all,
Who ne'er consented to our Father's fall?
Then Kings are slaves to those whom they Command,
And Tenants to their People's pleasure stand.
Add, that the Power for Property allow'd,
Is mischievously seated in the Crowd:
For who can be secure of private Right,
780 If Sovereign sway may be dissolv'd by might?
Nor is the People's Judgment always true:
The most may err as grossly as the few.
And faultless Kings run down, by Common Cry,
For Vice, Oppression, and for Tyranny.
What Standard is there in a fickle rout,
Which, flowing to the mark, runs faster out?
Nor only Crowds, but Sanhedrins may be
Infected with this public Lunacy:

And Share the madness of Rebellious times,
790 To Murder Monarchs for Imagin'd crimes.
If they may Give and Take whene'er they please,
Not Kings alone (the Godhead's Images,)
But Government itself at length must fall
To Nature's state; where all have Right to all.
Yet, grant our Lords the People Kings can make,
What Prudent men a settled Throne would shake?
For whatsoe'er their Sufferings were before,
That Change they Covet makes them suffer more.
All other Errors but disturb a State;
800 But Innovation is the Blow of Fate.
If ancient Fabrics nod, and threat to fall,
To Patch the Flaws, and Buttress up the Wall,
Thus far 'tis Duty; but here fix the Mark:
For all beyond it is to touch our Ark.
To change Foundations, cast the Frame anew,
Is work for Rebels who base Ends pursue:
At once Divine and Human Laws control;
And mend the Parts by ruin of the Whole.
The Tampering World is subject to this Curse,
810 To Physic their Disease into a worse.
  Now what Relief can Righteous *David* bring?
How Fatal 'tis to be too good a King!
Friends he has few, so high the Madness grows,
Who dare be such must be the People's Foes:
Yet some there were, ev'n in the worst of days;
Some let me name, and Naming is to praise.
In this short File *Barzillai* first appears;
Barzillai crown'd with Honour and with Years:
Long since, the rising Rebels he withstood
820 In Regions Waste beyond the *Jordan*'s Flood:
Unfortunately Brave to buoy the State;
But sinking underneath his Master's Fate:
In Exile with his Godlike Prince he Mourn'd;
For him he Suffer'd, and with him Return'd.
The Court he practis'd, not the Courtier's art:
Large was his Wealth, but larger was his Heart:

Which well the Noblest Objects knew to choose,
The Fighting Warrior, and Recording Muse.
His Bed could once a Fruitful Issue boast:
Now more than half a Father's Name is lost.
His Eldest Hope, with every Grace adorn'd,
By me (so Heav'n will have it) always Mourn'd,
And always honour'd, snatch'd in Manhood's prime
By' unequal Fates, and Providence's crime;
Yet not before the Goal of Honour won,
All parts fulfill'd of Subject and of Son;
Swift was the Race, but short the Time to run.
O Narrow Circle, but of Power Divine,
Scanted in Space, but perfect in thy Line!
By Sea, by Land, thy Matchless Worth was known;
Arms thy Delight, and War was all thy Own:
Thy force, Infus'd, the fainting *Tyrians* propp'd:
And Haughty *Pharaoh* found his Fortune stopp'd.
O Ancient Honour, O Unconquer'd Hand,
Whom Foes unpunish'd never could withstand!
But *Israel* was unworthy of thy Name:
Short is the date of all Immoderate Fame.
It looks as Heaven our Ruin had design'd,
And durst not trust thy Fortune and thy Mind.
Now, free from Earth, thy disencumbered Soul
Mounts up, and leaves behind the Clouds and Starry Pole:
From thence thy kindred legions mayst thou bring
To aid the guardian Angel of thy King.
Here stop my Muse, here cease thy painful flight;
No Pinions can pursue Immortal height:
Tell good *Barzillai* thou canst sing no more,
And tell thy Soul she should have fled before;
Or fled she with his life, and left this Verse
To hang on her departed Patron's Hearse?
Now take thy steepy flight from heaven, and see
If thou canst find on earth another *He*;
Another He would be too hard to find,
See then whom thou canst see not far behind.
Zadoc the Priest, whom, shunning Power and Place,

PLATE I. *Sir James Thornhill,* The
Glorification of the Protestant
Succession *c. 1710.*
*One of the most splendid examples
of baroque art employed in the
service of party politics. Thornhill,
like Dryden, shows that a political
movement has the approval of
heaven as well as earth. This
painting forms part of the ceiling
decoration of the Painted Hall,
Greenwich.*
*(By courtesy of the Ministry of
Public Buildings and Works)*

PLATE 2. *Claude Lorrain, Aeneas at Delos, 1672.*
This painting of Aeneas's visit to the Temple of Apollo at Delos, from Aeneid Book III, is a good indication of the way in which the later 17th century visualised the classical landscape of Virgil's poem. This is how Dryden may well have pictured the visit to the Temple of Apollo at Cumae, which he describes in the opening section of his translation of book VI of the Aeneid.
(By courtesy of the Trustees of the National Gallery, London)

His lowly mind advanc'd to *David*'s Grace·
With him the *Sagan* of *Jerusalem*,
Of hospitable Soul and noble Stem;
Him of the Western dome, whose weighty sense
Flows in fit words and heavenly eloquence.
870 The Prophets' Sons, by such example led,
To Learning and to Loyalty were bred:
For *Colleges* on bounteous Kings depend,
And never Rebel was to Arts a friend.
To these succeed the Pillars of the Laws,
Who best could plead and best can judge a Cause.
Next them a train of Loyal Peers ascend:
Sharp judging *Adriel* the Muses' friend,
Himself a Muse–in Sanhedrin's debate
True to his Prince; but not a Slave of State.
880 Whom *David*'s love with Honours did adorn,
That from his disobedient Son were torn.
Jotham of piercing wit and pregnant thought,
Endued by nature, and by learning taught
To move Assemblies, who but only tried
The worse awhile, then chose the better side;
Nor chose alone, but turn'd the balance too;
So much the weight of one brave man can do.
Hushai the friend of *David* in distress,
In public storms of manly steadfastness;
890 By foreign treaties he inform'd his Youth;
And join'd experience to his native truth.
His frugal care supplied the wanting Throne,
Frugal for that, but bounteous of his own:
'Tis easy conduct when Exchequers flow,
But hard the task to manage well the low:
For Sovereign power is too depress'd or high,
When Kings are forc'd to sell, or Crowds to buy.
Indulge one labour more, my weary Muse,
For *Amiel*, who can *Amiel*'s praise refuse?
900 Of ancient race by birth, but nobler yet
In his own worth, and without Title great:
The Sanhedrin long time as chief he rul'd,

Their Reason guided and their Passion cool'd;
So dexterous was he in the Crown's defence,
So form'd to speak a Loyal Nation's Sense,
That as their band was *Israel*'s Tribes in small,
So fit was he to represent them all.
Now rasher Charioteers the Seat ascend,
Whose loose Careers his steady Skill commend:
910 They like th' unequal Ruler of the Day,
Misguide the Seasons and mistake the Way;
While he withdrawn at their mad Labour smiles,
And safe enjoys the Sabbath of his Toils.

These were the chief, a small but faithful Band
Of Worthies, in the Breach who dar'd to stand,
And tempt th' united Fury of the Land.
With grief they view'd such powerful Engines bent,
To batter down the lawful Government.
A numerous Faction with pretended frights,
920 In Sanhedrins to plume the Regal Rights.
The true Successor from the Court remov'd:
The Plot, by hireling Witnesses improv'd.
These Ills they saw, and as their Duty bound,
They show'd the King the danger of the Wound:
That no Concessions from the Throne would please,
But Lenitives fomented the Disease:
That *Absalom*, ambitious of the Crown,
Was made the Lure to draw the People down:
That false *Achitophel*'s pernicious Hate,
930 Had turn'd the Plot to Ruin Church and State:
The Council violent, the Rabble worse
That *Shimei* taught *Jerusalem* to Curse.

With all these loads of Injuries oppress'd,
And long revolving, in his careful Breast,
Th' event of things; at last his patience tir'd,
Thus from his Royal Throne by Heav'n inspir'd,
The Godlike *David* spoke: with awful fear
His Train their Maker in their Master hear.

'Thus long have I, by native mercy sway'd,
940 My wrongs dissembl'd, my revenge delay'd:

So willing to forgive th' Offending Age,
So much the Father did the King assuage.
But now so far my Clemency they slight,
Th' Offenders question my Forgiving Right.
That one was made for many, they contend:
But 'tis to Rule, for that's a Monarch's End.
They call my tenderness of Blood, my Fear:
Though Manly tempers can the longest bear.
Yet, since they will divert my Native course,
'Tis time to show I am not Good by Force.
Those heap'd Affronts that haughty Subjects bring,
Are burdens for a Camel, not a King:
Kings are the public Pillars of the State,
Born to sustain and prop the Nation's weight:
If my Young *Samson* will pretend a Call
To shake the Column, let him share the Fall:
But oh, that yet he would repent and live!
How easy 'tis for Parents to forgive!
With how few Tears a Pardon might be won
From Nature, pleading for a Darling Son!
Poor pitied Youth, by my Paternal care,
Rais'd up to all the Height his Frame could bear:
Had God ordain'd his fate for Empire born,
He would have given his Soul another turn:
Gull'd with a Patriot's name, whose Modern sense
Is one that would by Law supplant his Prince:
The People's Brave, the Politicians' Tool:
Never was Patriot yet, but was a Fool.
Whence comes it that Religion and the Laws
Should more be *Absalom*'s than *David*'s Cause?
His old Instructor, ere he lost his Place,
Was never thought endued with so much Grace.
Good Heav'ns, how Faction can a Patriot Paint!
My Rebel ever proves my People's Saint.
Would *They* impose an Heir upon the Throne?
Let Sanhedrins be taught to give their Own.
A King's at least a part of Government,
And mine as requisite as their Consent:

Without my Leave a future King to choose,

980   Infers a Right the Present to Depose.
True, they Petition me t' approve their Choice,
But *Esau*'s Hands suit ill with *Jacob*'s Voice.
My Pious Subjects for my Safety pray,
Which to Secure they take my Power away.
From Plots and Treasons Heaven preserve my years,
But save me most from my Petitioners.
Unsatiate as the barren Womb or Grave;
God cannot Grant so much as they can Crave.
What then is left but with a Jealous Eye

990   To guard the Small remains of Royalty?
The Law shall still direct my peaceful Sway,
And the same Law teach Rebels to Obey:
Votes shall no more Establish'd Power control,
Such Votes as make a Part exceed the Whole:
No groundless Clamours shall my Friends remove,
Nor Crowds have Power to Punish ere they Prove:
For Gods, and Godlike Kings their Care express,
Still to Defend their Servants in distress.
Oh that my Power to Saving were confin'd:

1000   Why am I forc'd, like Heaven, against my mind,
To make Examples of another Kind?
Must I at length the Sword of Justice draw?
Oh curs'd Effects of necessary Law!
How ill my Fear they by my Mercy scan,
Beware the Fury of a Patient Man.
Law they require, let Law then show her Face;
They could not be content to look on Grace,
Her hinder parts, but with a daring Eye
To tempt the terror of her Front, and Die.

1010   By their own arts 'tis Righteously decreed,
Those dire Artificers of Death shall bleed.
Against themselves their Witnesses will Swear,
Till Viper-like their Mother Plot they tear:
And suck for Nutriment that bloody gore
Which was their Principle of Life before.
Their *Belial* with their *Belzebub* will fight;

Thus on my Foes, my Foes shall do me Right:
Nor doubt th' event: for Factious crowds engage
In their first Onset, all their Brutal Rage;
1020   Then, let 'em take an unresisted Course,
Retire and Traverse, and Delude their Force:
But when they stand all Breathless, urge the fight,
And rise upon 'em with redoubled might:
For Lawful Power is still superior found,
When long driven back, at length it stands the ground.'
    He said. Th' Almighty, nodding, gave Consent;
And Peals of Thunder shook the Firmament.
Henceforth a Series of new time began,
The mighty Years in long Procession ran:
1030   Once more the Godlike *David* was Restor'd,
And willing Nations knew their Lawful Lord.

Prologue to the Duchess
on her Return from Scotland

When Factious Rage to cruel Exile, drove
The Queen of Beauty, and the Court of Love;
The Muses Droop'd with their forsaken Arts,
And the sad *Cupids* broke their useless Darts.
Our fruitful Plains to Wilds and Deserts turn'd,
Like *Eden*'s Face when banish'd Man it mourn'd:
Love was no more when Loyalty was gone,
The great Supporter of his Awful Throne.
Love could no longer after Beauty stay,
But wander'd Northward to the verge of day,
As if the Sun and He had lost their way.
But now th' Illustrious Nymph return'd again,
Brings every Grace triumphant in her Train:
The wond'ring *Nereids*, though they rais'd no storm,
Foreslow'd her passage to behold her form:
Some cried a *Venus*, some a *Thetis* pass'd:
But this was not so fair, nor that so chaste.
Far from her sight flew Faction, Strife and Pride:
And Envy did but look on her, and died.
Whate'er we suffer'd from our sullen Fate,
Her sight is purchas'd at an easy rate:
Three gloomy Years against this day were set:
But this one mighty Sum has clear'd the Debt.
Like *Joseph*'s Dream, but with a better doom;
The Famine past, the Plenty still to come.
For her the weeping Heav'ns become serene,
For her the Ground is clad in cheerful green:
For her the Nightingales are taught to sing,
And Nature has for her delay'd the Spring.

118

30　The Muse resumes her long-forgotten Lays,
And Love, restor'd, his Ancient Realm surveys;
Recalls our Beauties, and revives our Plays.
His Waste Dominions peoples once again,
And from Her presence dates his Second Reign.
But awful Charms on her fair Forehead sit,
Dispensing what she never will admit.
Pleasing, yet cold, like *Cynthia*'s silver Beam,
The People's Wonder, and the Poets' Theme.
Distemper'd Zeal, Sedition, canker'd Hate,
40　No more shall vex the Church, and tear the State;
No more shall Faction civil Discords move,
Or only discords of too tender love:
Discord like that of Music's various parts,
Discord that makes the harmony of Hearts,
Discord that only this dispute shall bring,
Who best shall love the Duke, and serve the King.

Mac Flecknoe

All human things are subject to decay,
And, when Fate summons, Monarchs must obey:
This *Flecknoe* found, who, like *Augustus*, young
Was call'd to Empire, and had govern'd long;
In Prose and Verse was own'd, without dispute,
Through all the Realms of *Nonsense*, absolute.
This aged Prince, now flourishing in Peace,
And blest with issue of a large increase,
Worn out with business, did at length debate
To settle the succession of the State;
And, pond'ring which of all his Sons was fit
To Reign and wage immortal War with Wit,
Cry'd, ' 'Tis resolv'd; for Nature pleads that He
Should only rule who most resembles me:
Shadwell alone my perfect image bears,
Mature in dullness from his tender years;
Shadwell alone, of all my Sons, is he
Who stands confirm'd in full stupidity.
The rest to some faint meaning make pretence,
But *Shadwell* never deviates into sense.
Some Beams of Wit on other souls may fall,
Strike through and make a lucid interval;
But *Shadwell*'s genuine night admits no ray,
His rising Fogs prevail upon the Day.
Besides, his goodly Fabric fills the eye,
And seems design'd for thoughtless Majesty;
Thoughtless as Monarch Oaks that shade the plain,
And, spread in solemn state, supinely reign.
Heywood and *Shirley* were but Types of thee,
Thou last great Prophet of Tautology.
Even I, a dunce of more renown than they,
Was sent before but to prepare thy way;

And coarsely clad in *Norwich* Drugget came
To teach the Nations in thy greater name.
My warbling Lute, the Lute I whilom strung
When to King *John* of *Portugal* I sung,
Was but the prelude to that glorious day,
When thou on silver *Thames* did'st cut thy way,
With well-tim'd Oars before the Royal Barge,
40   Swell'd with the Pride of thy Celestial charge;
And big with Hymn, Commander of an Host,
The like was ne'er in *Epsom* Blankets toss'd.
Methinks I see the new *Arion* Sail,
The Lute still trembling underneath thy nail.
At thy well-sharpen'd thumb from Shore to Shore
The Treble squeaks for fear, the Basses roar;
Echoes from *Pissing-Alley Shadwell* call,
And *Shadwell* they resound from *Aston Hall*.
About thy boat the little Fishes throng,
50   As at the Morning Toast that Floats along.
Sometimes, as Prince of thy Harmonious band,
Thou wield'st thy Papers in thy threshing hand.
St André's feet ne'er kept more equal time,
Not ev'n the feet of thy own *Psyche*'s rhyme,
Though they in number as in sense excel;
So just, so like tautology, they fell,
That, pale with envy, *Singleton* forswore
The Lute and Sword which he in Triumph bore,
And vow'd he ne'er would act *Villerius* more.'
60   Here stopp'd the good old *Sire*, and wept for joy
In silent raptures of the hopeful boy.
All arguments, but most his Plays, persuade
That for anointed dullness he was made.

Close to the Walls which fair *Augusta* bind,
(The fair *Augusta* much to fears inclin'd)
An ancient fabric, rais'd t'inform the sight,
There stood of yore, and *Barbican* it hight:
A watch Tower once; but now, so Fate ordains,
Of all the Pile an empty name remains.
70   From its old Ruins Brothel-houses rise,

Scenes of lewd loves and of polluted joys;
Where their vast Courts the Mother-Strumpets keep,
And, undisturb'd by Watch, in silence sleep.
Near these a Nursery erects its head,
Where Queens are form'd, and future Heroes bred;
Where unfledg'd Actors learn to laugh and cry,
Where infant Punks their tender Voices try,
And little *Maximins* the Gods defy.
Great *Fletcher* never treads in Buskins here,
80   Nor greater *Jonson* dares in Socks appear;
But gentle *Simkin* just reception finds
Amidst this Monument of vanish'd minds;
Pure Clinches the suburban Muse affords,
And *Panton* waging harmless War with words.
Here *Flecknoe*, as a place to Fame well known,
Ambitiously design'd his *Shadwell*'s Throne;
For ancient *Dekker* prophesied long since
That in this Pile should Reign a mighty Prince,
Born for a scourge of Wit, and flail of Sense;
90   To whom true dullness should some *Psyches* owe,
But Worlds of *Misers* from his pen should flow;
Humorists and *Hypocrites* it should produce,
Whole *Raymond* families, and Tribes of *Bruce*.

    Now Empress *Fame* had publish'd the Renown
Of *Shadwell*'s Coronation through the Town.
Rous'd by report of Fame, the Nations meet
From near *Bun-Hill*, and distant *Watling-Street*.
No *Persian* Carpets spread th' Imperial way,
But scatter'd Limbs of mangled Poets lay;
100   From dusty shops neglected Authors come,
Martyrs of Pies, and Relics of the Bum.
Much *Heywood, Shirley, Ogilby* there lay,
But loads of *Shadwell* almost chok'd the way.
Bilk'd *Stationers* for Yeomen stood prepar'd,
And *Herringman* was Captain of the Guard.
The hoary Prince in Majesty appear'd,
High on a Throne of his own Labours rear'd.
At his right hand our young *Ascanius* sate,

Rome's other hope, and pillar of the State.
110 His Brows thick fogs, instead of glories, grace,
And lambent dullness play'd around his face.
As *Hannibal* did to the Altars come,
Sworn by his *Sire* a mortal Foe to *Rome*,
So *Shadwell* swore, nor should his Vow be vain,
That he till Death true dullness would maintain,
And, in his father's Right, and Realm's defence,
Ne'er to have peace with Wit, nor truce with Sense.
The King himself the sacred Unction made,
As King by Office, and as Priest by Trade.
120 In his sinister hand, instead of Ball,
He plac'd a mighty Mug of potent Ale;
Love's Kingdom to his right he did convey,
At once his Sceptre and his rule of Sway;
Whose righteous Lore the Prince had practis'd young,
And from whose Loins recorded *Psyche* sprung.
His Temples, last, with Poppies were o'erspread,
That nodding seem'd to consecrate his head.
Just at that point of time, if Fame not lie,
On his left hand twelve reverend *Owls* did fly.
130 So *Romulus*, 'tis sung, by *Tiber*'s *Brook*,
Presage of Sway from twice six Vultures took.
Th' admiring throng loud acclamations make,
And Omens of his future Empire take.
The *Sire* then shook the honours of his head,
And from his brows damps of oblivion shed
Full on the filial dullness. Long he stood, ⎫
Repelling from his Breast the raging God; ⎬
At length burst out in this prophetic mood: ⎭
        'Heavens bless my Son, from *Ireland* let him reign
140 To far *Barbadoes* on the Western main;
Of his Dominion may no end be known,
And greater than his Father's be his Throne.
Beyond *Love's Kingdom* let him stretch his Pen;'
He paus'd, and all the people cry'd, 'Amen.'
Then thus continu'd he: 'My Son, advance
Still in new Impudence, new Ignorance.

Success let others teach, learn thou from me
Pangs without birth and fruitless Industry.
Let *Virtuosos* in five years be Writ,
150 Yet not one thought accuse thy toil of wit.
Let gentle *George* in triumph tread the Stage,
Make *Dorimant* betray, and *Loveit* rage;
Let *Cully, Cockwood, Fopling*, charm the Pit,
And in their folly show the Writer's wit;
Yet still thy fools shall stand in thy defence,
And justify their Author's want of sense.
Let 'em be all by thy own model made
Of dullness, and desire no foreign aid;
That they to future ages may be known,
160 Not Copies drawn, but Issue of thy own.
Nay, let thy men of wit too be the same,
All full of thee, and differing but in name;
But let no alien *Sedley* interpose,
To lard with wit thy hungry *Epsom* prose.
And when false flowers of *Rhetoric* thou would'st cull,
Trust Nature, do not labour to be dull,
But write thy best, and top; and in each line
Sir *Formal's* oratory will be thine:
Sir *Formal*, though unsought, attends thy quill,
170 And does thy *Northern Dedications* fill.
Nor let false friends seduce thy mind to fame
By arrogating *Jonson's* Hostile name.
Let Father *Flecknoe* fire thy mind with praise,
And Uncle *Ogilby* thy envy raise;
Thou art my blood, where *Jonson* has no part:
What share have we in Nature or in Art?
Where did his wit on learning fix a brand,
And rail at Arts he did not understand?
Where made he love in Prince *Nicander's* vein,
180 Or swept the dust in *Psyche's* humble strain?
Where sold he Bargains, "Whip-stitch, kiss my Arse,"
Promis'd a Play and dwindled to a Farce?
When did his Muse from *Fletcher* scenes purloin,
As thou whole *Eth'rege* dost transfuse to thine?

But so transfus'd as Oil on Waters flow,
His always floats above, thine sinks below.
This is thy Province, this thy wondrous way,
New Humours to invent for each new Play:
This is that boasted Bias of thy mind,
190   By which one way, to dullness, 'tis inclined;
Which makes thy writings lean on one side still,
And in all changes that way bends thy will.
Nor let thy mountain belly make pretence
Of likeness; thine's a tympany of sense.
A Tun of Man in thy Large bulk is writ,
But sure thou'rt but a Kilderkin of wit.
Like mine thy gentle numbers feebly creep,
Thy Tragic Muse gives smiles, thy Comic sleep.
With whate'er gall thou sett'st thyself to write,
200   Thy inoffensive Satires never bite
In thy felonious heart though Venom lies,
It does but touch thy *Irish* pen, and dies.
Thy Genius calls thee not to purchase fame
In keen Iambics, but mild Anagram;
Leave writing Plays, and choose for thy command
Some peaceful Province in Acrostic Land.
There thou may'st Wings display and Altars raise,
And torture one poor word Ten thousand ways.
Or, if thou would'st thy different talents suit,
210   Set thy own Songs, and sing them to thy lute.'
He said, but his last words were scarcely heard,
For *Bruce* and *Longvil* had a *Trap* prepar'd,
And down they sent the yet declaiming Bard.
Sinking he left his Drugget robe behind,
Borne upwards by a subterranean wind.
The Mantle fell to the young Prophet's part,
With double portion of his Father's Art.

310   Next these, a Troop of busy Spirits press,
         Of little Fortunes, and of Conscience Less;
         With them the Tribe whose Luxury had drain'd
         Their Banks, in former Sequestrations gain'd:
         Who Rich and Great by past Rebellions grew,
         And long to fish the troubled Streams anew.
         Some future Hopes, some present Payment draws
         To Sell their Conscience and espouse the Cause;
         Such Stipends those vile Hirelings best befit,
         Priests without Grace, and Poets without Wit.
320   Shall that false *Hebronite* escape our Curse,
         Judas, that keeps the Rebels' Pension-Purse,
         Judas, that pays the Treason-writer's Fee,
         Judas, that well deserves his Namesake's Tree;
         Who at *Jerusalem*'s own Gates Erects
         His College for a Nursery of Sects;
         Young Prophets with an early Care secures,
         And with the Dung of his own Arts manures?
         What have the Men of *Hebron* here to do?
         What part in *Israel*'s Promis'd Land have you?
330   Here *Phaleg*, the Lay *Hebronite*, is come,
         'Cause like the rest he could not live at Home;
         Who from his own Possessions could not drain
         An *Omer* even of *Hebronitish* Grain,
         Here Struts it like a Patriot, and talks high
         Of Injur'd Subjects, alter'd Property:
         An Emblem of that buzzing Insect Just,
         That mounts the Wheel, and thinks she raises Dust.
         Can dry Bones live, or *Skeletons* produce

The Vital Warmth of Cuckoldising Juice?
340 Slim *Phaleg* could, and, at the Table fed,
Return'd the grateful product to the Bed.
A Waiting-man to Trav'lling Nobles chose,
He his own Laws would Saucily impose,
Till Bastinado'd back again he went,
To Learn those Manners he to Teach was sent.
Chastis'd, he ought to have retreated Home,
But He reads Politics to *Absalom*.
For never *Hebronite*, though Kick'd and Scorn'd,
To his own Country willingly return'd.
350 – But leaving famish'd *Phaleg* to be fed
And to talk Treason for his daily Bread,
Let *Hebron*, nay let Hell, produce a Man
So made for Mischief as *Ben-Jochanan*.
A *Jew* of Humble Parentage was He,
By Trade a Levite, though of low Degree:
His Pride no higher than the Desk aspir'd,
But for the Drudgery of Priests was hir'd
To Read and Pray in Linen Ephod brave,
And pick up single Shekels from the Grave.
360 Married at last, and finding Charge come faster,
He could not live by God, but chang'd his Master:
Inspir'd by Want, was made a Factious Tool,
They Got a Villain, and we lost a Fool.
Still Violent, whatever Cause he took,
But most against the Party he forsook,
For Renegadoes, who ne'er turn by halves,
Are bound in Conscience to be double Knaves.
So this Prose-Prophet took most monstrous Pains
To let his Masters see he earn'd his Gains.
370 But as the Devil owes all his Imps a Shame,
He chose th' *Apostate* for his proper Theme;
With little Pains he made the Picture true,
And from Reflexion took the Rogue he drew.
A wondrous Work to prove the *Jewish* Nation,
In every Age a Murmuring Generation;
To trace 'em from their Infancy of Sinning,

And show 'em Factious from their First Beginning.
To prove they could Rebel, and Rail, and Mock,
Much to the Credit of the Chosen Flock;
380   A strong Authority which must Convince,
That Saints own no Allegiance to their Prince.
As 'tis a Leading-Card to make a Whore,
To prove her Mother had turn'd up before.
But, tell me, did the Drunken Patriarch Bless
The Son that show'd his Father's Nakedness?
Such Thanks the present Church thy Pen will give,
Which proves Rebellion was so Primitive.
Must Ancient Failings be Examples made?
Then Murderers from *Cain* may learn their Trade.
390   As thou the Heathen and the Saint hast drawn,
Methinks th' Apostate was the better man:
And thy hot *Father* (waiving my respect)
Not of a mother Church, but of a Sect.
And Such he needs must be of thy Inditing,
This Comes of drinking Asses' milk and writing.
If *Balack* should be call'd to leave his place
(As profit is the loudest call of Grace,)
His Temple dispossess'd of one, would be
Replenish'd with seven Devils more by thee.
400   *Levi*, thou art a load, I'll lay thee down,
And show Rebellion bare, without a Gown;
Poor Slaves in metre, dull and addle-pated,
Who Rhyme below ev'n *David*'s Psalms translated.
Some in my Speedy pace I must outrun,
As lame *Mephibosheth* the Wizard's Son;
To make quick way I'll Leap o'er heavy blocks,
Shun rotten *Uzza* as I would the Pox;
And hasten *Og* and *Doeg* to rehearse,
Two Fools that Crutch their Feeble sense on Verse;
410   Who by my Muse, to all succeeding times,
Shall live in spite of their own Dogg'rel Rhymes.
    Doeg, though without knowing how or why,
Made still a blund'ring kind of Melody;
Spurr'd boldly on, and Dash'd through Thick and Thin,

PLATE 3. A. Storck, Anglo–Dutch
Naval Battle, 1666.
One of the best realistic paintings
of the naval war between England
and Holland. The fleets are
delivering a broadside attack in
two parallel lines, the Dutch fleet
being on the left hand side. This
type of engagement is described
in Annus Mirabilis, lines 229–240.
(By courtesy of the National
Maritime Museum, Greenwich)

PLATE 4. *Antonio Verrio*, The Sea
Triumph of Charles II.
*An allegorical representation of
England's naval victories, mingling
history and classical mythology for
purposes of panegyric, as Dryden
does in* Annus Mirabilis.
*(By gracious permission of
Her Majesty the Queen)*

Through Sense and Nonsense, never out nor in;
Free from all meaning, whether good or bad,
And in one word, Heroically mad:
He was too warm on Picking work to dwell,
But Faggoted his Notions as they fell,
And if they Rhymed and Rattled all was well.
Spiteful he is not, though he wrote a Satire,
For still there goes some *thinking* to ill-Nature:
He needs no more than Birds and Beasts to think,
All his occasions are to eat and drink.
If he call Rogue and Rascal from a Garret,
He means you no more Mischief than a Parrot:
The words for Friend and Foe alike were made,
To Fetter 'em in Verse is all his Trade.
For Almonds he'll cry Whore to his own Mother:
And call Young *Absalom* King *David*'s Brother.
Let him be Gallows-Free by my consent,
And nothing suffer since he nothing meant;
Hanging supposes human Soul and Reason,
This Animal's below committing Treason:
Shall he be hang'd who never could Rebel?
That's a preferment for *Achitophel*.
The Woman that Committed Buggery,
Was rightly Sentenc'd by the Law to die;
But 'twas hard Fate that to the Gallows led,
The Dog that never heard the Statute read.
Railing in other Men may be a crime,
But ought to pass for mere instinct in him;
Instinct he follows and no farther knows,
For to write Verse with him is to *Transprose*.
'Twere pity treason at his Door to lay,
Who makes Heaven's gate a Lock to its own Key:
Let him rail on, let his invective muse
Have four and Twenty letters to abuse,
Which if he Jumbles to one line of Sense,
Indict him of a Capital Offence.
In Fireworks give him leave to vent his Spite,
Those are the only Serpents he can write;

420

430

440

450

The height of his Ambition is we know
But to be Master of a Puppet-show:
On that one Stage his works may yet appear,
And a month's Harvest keeps him all the Year.
  Now stop your noses, Readers, all and some,
For here's a tun of Midnight-work to come,
Og from a Treason Tavern rolling home.
460   Round as a Globe, and Liquor'd ev'ry chink,
Goodly and Great he sails behind his Link;
With all this Bulk there's nothing lost in *Og*
For ev'ry inch that is not Fool is Rogue:
A Monstrous mass of foul corrupted matter,
As all the Devils had spew'd to make the batter.
When wine has given him courage to Blaspheme,
He Curses God, but God before Curs'd him;
And if man could have reason none has more,
That made his Paunch so rich and him so poor.
470   With wealth he was not trusted, for Heav'n knew
What 'twas of Old to pamper up a *Jew*;
To what would he on Quail and Pheasant swell,
That ev'n on Tripe and Carrion could rebel?
But though Heav'n made him poor (with rev'rence
        speaking)
He never was a Poet of God's making;
The Midwife laid her hand on his Thick Skull,
With this Prophetic blessing—*Be thou Dull;*
Drink, Swear and Roar, forbear no lewd delight
Fit for thy Bulk, do anything but write:
480   Thou art of lasting Make like thoughtless men,
A strong Nativity—but for the Pen;
Eat Opium, mingle Arsenic in thy Drink,
Still thou may'st live, avoiding Pen and Ink.
I see, I see, 'tis Counsel given in vain,
For Treason botch'd in Rhyme will be thy bane;
Rhyme is the Rock on which thou art to wreck,
'Tis fatal to thy Fame and to thy Neck:
Why should thy Metre good King *David* blast?
A Psalm of his will Surely be thy last.

Dar'st thou presume in verse to meet thy foes,
Thou whom the Penny Pamphlet foil'd in prose?
Doeg, whom God for Mankind's mirth has made,
O'er-tops thy talent in thy very Trade;
Doeg to thee, thy paintings are so Coarse,
A Poet is, though he's the Poet's Horse.
A Double Noose thou on thy Neck dost pull,
For Writing Treason, and for Writing dull;
To die for Faction is a Common evil,
But to be hang'd for Nonsense is the Devil:

Had'st thou the Glories of thy King express'd,
Thy praises had been Satire at the best;
But thou in Clumsy verse, unlick'd, unpointed,
Hast Shamefully defied the Lord's Anointed:
I will not rake the Dunghill of thy Crimes,
For who would read thy Life that reads thy Rhymes?
But of King *David*'s Foes be this the Doom,
May all be like the young man *Absalom*;
And for my Foes may this their Blessing be,
To Talk like *Doeg*, and to Write like Thee.

To my Ingenious Friend,
Mr. Henry Higden, Esq.;
on his translation of
The Tenth Satire of Juvenal

The *Grecian* Wits, who *Satire* first began,
Were Pleasant *Pasquins* on the Life of Man:
At Mighty Villains, who the State oppress'd,
They durst not Rail; perhaps, they Laugh'd at least,
And turn'd 'em out of Office with a Jest.
No Fool could peep abroad, but ready stand
The *Drolls* to clap a *Bauble* in his Hand:
Wise *Legislators* never yet could draw
A *Fop* within the Reach of Common Law;
10   For Posture, Dress, Grimace, and Affectation,
Though Foes to *Sense*, are Harmless to the *Nation*.
Our last Redress is Dint of *Verse* to try;
And *Satire* is our *Court* of *Chancery*.
This Way took *Horace* to reform an Age
Not Bad enough to need an Author's Rage:
But Yours, who liv'd in more degen'rate Times,
Was forc'd to fasten Deep, and worry Crimes:
Yet You, my Friend, have temper'd him so well,
You make him Smile in spite of all his Zeal:
20   An Art peculiar to yourself alone,
To join the Virtues of Two Styles in One.

   Oh! were your Author's Principle receiv'd,
Half of the lab'ring World would be reliev'd;
For not to Wish, is not to be Deceiv'd!
Revenge would into *Charity* be chang'd,
Because it costs too Dear to be *Reveng'd*:
It costs our *Quiet* and *Content of Mind*;

132

And when 'tis compass'd, leaves a Sting behind.
Suppose I had the better End o' th' Staff,
Why should I help th' ill-natur'd World to laugh?
'Tis all alike to them, who gets the Day;
They Love the Spite and Mischief of the Fray.
No; I have Cur'd myself of that *Disease*;
Nor will I be provok'd, but when I please:
But let me half that *Cure* to You restore;
You gave the *Salve*, I laid it to the *Sore*.

Our kind Relief against a Rainy Day, ⎫
Beyond a Tavern, or a tedious Play; ⎬
We take your Book, and laugh our Spleen away. ⎭
If all Your *Tribe* (too studious of *Debate*)
Would cease false Hopes and Titles to create,
Led by the *Rare Example* you begun,
Clients would fail, and *Lawyers* be undone.

To Sir George Etherege

To you who live in chill Degree,
(As Map informs) of Fifty three;
And do not much for Cold atone
By bringing thither Fifty one:
(Methinks) all Climes should be alike,
From Tropic, e'en to Pole Arctic;
Since you have such a Constitution,
As cannot suffer Diminution;
You can be old in grave Debate,
10 And young in Love's Affairs of State,
And both to Wives and Husbands show
The vigour of a Plenipo------
Like mighty Missioner you come,
Ad partes infidelium;
A work of wondrous Merit sure,
So far to go, so much endure,
And all to preach to German Dame,
Where sound of *Cupid* never came.
Less had you done, had you been sent,
20 As far as *Drake*, or *Pinto* went,
For Cloves and Nutmegs to the Line-a,
Or even for Oranges to *China*;
That had indeed been Charity
Where Lovesick Ladies helpless lie
Chopp'd, and for want of Liquor dry;
But you have made your Zeal appear,
Within the Circle of the Bear;
What Region of the World so dull,
That is not of your Labours full.
30 *Triptolemus* (so Sing the Nine)
Strew'd plenty from his Cart Divine;
But (spite of all those Fable-makers)

He never sow'd on Almaine Acres;
No, that was left by fate's Decree,
To be perform'd and sung by thee.
Thou break'st through Forms, with as much Ease
As the French King through Articles;
In grand Affairs thy days are spent
In waging weighty Compliment,
With such as Monarchs represent;
They whom such vast Fatigues attend,
Want some soft minutes to unbend,
To show the World, that now and then
Great Ministers are mortal Men.
Then Rhenish Rummers walk the Round,
In Bumpers every King is Crown'd;
Besides Three holy Mitr'd Hectors,
And the whole College of Electors;
No health of Potentate is sunk,
That pays to make his Envoy Drunk.
These Dutch delights I mention'd last
Suit not, I know, your English Taste,
For Wine, to leave a Whore, or Play,
Was ne'er your Excellency's way;
Nor need the Title give offence,
For here you were his Excellence;
For Gaming, Writing, Speaking, Keeping,
His Excellence for all but sleeping.
Now if you tope in Form, and Treat,
'Tis the sour Sauce, to the sweet Meat,
The Fine you pay for being Great.
Nay, there's a harder Imposition,
Which is (indeed) the Court Petition,
That setting Worldly Pomp aside,
(Which Poet has at Font defied.)
You would be pleas'd in humble way,
To write a trifle call'd a Play:
This truly is, a Degradation,
But would oblige the Crown and Nation,
Next to your Wise Negotiation:

40

50

60

70

If you pretend, as well you may,
Your high Degree, your Friends will say,
The Duke St. *Aignan* made a Play;
If Gallic Peer affect you scarce,
His Grace of B.----- has made a Farce,
And you whose comic Wit is Terse all,
Can hardly fall below Rehearsal.
Then finish what you once began,
But scribble faster if you can;
For yet no George, to our discerning,
E'er Writ without a Ten years warning.

80

A Discourse Concerning the Original and Progress of Satire

And, indeed, a provocation is almost necessary, in behalf of the World ... in relation to a multitude of Scribblers, who daily pester the World with their insufferable Stuff, that they might be discourag'd from Writing any more. I complain not of their Lampoons and Libels, though I have been the Public Mark for many years. I am vindictive enough to have repell'd force by force, if I could imagine that any of them had ever reach'd me; but they either shot at Rovers, and therefore miss'd, or their Powder was so weak, that I might safely stand
10 them, at the nearest distance. I answer'd not the *Rehearsal*, because I knew the Author sat to himself when he drew the Picture, and was the very *Bayes* of his own Farce. Because also I knew, that my Betters were more concern'd than I was in that Satire: and lastly, because Mr *Smith*, and Mr *Johnson*, the main Pillars of it, were two such Languishing Gentlemen in their Conversation, that I could liken them to nothing but to their own Relations, those Noble Characters of Men of Wit and Pleasure about the Town. The like Considerations have hinder'd me from dealing with the lamentable Companions of their
20 Prose and Doggerel. I am so far from defending my Poetry against them, that I will not so much as expose theirs. And for my Morals, if they are not proof against their attacks, let me be thought by Posterity what those Authors would be thought, if any Memory of them or of their Writings could endure so long, as to another Age. But these dull Makers of Lampoons, as harmless as they have been to me, are yet of dangerous Example to the Public. Some Witty Men may perhaps succeed to their Designs, and mixing Sense with Malice, blast the Reputation of the most Innocent amongst Men, and the most Virtuous
30 amongst Women.

Heaven be prais'd, our common Libellers are as free from the imputation of Wit, as of Morality; and therefore whatever Mischief they have design'd, they have perform'd but little of it. Yet these ill Writers, in all justice, ought themselves to be expos'd, as *Persius* has given us a fair Example in his First Satire, which is levell'd particularly at them. And none is so fit to Correct their Faults, as he who is not only clear from any in his own Writings, but is also so just, that he will never defame the good, and is arm'd with the power of Verse, to Punish
40 and make Examples of the bad.

*

Thus, my Lord, I have as briefly as I could, given your Lordship, and by you the World, a rude Draught of what I have been long labouring in my Imagination. And what I had intended to have put in practice (though far unable for the attempt of such a Poem), and to have left the Stage, to which my Genius never much inclin'd me, for a Work which would have taken up my Life in the performance of it. This too, I had intended chiefly for the Honour of my Native Country, to which a Poet is particularly oblig'd. Of two Subjects, both
50 relating to it, I was doubtful, whether I should choose that of King *Arthur* Conquering the *Saxons*, which being farther distant in Time, gives the greater Scope to my Invention: or that of *Edward* the Black Prince in subduing *Spain*, and Restoring it to the Lawful Prince, though a Great Tyrant, *Don Pedro* the Cruel, which for the compass of Time, including only the Expedition of one Year; for the greatness of the Action, and its answerable Event; for the Magnanimity of the English Hero, oppos'd to the Ingratitude of the person whom he restor'd; and for the many Beautiful Episodes, which I had interwoven
60 with the principal Design, together with the Characters of the chiefest *English* Persons; wherein, after *Virgil* and *Spenser*, I would have taken occasion to represent my living Friends and Patrons of the Noblest Families, and also shadow'd the Events of future Ages, in the Succession of our Imperial Line. With these helps, and those of the Machines, which I have mention'd, I might perhaps have done as well as some of my Predecessors, or at least chalk'd out a way, for others to amend my Errors in a like Design. But being encourag'd only with fair Words, by King *Charles* II, my little Salary ill paid, and no
70 prospect of a future Subsistence, I was then Discourag'd in the

beginning of my Attempt; and now Age has overtaken me, and Want, a more insufferable Evil, through the Change of the Times, has wholly disenabl'd me.

*

If we take Satire in the general signification of the Word, as it is us'd in all Modern Languages, for an Invective, 'tis certain that it is almost as old as Verse; and though Hymns, which are praises of God, may be allow'd to have been before it, yet the defamation of others was not long after it. After God had Curs'd *Adam* and *Eve* in Paradise, the Husband and Wife 80 excus'd themselves, by laying the blame on one another, and gave a beginning to those Conjugal Dialogues in Prose, which the Poets have perfected in Verse. The Third Chapter of *Job* is one of the first Instances of this Poem in Holy Scripture: unless we will take it higher, from the latter end of the second, where his Wife advises him to curse his Maker.

This Original, I confess, is not much to the Honour of Satire, but here it was Nature, and that deprav'd. When it became an Art, it bore better Fruit. Only we have learnt thus much already, that Scoffs and Revilings are of the growth of 90 all Nations; and consequently that neither the *Greek* Poets borrow'd from other People their Art of Railing, neither needed the *Romans* to take it from them.

*

In a word, that former sort of Satire, which is known in *England* by the Name of Lampoon, is a dangerous sort of Weapon, and for the most part Unlawful. We have no Moral right on the Reputation of other Men. 'Tis taking from them, what we cannot restore to them. There are only two Reasons, for which we may be permitted to write Lampoons, and I will not promise that they can always justify us. The first is Revenge, 100 when we have been affronted in the same Nature, or have been any ways notoriously abus'd, and can make ourselves no other Reparation. And yet we know, that, in Christian Charity, all Offences are to be forgiven, as we expect the like Pardon for those which we daily commit against Almighty God. And this Consideration has often made me tremble when I was saying our Saviour's Prayer; for the plain Condition of the forgiveness which we beg, is the pardoning of others the Offences which they have done to us. For which Reason I have many times avoided the Commission of that Fault, even when

110 I have been notoriously provok'd. Let not this, my Lord, pass for Vanity in me, for 'tis Truth. More Libels have been written against me, than almost any Man now living: and I had Reason on my side, to have defended my own Innocence. I speak not of my Poetry, which I have wholly given up to the Critics; let them use it as they please; Posterity, perhaps, may be more favourable to me, for Interest and Passion will lie buried in another Age, and Partiality and Prejudice be forgotten. I speak of my Morals, which have been sufficiently aspers'd: that only sort of Reputation ought to be dear to every honest Man,
120 and is to me. But let the World witness for me, that I have been often wanting to myself in that particular; I have seldom answer'd any scurrilous Lampoon, when it was in my power to have expos'd my Enemies: and being naturally vindictive, have suffer'd in silence, and possess'd my Soul in quiet.

Anything, though never so little, which a Man speaks of himself, in my Opinion, is still too much, and therefore I will waive this Subject, and proceed to give the second Reason, which may justify a Poet, when he writes against a particular Person; and that is, when he is become a Public Nuisance.
130 All those, whom *Horace* in his Satires, and *Persius* and *Juvenal* have mention'd in theirs, with a Brand of infamy, are wholly such. 'Tis an Action of Virtue to make Examples of vicious Men. They may and ought to be upbraided with their Crimes and Follies, both for their own amendment, if they are not yet incorrigible, and for the Terror of others, to hinder them from falling into those Enormities, which they see are so severely punish'd in the Persons of others. The first Reason was only an Excuse for Revenge, but this second is absolutely of a Poet's Office to perform. But how few Lampooners are
140 there now living who are capable of this Duty! When they come in my way, 'tis impossible sometimes to avoid reading them. But, good God, how remote they are in common Justice, from the choice of such Persons as are the proper Subject of Satire! And how little Wit they bring, for the support of their injustice! The weaker Sex is their most ordinary Theme, and the best and fairest are sure to be the most severely handled. Amongst Men, those who are prosperously unjust, are Entitled to a Panegyric. But afflicted Virtue is insolently stabb'd with all manner of Reproaches. No Decency is consider'd, no fulsome-
150 ness omitted; no Venom is wanting, as far as dullness can supply

it. For there is a perpetual Dearth of Wit; a Barrenness of good Sense, and Entertainment. The neglect of the Readers will soon put an end to this sort of scribbling. There can be no pleasantry where there is no Wit: no Impression can be made, where there is no Truth for the Foundation. To conclude, they are like the Fruits of the Earth in this unnatural Season. The Corn which held up its Head, is spoil'd with rankness, but the greater part of the Harvest is laid along; and little of good Income and wholesome Nourishment is receiv'd into the Barns.

*

160   How easy it is to call Rogue and Villain, and that wittily! But how hard to make a Man appear a Fool, a Blockhead, or a Knave, without using any of those opprobrious terms! To spare the grossness of the Names, and to do the thing yet more severely, is to draw a full Face, and to make the Nose and Cheeks stand out, and yet not to employ any depth of Shadowing. This is the Mystery of that Noble Trade, which yet no Master can teach his Apprentice. He may give the Rules, but the Scholar is never the nearer in his practice. Neither is it true that this fineness of Raillery is offensive. A witty man is
170 tickl'd while he is hurt in this manner; and a Fool feels it not. The occasion of an Offence may possibly be given, but he cannot take it. If it be granted that in effect this way does more Mischief; that a Man is secretly wounded, and though he be not sensible himself, yet the malicious World will find it for him, yet there is still a vast difference betwixt the slovenly Butchering of a Man, and the fineness of a stroke that separates the Head from the Body, and leaves it standing in its place. A man may be capable, as *Jack Ketch*'s Wife said of his Servant, of a plain piece of Work, a bare Hanging; but to make a Malefactor die sweetly,
180 was only belonging to her Husband. I wish I could apply it to myself, if the Reader would be kind enough to think it belongs to me. The Character of *Zimri* in my *Absalom*, is, in my Opinion, worth the whole Poem. 'Tis not bloody, but 'tis ridiculous enough. And he for whom it was intended, was too witty to resent it as an injury. If I had rail'd, I might have suffer'd for it justly, but I manag'd my own Work more happily, perhaps more dextrously. I avoided the mention of great Crimes, and applied myself to the representing of Blind-sides, and little Extravagances, to which the wittier a Man is, he is generally
190 the more obnoxious. It succeeded as I wish'd; the Jest went round, and he was laugh'd at in his turn who began the Frolic.

The Dedication of the Aeneis

TO THE MOST HONOURABLE
John, Lord Marquess of *Normanby*,
EARL of *MULGRAVE*, &c. AND Knight of
the *Most Noble Order of the Garter*

A Heroic Poem, truly such, is undoubtedly the greatest Work which the Soul of Man is capable to perform. The Design of it, is to form the Mind to Heroic Virtue by Example; 'tis convey'd in Verse, that it may delight, while it instructs. The Action of it is always one, entire, and great. The least and most trivial Episodes, or under-actions, which are interwoven in it, are parts either necessary, or convenient to carry on the main Design. Either so necessary, that without them the Poem must be Imperfect, or so convenient, that no others can be imagin'd
10 more suitable to the place in which they are. There is nothing to be left void in a firm Building; even the Cavities ought not to be fill'd with Rubbish, which is of a perishable kind, destructive to the strength: but with Brick or Stone, though of less pieces, yet of the same Nature, and fitted to the Crannies. Even the least portions of them must be of the Epic kind; all things must be Grave, Majestical, and Sublime. Nothing of a Foreign Nature, like the trifling *Novels*, which *Ariosto* and others have inserted in their Poems. By which the Reader is misled into another sort of Pleasure, opposite to that which is
20 design'd in an Epic Poem. One raises the Soul and hardens it to Virtue, the other softens it again and unbends it into Vice. One conduces to the Poet's aim, the completing of his Work, which he is driving on, labouring and hast'ning in every Line: the other slackens his pace, diverts him from his Way, and locks him up like a Knight Errant in an Enchanted Castle, when he should be pursuing his first Adventure.

*

The shining quality of an Epic Hero, his Magnanimity, his Constancy, his Patience, his Piety, or whatever Characteristical

Virtue his Poet gives him, raises first our Admiration. We are
30 naturally prone to imitate what we admire: and frequent Acts
produce a habit. If the Hero's chief quality be vicious, as for
Example, the Choler and obstinate desire of Vengeance in
Achilles, yet the Moral is Instructive. And besides, we are
inform'd in the very proposition of the *Iliads*, that this anger was
pernicious, that it brought a thousand ills on the *Grecian* Camp.
The Courage of *Achilles* is propos'd to imitation, not his Pride
and Disobedience to his General, nor his brutal Cruelty to his
dead Enemy, nor the selling his Body to his Father. We abhor
these Actions while we read them, and what we abhor we
40 never imitate. The Poet only shows them like Rocks or Quick-
sands, to be shunn'd.

By this Example the Critics have concluded that it is not
necessary the Manners of the Hero should be virtuous. They
are Poetically good if they are of a Piece. Though where a
Character of perfect Virtue is set before us, 'tis more lovely,
for there the whole Hero is to be imitated. This is the *Aeneas*
of our Author: this is that Idea of perfection in an Epic Poem,
which Painters and Statuaries have only in their minds; and
which no hands are able to express. These are the Beauties of a
50 God in a Human Body.

*

Long before I undertook this Work, I was no stranger to
the Original. I had also studied *Virgil*'s Design, his disposition of
it, his Manners, his judicious management of the Figures, the
sober retrenchments of his Sense, which always leaves some-
what to gratify our imagination, on which it may enlarge at
pleasure; but above all, the Elegance of his Expressions, and
the harmony of his Numbers. For, as I have said in a former
Dissertation, the words are in Poetry, what the Colours are
in Painting. If the Design be good, and the Draught be true,
60 the Colouring is the first Beauty that strikes the Eye. *Spenser*
and *Milton* are the nearest in English to *Virgil* and *Horace* in
the Latin; and I have endeavour'd to form my Style by imitating
their Masters. I will farther own to you, my Lord, that my
chief Ambition is to please those Readers, who have discern-
ment enough to prefer *Virgil* before any other Poet in the Latin
Tongue. Such Spirits as he desir'd to please, such would I
choose for my Judges, and would stand or fall by them alone.
Segrais has distinguish'd the Readers of Poetry, according to

their capacity of judging, into three Classes. (He might have said the same of Writers too if he had pleas'd.) In the lowest Form he places those whom he calls *Les Petits Esprits*: such things as are our Upper-Gallery Audience in a Playhouse; who like nothing but the Husk and Rind of Wit; prefer a Quibble, a Conceit, an Epigram, before solid Sense, and Elegant Expression. These are Mob-Readers. If *Virgil* and *Martial* stood for Parliament-Men, we know already who would carry it. But though they make the greatest appearance in the Field, and cry the loudest, the best on 't is, they are but a sort of *French Huguenots*, or *Dutch Boers*, brought over in Herds, but not Naturalis'd: who have not Land of two Pounds *per Annum* in *Parnassus*, and therefore are not privileg'd to Poll. Their Authors are of the same level; fit to represent them on a Mountebank's Stage, or to be Masters of the Ceremonies in a Bear-Garden. Yet these are they who have the most Admirers. But it often happens, to their mortification, that as their Readers improve their Stock of Sense, (as they may by reading better Books, and by Conversation with Men of Judgment,) they soon forsake them. And when the Torrent from the Mountains falls no more, the swelling Writer is reduc'd into his shallow Bed, like the *Mançanares* at *Madrid*, with scarce water to moisten his own Pebbles. There are a middle sort of Readers (as we hold there is a middle state of Souls) such as have a farther insight than the former, yet have not the capacity of judging right; (for I speak not of those who are brib'd by a Party, and know better if they were not corrupted;) but I mean a Company of warm young Men, who are not yet arriv'd so far as to discern the difference betwixt Fustian, or ostentatious Sentences, and the true sublime. These are above liking *Martial*, or *Owen*'s Epigrams, but they would certainly set *Virgil* below *Statius*, or *Lucan*. I need not say their Poets are of the same Paste with their Admirers. They affect greatness in all they write, but 'tis a bladder'd greatness, like that of the vain Man whom *Seneca* describes: an ill habit of Body, full of Humours, and swell'd with Dropsy. Even these too desert their Authors, as their Judgment ripens. The young Gentlemen themselves are commonly misled by their *Pedagogue* at School, their Tutor at the University, or their Governor in their Travels. And many of those three sorts are the most positive Blockheads in the World. How many of those flatulent Writers have I known, who have

144

110   sunk in their Reputation, after Seven or Eight Editions of their
Works? For indeed they are Poets only for young Men. They
had great success at their first appearance, but not being of
God, as a Wit said formerly, they could not stand.

    I have already nam'd two sorts of Judges, but *Virgil* wrote
for neither of them: and by his Example, I am not ambitious
of pleasing the lowest, or the middle form of Readers.

    He chose to please the most Judicious: Souls of the highest
Rank, and truest Understanding. These are few in number,
but whoever is so happy as to gain their approbation, can never
120   lose it, because they never give it blindly. Then they have a
certain Magnetism in their Judgment, which attracts others to
their Sense. Every day they gain some new Proselyte, and in
time become the Church. For this Reason, a well-weigh'd
Judicious Poem, which at its first appearance gains no more
upon the World than to be just receiv'd, and rather not blam'd,
than much applauded, insinuates itself by insensible degrees
into the liking of the Reader. The more he studies it, the more
it grows upon him; every time he takes it up, he discovers some
new Graces in it. And whereas Poems which are produc'd
130   by the vigour of Imagination only, have a gloss upon them at
the first, which Time wears off, the Works of Judgment are
like the Diamond, the more they are polish'd, the more lustre
they receive.

*

    On the whole Matter, I thought fit to steer betwixt the two
Extremes, of Paraphrase, and literal Translation: to keep as
near my Author as I could, without losing all his Graces, the
most Eminent of which are in the Beauty of his words. And those
words, I must add, are always Figurative. Such of these as
would retain their Elegance in our Tongue, I have endeavour'd
140   to graft on it; but most of them are of necessity to be lost,
because they will not shine in any but their own. Virgil has
sometimes two of them in a Line; but the scantiness of our
Heroic Verse is not capable of receiving more than one, and
that too must expiate for many others which have none. Such
is the difference of the Languages, or such my want of skill in
choosing words. Yet I may presume to say, and I hope with as
much reason as the *French* Translator, that taking all the
Materials of this divine Author, I have endeavour'd to make
Virgil speak such *English*, as he would himself have spoken,

150　if he had been born in *England*, and in this present Age. I acknow-
ledge, with *Segrais*, that I have not succeeded in this attempt,
according to my desire, yet I shall not be wholly without
praise, if in some sort I may be allow'd to have copied the
Clearness, the Purity, the Easiness and the Magnificence of his
Style.

The Sixth Book of the Aeneis

The Argument

The Sibyl foretells Aeneas the Adventures he should meet with in Italy. She attends him to Hell; describing to him the various Scenes of that Place, and conducting him to his Father Anchises. Who instructs him in those sublime Mysteries of the Soul of the World, and the Transmigration: And shows him that glorious Race of Heroes, which was to descend from him and his Posterity.

He said, and wept: then spread his Sails before
The Winds, and reach'd at length the *Cumaean* Shore:
Their Anchors dropp'd, his Crew the Vessels moor.
They turn their Heads to Sea; their Sterns to Land;
And greet with greedy Joy th' *Italian* Strand.
Some strike from clashing Flints their fiery Seed;
Some gather Sticks, the kindled Flames to feed:
Or search for hollow Trees, and fell the Woods,
Or trace through Valleys the discover'd Floods.
10 Thus, while their sev'ral Charges they fulfil,
The Pious Prince ascends the sacred Hill
Where *Phoebus* is ador'd; and seeks the Shade,
Which hides from sight, his venerable Maid.
Deep in a Cave the Sibyl makes abode;
Thence full of Fate returns, and of the God.
Through *Trivia*'s Grove they walk; and now behold,
And enter now, the Temple roof'd with Gold.
When *Daedalus*, to fly the *Cretan* Shore,
His heavy Limbs on jointed Pinions bore,
20 (The first who sail'd in Air,) 'tis sung by Fame,
To the *Cumaean* Coast at length he came;
And, here alighting, built this costly Frame.
Inscrib'd to *Phoebus*, here he hung on high
The steerage of his Wings, that cut the Sky:

Then o'er the lofty Gate his Art emboss'd
Androgeos' Death, and Off'rings to his Ghost.
Seven Youths from *Athens* yearly sent, to meet
The Fate appointed by revengeful *Crete*.
And next to those the dreadful Urn was plac'd,
30   In which the destin'd Names by Lots were cast:
The mournful Parents stand around in Tears;
And rising *Crete* against their Shore appears.
There too, in living Sculpture, might be seen
The mad Affection of the *Cretan* Queen:
Then how she cheats her bellowing Lover's Eye:
The rushing leap, the doubtful Progeny,
The lower part a Beast, a Man above,
The Monument of their polluted Love.
Nor far from thence he grav'd the wond'rous Maze;
40   A thousand Doors, a thousand winding Ways;
Here dwells the Monster, hid from Human View,
Not to be found, but by the faithful Clue:
Till the kind Artist, mov'd with Pious Grief,
Lent to the loving Maid this last Relief.
And all those erring Paths describ'd so well,
That *Theseus* conquer'd, and the Monster fell.
Here hapless *Icarus* had found his part;
Had not the Father's Grief restrain'd his Art.
He twice essay'd to cast his Son in Gold;
50   Twice from his Hands he dropp'd the forming Mould.
   All this with wond'ring Eyes *Aeneas* view'd:
Each varying Object his Delight renew'd.
Eager to read the rest, *Achates* came,
And by his side the mad divining Dame; $\Big\}$
The Priestess of the God, *Deiphobe* her Name.
'Time suffers not,' she said, 'to feed your Eyes
With empty Pleasures: haste the Sacrifice.
Seven Bullocks yet unyok'd, for *Phoebus* choose,
And for *Diana* seven unspotted Ewes.'
60   This said, the Servants urge the Sacred Rites;
While to the Temple she the Prince invites.
A spacious Cave, within its farmost part,

Was hew'd and fashion'd by laborious Art,
Through the Hill's hollow sides: before the place,
A hundred Doors a hundred Entries grace:
As many Voices issue; and the sound
Of Sibyl's Words as many times rebound.
Now to the Mouth they come: aloud she cries,
'This is the time, inquire your Destinies.

70 He comes, behold the God!' Thus while she said,
(And shiv'ring at the sacred Entry stayed)
Her Colour chang'd, her Face was not the same,
And hollow Groans from her deep Spirit came.
Her Hair stood up; convulsive Rage possess'd
Her trembling Limbs, and heav'd her lab'ring Breast.
Greater than Human Kind she seem'd to look:
And with an Accent more than Mortal spoke.
Her staring Eyes with sparkling Fury roll;
When all the God came rushing on her Soul.

80 Swiftly she turn'd, and foaming as she spoke,
'Why this Delay,' she cried; 'the Powers invoke.
Thy Prayers alone can open this abode,
Else vain are my Demands, and dumb the God.'
She said no more: the trembling *Trojans* hear;
O'erspread with a damp Sweat, and holy Fear.
The Prince himself, with awful Dread possess'd,
His Vows to great *Apollo* thus address'd.

  'Indulgent God, propitious Power to *Troy*,
Swift to relieve, unwilling to destroy;
90 Directed by whose Hand, the *Dardan* Dart
Pierc'd the proud *Grecian*'s only Mortal part:
Thus far, by Fate's Decrees, and thy Commands,
Through ambient Seas, and through devouring Sands,
Our exil'd Crew has sought th' *Ausonian* Ground:
And now, at length, the flying Coast is found.
Thus far the Fate of *Troy*, from place to place,
With Fury has pursu'd her wand'ring Race:
Here cease ye Powers, and let your Vengeance end,
Troy is no more, and can no more offend.
100 And thou, O sacred Maid, inspir'd to see

149

Th' Event of things in dark Futurity;
Give me, what Heav'n has promis'd to my Fate,
To conquer and command the *Latian* State:
To fix my wand'ring Gods; and find a place
For the long Exiles of the *Trojan* Race.
Then shall my grateful Hands a Temple rear
To the twin Gods, with Vows and solemn Prayer;
And Annual Rites, and Festivals, and Games,
Shall be perform'd to their auspicious Names.
110   Nor shalt thou want thy Honours in my Land,
For there thy faithful Oracles shall stand,
Preserv'd in Shrines: and every Sacred Lay,
Which, by thy Mouth, *Apollo* shall convey.
All shall be treasur'd, by a chosen Train
Of holy Priests, and ever shall remain.
But, oh! commit not they prophetic Mind
To flitting Leaves, the sport of ev'ry Wind:
Lest they disperse in Air our empty Fate:
Write not, but, what the Powers ordain, relate.'
120   Struggling in vain, impatient of her Load,
And lab'ring underneath the pond'rous God,
The more she strove to shake him from her Breast,
With more, and far superior Force he press'd:
Commands his Entrance, and without Control,
Usurps her Organs, and inspires her Soul.
Now, with a furious Blast, the hundred Doors
Ope of themselves; a rushing Whirlwind roars
Within the Cave; and Sibyl's Voice restores.
   'Escap'd the Dangers of the watery Reign,
130   Yet more, and greater Ills, by Land remain.
The Coast so long desir'd (nor doubt th' Event)
Thy Troops shall reach, but having reach'd, repent.
Wars, horrid Wars I view; a field of Blood;
And *Tiber* rolling with a Purple Flood.
Simois nor *Xanthus* shall be wanting there;
A new *Achilles* shall in Arms appear:
And he, too, Goddess-born: fierce *Juno*'s Hate,
Added to hostile Force, shall urge thy Fate.

To what strange Nations shalt not thou resort,
140 Driven to solicit Aid at every Court!
The Cause the same which *Ilium* once oppress'd,
A foreign Mistress, and a foreign Guest.
But thou, secure of Soul, unbent with Woes,
The more thy Fortune frowns, the more oppose.
The dawnings of thy Safety shall be shown,
From whence thou least shalt hope, a *Grecian* Town.'

Thus from the dark Recess, the Sibyl spoke,
And the resisting Air the Thunder broke;
The Cave rebellow'd; and the Temple shook.
150 Th' ambiguous God, who rul'd her lab'ring Breast
In these mysterious Words his Mind express'd:
Some Truths reveal'd, in Terms involv'd the rest.
At length her Fury fell; her foaming ceas'd,
And, ebbing in her Soul, the God decreas'd.
Then thus the Chief: 'No Terror to my view,
No frightful Face of Danger can be new.
Inur'd to suffer, and resolv'd to dare,
The Fates, without my Power, shall be without my Care.
This let me crave, since near your Grove the Road
160 To Hell lies open, and the dark Abode,
Which *Acheron* surrounds, th' unnavigable Flood:
Conduct me through the Regions void of Light,
And lead me longing to my Father's sight.
For him, a thousand Dangers I have sought;
And, rushing where the thickest *Grecians* fought,
Safe on my Back the sacred Burden brought.
He, for my sake, the raging Ocean tried,
And Wrath of Heav'n; my still auspicious Guide;
And bore beyond the strength decrepit Age supplied.
170 Oft since he breathed his last, in dead of Night,
His reverend Image stood before my sight;
Enjoin'd to seek below, his holy Shade;
Conducted there, by your unerring aid.
But you, if pious Minds by Prayers are won,
Oblige the Father, and protect the Son.
Yours is the Power; nor *Proserpine* in vain

Has made you Priestess of her nightly Reign.
If *Orpheus*, arm'd with his enchanting Lyre,
The ruthless King with Pity could inspire;
And from the Shades below redeem his Wife:
If *Pollux*, off'ring his alternate Life,
Could free his Brother; and can daily go
By turns aloft, by turns descend below:
Why name I *Theseus*, or his greater Friend,
Who trod the downward Path, and upward could ascend!
Not less than theirs, from *Jove* my Lineage came:
My Mother greater, my Descent the same.'
So pray'd the *Trojan* Prince; and while he pray'd
His Hand upon the holy Altar laid.

Then thus replied the Prophetess Divine:
'O Goddess-born! of Great *Anchises'* Line;
The Gates of Hell are open Night and Day;
Smooth the Descent, and easy is the Way:
But, to return and view the cheerful Skies;
In this the Task, and mighty Labour lies.
To few great *Jupiter* imparts this Grace:
And those of shining Worth, and Heav'nly Race.
Betwixt those Regions, and our upper Light,
Deep Forests, and impenetrable Night
Possess the middle space: th' Infernal Bounds
Cocytus, with his sable Waves, surrounds.
But if so dire a Love your Soul invades,
As twice below to view the trembling Shades;
If you so hard a Toil will undertake,
As twice to pass th' unnavigable Lake;
Receive my Counsel. In the Neighb'ring Grove
There stands a Tree; the Queen of *Stygian Jove*
Claims it her own; thick Woods, and gloomy Night,
Conceal the happy Plant from Human sight.
One Bough it bears; but, wond'rous to behold;
The ductile Rind, and Leaves, of Radiant Gold;
This, from the vulgar Branches must be torn,
And to fair *Proserpine*, the Present borne:

180

190

200

210

Ere leave be giv'n to tempt the nether Skies:
The first thus rent, a second will arise;
And the same Metal the same room supplies.
Look round the Wood, with lifted Eyes, to see
The lurking Gold upon the fatal Tree:
Then rend it off, as holy Rites command:
220   The willing Metal will obey thy hand,
Following with ease, if, favour'd by thy Fate,
Thou art foredoom'd to view the *Stygian* State:
If not, no labour can the Tree constrain:
And strength of stubborn Arms, and Steel are vain.
Besides you know not, while you here attend
Th' unworthy Fate of your unhappy Friend:
Breathless he lies: and his unburied Ghost,
Depriv'd of Fun'ral Rites, pollutes your Host.
Pay first his Pious Dues: and for the dead,
230   Two sable Sheep around his Hearse be led.
Then, living Turfs upon his Body lay;
This done, securely take the destin'd Way,
To find the Regions destitute of Day.'

    She said: and held her Peace. *Aeneas* went
Sad from the Cave, and full of Discontent;
Unknowing whom the sacred Sibyl meant.
Achates, the Companion of his Breast,
Goes grieving by his side; with equal Cares oppress'd.
Walking, they talk'd, and fruitlessly divin'd
240   What Friend, the Priestess by those Words design'd.
But soon they found an Object to deplore;
Misenus lay extended on the Shore.
Son to the God of Winds; none so renown'd,
The Warrior Trumpet in the Field to sound:
With breathing-Brass to kindle fierce Alarms;
And rouse to dare their Fate, in honourable Arms.
He serv'd great *Hector*; and was ever near;
Not with his Trumpet only, but his Spear.
But, by *Pelides'* Arms, when *Hector* fell,
250   He chose *Aeneas*, and he chose as well.
Swoll'n with Applause, and aiming still at more,

He now provokes the Sea Gods from the Shore;
With Envy *Triton* heard the Martial sound,
And the bold Champion, for his Challenge, drown'd.
Then cast his mangled Carcass on the Strand:
The gazing Crowd around the Body stand.
All weep, but most *Aeneas* mourns his Fate;
And hastens to perform the Funeral state.
In Altar-wise, a stately Pile they rear;
260   The Basis broad below, and top advanc'd in Air.
An ancient Wood, fit for the Work design'd,
(The shady Covert of the Savage Kind)
The *Trojans* found: the sounding axe is plied:
Firs, Pines, and Pitch-Trees, and the tow'ring Pride
Of Forest Ashes, feel the fatal Stroke:
And piercing Wedges cleave the stubborn Oak.
Huge Trunks of Trees, fell'd from the steepy Crown
Of the bare Mountains, roll with Ruin down.
Arm'd like the rest, the *Trojan* Prince appears:
270   And, by his pious Labour, urges theirs.
    Thus while he wrought, revolving in his Mind,
The ways to compass what his Wish design'd,
He cast his Eyes upon the gloomy Grove;
And then with Vows implor'd the Queen of Love.
'Oh may thy Power, propitious still to me,
Conduct my steps to find the fatal Tree,
In this deep Forest; since the Sibyl's Breath
Foretold, alas! too true, *Misenus'* Death.'
Scarce had he said, when full before his sight
280   Two Doves, descending from their Airy Flight,
Secure upon the grassy Plain alight.
He knew his Mother's Birds: and thus he pray'd:
'Be you my Guides, with your auspicious Aid:
And lead my Footsteps, till the Branch be found,
Whose glittering Shadow gilds the sacred Ground:
And thou, great Parent! with Celestial Care,
In this Distress, be present to my Prayer.'
Thus having said, he stopp'd: with watchful sight,
Observing still the motions of their Flight,

What course they took, what happy Signs they show.
They fed, and flutt'ring by degrees withdrew
Still farther from the Place; but still in view.
Hopping, and flying, thus they led him on
To the slow Lake; whose baleful Stench to shun,
They wing'd their Flight aloft; then, stooping low,
Perch'd on the double Tree, that bears the golden Bough.
Through the green Leaves the glitt'ring Shadows glow;
As on the sacred Oak, the wintry Mistletoe:
Where the proud Mother views her precious Brood;

And happier Branches, which she never sow'd.
Such was the glitt'ring; such the ruddy Rind,
And dancing Leaves, that wanton'd in the Wind.
He seiz'd the shining Bough with gripping hold;
And rent away, with ease, the ling'ring Gold.
Then to the Sibyl's Palace bore the Prize.
Meantime, the *Trojan* Troops, with weeping Eyes,
To dead *Misenus* pay his Obsequies.

First, from the Ground, a lofty Pile they rear,
Of Pitch-trees, Oaks, and Pines, and unctuous Fir:

The Fabric's Front with Cypress Twigs they strew;
And stick the sides with Boughs of baleful Yew.
The topmost part, his glitt'ring Arms adorn;
Warm Waters, then, in brazen Cauldrons borne,
Are pour'd to wash his Body, Joint by Joint:
And fragrant Oils the stiffen'd Limbs anoint.
With Groans and Cries *Misenus* they deplore:
Then on a Bier, with Purple cover'd o'er,
The breathless Body, thus bewail'd, they lay:
And fire the Pile, their Faces turn'd away:

(Such reverend Rites their Fathers us'd to pay.)
Pure Oil, and Incense, on the Fire they throw:
And Fat of Victims, which his Friends bestow.
These Gifts, the greedy Flames to Dust devour;
Then, on the living Coals, red Wine they pour:
And last, the Relics by themselves dispose;
Which in a brazen Urn the Priests enclose.
Old *Choryneus* compass'd thrice the Crew;

And dipp'd an Olive Branch in holy Dew;
Which thrice he sprinkl'd round; and thrice aloud
330   Invok'd the dead, and then dismiss'd the Crowd
     But good *Aeneas* order'd on the Shore
A stately Tomb; whose top a Trumpet bore:
A Soldier's Falchion, and a Seaman's Oar.
Thus was his Friend interr'd: and deathless Fame
Still to the lofty Cape consigns his Name.

     These Rites perform'd, the Prince without delay
Hastes to the nether World, his destin'd Way.
Deep was the Cave; and downward as it went
From the wide Mouth, a rocky rough Descent;
340   And here th' access a gloomy Grove defends;
And there th' unnavigable Lake extends.
O'er whose unhappy Waters, void of Light,
No Bird presumes to steer his Airy Flight;
Such deadly Stenches from the depth arise,
And steaming Sulphur, that infects the Skies.
From hence the *Grecian* Bards their Legends make,
And give the name *Avernus* to the Lake.
Four sable Bullocks, in the Yoke untaught,
For Sacrifice the pious Hero brought.
350   The Priestess pours the Wine betwixt their Horns:
Then cuts the curling Hair; that first Oblation burns.
Invoking *Hecate* hither to repair;
(A powerful Name in Hell, and upper Air.)
The sacred Priests with ready Knives bereave
The Beasts of Life; and in full Bowls receive
The streaming Blood: a Lamb to Hell and Night,
(The sable Wool without a streak of white)
Aeneas offers: and, by Fate's decree,
A barren Heifer, *Proserpine* to thee.
360   With Holocausts he *Pluto*'s Altar fills:
Seven brawny Bulls with his own Hand he kills:
Then on the broiling Entrails Oil he pours;
Which, ointed thus, the raging Flame devours.
Late, the Nocturnal Sacrifice begun;
Nor ended, till the next returning Sun.

Then Earth began to bellow, Trees to dance;
And howling Dogs in glimm'ring Light advance;
Ere *Hecate* came: 'Far hence be Souls profane,'
The Sibyl cried, 'and from the Grove abstain.
370 Now, *Trojan*, take the way thy Fates afford:
Assume thy Courage, and unsheathe thy Sword.'
She said, and pass'd along the gloomy Space:
The Prince pursu'd her Steps with equal pace.

Ye Realms, yet unreveal'd to human sight,
Ye Gods, who rule the Regions of the Night,
Ye gliding Ghosts, permit me to relate
The mystic Wonders of your silent State.

Obscure they went through dreary Shades, that led
Along the waste Dominions of the dead:
380 Thus wander Travellers in Woods by Night,
By the Moon's doubtful and malignant Light:
When *Jove* in dusky Clouds involves the Skies;
And the faint Crescent shoots by fits before their Eyes.

Just in the Gate, and in the Jaws of Hell,
Revengeful Cares, and sullen Sorrows dwell;
And pale Diseases, and repining Age;
Want, Fear, and Famine's unresisted rage.
Here Toils, and Death, and Death's half-brother, Sleep,
Forms terrible to view, their Sentry keep:
390 With anxious Pleasures of a guilty Mind,
Deep Frauds before, and open Force behind:
The Furies' Iron Beds, and Strife that shakes
Her hissing Tresses, and unfolds her Snakes.
Full in the midst of this infernal Road,
An Elm displays her dusky Arms abroad;
The God of Sleep there hides his heavy Head:
And empty Dreams on ev'ry Leaf are spread.
Of various Forms unnumber'd Spectres more;
Centaurs, and double Shapes, besiege the Door:
400 Before the Passage horrid *Hydra* stands,
And *Briareus* with all his hundred Hands:
Gorgons, Geryon with his triple Frame;
And vain *Chimaera* vomits empty Flame.

The Chief unsheath'd his shining Steel, prepar'd,
Though seiz'd with sudden Fear, to force the Guard.
Off'ring his brandish'd Weapon at their Face;
Had not the Sibyl stopp'd his eager Pace,
And told him what those empty Phantoms were;
Forms without Bodies, and impassive Air.
410   Hence to deep *Acheron* they take their way;
Whose troubled Eddies, thick with Ooze and Clay,
Are whirl'd aloft, and in *Cocytus* lost:
There *Charon* stands, who rules the dreary Coast:
A sordid God; down from his hoary Chin
A length of Beard descends; uncomb'd, unclean:
His Eyes, like hollow Furnaces on Fire:
A Girdle, foul with grease, binds his obscene Attire.
He spreads his Canvas, with his Pole he steers;
The Freights of flitting Ghosts in his thin Bottom bears.
420   He look'd in Years; yet in his Years were seen
A youthful Vigour, and Autumnal green.
An Airy Crowd came rushing where he stood;
Which fill'd the Margin of the fatal Flood.
Husbands and Wives, Boys and unmarried Maids;
And mighty Heroes' more Majestic Shades.
And Youths, entomb'd before their Fathers' Eyes,
With hollow Groans, and Shrieks, and feeble Cries:
Thick as the Leaves in Autumn strew the Woods:
Or Fowls, by Winter forc'd, forsake the Floods,
430   And wing their hasty flight to happier Lands: ⎫
Such, and so thick, the shiv'ring Army stands: ⎬
And press for passage with extended hands.   ⎭

    Now these, now those, the surly Boatman bore:
The rest he drove to distance from the Shore.
The Hero, who beheld with wond'ring Eyes,
The Tumult mix'd with Shrieks, Laments, and Cries;
Ask'd of his Guide, what the rude Concourse meant?
Why to the Shore the thronging People bent?
What Forms of Law, among the Ghosts were us'd?
440   Why some were ferried o'er, and some refus'd?
    'Son of *Anchises*, Offspring of the Gods,'

The Sibyl said; 'you see the *Stygian* Floods,
The Sacred Stream, which Heav'n's Imperial State
Attests in Oaths, and fears to violate.
The Ghosts rejected, are th' unhappy Crew
Depriv'd of Sepulchres, and Fun'ral due.
The Boatman *Charon*; those, the bury'd host,
He Ferries over to the Farther Coast.
Nor dares his Transport Vessel cross the Waves,
450   With such whose Bones are not compos'd in Graves.
A hundred years they wander on the Shore,
At length, their Penance done, are wafted o'er.'
 The *Trojan* Chief his forward pace repress'd;
Revolving anxious Thoughts within his Breast.
He saw his Friends, who whelm'd beneath the Waves,
Their Fun'ral Honours claim'd, and ask'd their quiet Graves.
The lost *Leucaspis* in the Crowd he knew;
And the brave Leader of the *Lycian* Crew:
Whom on the *Tyrrhene* Seas, the Tempests met;
460   The Sailors master'd, and the Ship o'erset.
Amidst the Spirits *Palinurus* press'd;
Yet fresh from life; a new admitted Guest.
Who, while he steering view'd the Stars, and bore
His Course from *Afric*, to the *Latian* Shore,
Fell headlong down. The *Trojan* fix'd his view;
And scarcely through the gloom the sullen Shadow knew.
Then thus the Prince, 'What envious Power, O Friend,
Brought your lov'd life to this disastrous end?
For *Phoebus*, ever true in all he said,
470   Has, in your fate alone, my Faith betray'd.
The God foretold you should not die, before
You reach'd, secure from Seas, th' *Italian* Shore.
Is this th' unerring Power?' The Ghost replied,
'Nor *Phoebus* flatter'd, nor his Answers lied;
Nor envious Gods have sent me to the Deep:
But while the Stars, and course of Heav'n I keep,
My wearied Eyes were seiz'd with fatal sleep.
I fell; and with my weight, the Helm constrain'd,
Was drawn along, which yet my grip retain'd.

480   Now by the Winds, and raging Waves, I swear,
      Your Safety, more than mine, was then my Care:
      Lest, of the Guide bereft, the Rudder lost,
      Your Ship should run against the rocky Coast.
      Three blust'ring Nights, borne by the Southern blast,
      I floated; and discover'd Land at last:
      High on a Mounting Wave, my head I bore:
      Forcing my Strength, and gath'ring to the Shore:
      Panting, but past the danger, now I seiz'd
      The Craggy Cliffs, and my tir'd Members eas'd:
490   While, cumber'd with my dropping Clothes, I lay,
      The cruel Nation, covetous of Prey,
      Stain'd with my Blood th' unhospitable Coast:
      And now, by Winds and Waves, my lifeless Limbs are toss'd.
      Which O avert, by yon Etherial Light
      Which I have lost, for this eternal Night:
      Or if by dearer ties you may be won,
      By your dead Sire, and by your living Son,
      Redeem from this Reproach my wand'ring Ghost;
      Or with your Navy seek the *Velin* Coast:
500   And in a peaceful Grave my Corpse compose:
      Or, if a nearer way your Mother shows,
      Without whose Aid you durst not undertake
      This frightful Passage o'er the *Stygian* Lake;
      Lend to this Wretch your Hand, and waft him o'er
      To the sweet Banks of yon forbidden Shore.'
      Scarce had he said, the Prophetess began;
      'What Hopes delude thee, miserable Man?
      Think'st thou thus unentomb'd to cross the Floods,
      To view the Furies, and Infernal Gods;
510   And visit, without Leave, the dark abodes?
      Attend the term of long revolving Years:
      Fate, and the dooming Gods, are deaf to Tears.
      This Comfort of thy dire Misfortune take;
      The Wrath of Heav'n, inflicted for thy sake,
      With Vengeance shall pursue th' inhuman Coast.
      Till they propitiate thy offended Ghost,
      And raise a Tomb, with Vows, and solemn Prayer;

And *Palinurus'* name the Place shall bear.'
This calm'd his Cares: sooth'd with his future Fame;
And pleas'd to hear his propagated Name.
　　Now nearer to the *Stygian* Lake they draw:
Whom from the Shore, the surly Boatman saw:
Observ'd their Passage through the shady Wood;
And mark'd their near Approaches to the Flood:
Then thus he call'd aloud, inflam'd with Wrath;
'Mortal, whate'er, who this forbidden Path
In Arms presum'st to tread, I charge thee stand,
And tell thy Name, and Business in the Land.
Know this, the Realm of Night; the *Stygian* Shore:
My Boat conveys no living Bodies o'er:
Nor was I pleas'd great *Theseus* once to bear;
Who forc'd a Passage with his pointed Spear;
Nor strong *Alcides*: Men of mighty Fame;
And from th' immortal Gods their Lineage came.
In Fetters one the barking Porter tied,
And took him trembling from his Sov'reign's side:
Two sought by Force to seize his beauteous Bride.'
To whom the Sibyl thus, 'Compose thy Mind:
Nor Frauds are here contriv'd, nor Force design'd.
Still may the Dog the wand'ring Troops constrain
Of Airy Ghosts; and vex the guilty Train;
And with her grisly Lord his lovely Queen remain.
The *Trojan* Chief, whose Lineage is from *Jove*,
Much fam'd for Arms, and more for filial Love,
Is sent to seek his Sire, in your *Elysian* Grove.
If neither Piety, nor Heav'n's Command,
Can gain his Passage to the *Stygian* Strand,
This fatal Present shall prevail, at least;'
Then show'd the shining Bough, conceal'd within her Vest.
No more was needful: for the gloomy God
Stood mute with Awe, to see the Golden Rod:
Admir'd the destin'd Off'ring to his Queen;
(A venerable Gift so rarely seen.)
His Fury thus appeas'd, he puts to Land:
The Ghosts forsake their Seats at his Command:

He clears the Deck, receives the mighty Freight,
The leaky Vessel groans beneath the weight.
Slowly she sails; and scarcely stems the Tides:
The pressing Water pours within her sides.
His Passengers at length are wafted o'er;
Expos'd in muddy Weeds, upon the miry Shore.
   No sooner landed, in his Den they found
The triple Porter of the *Stygian* Sound:
Grim *Cerberus*; who soon began to rear
His crested Snakes, and arm'd his bristling Hair.
The prudent Sibyl had before prepar'd
A Sop, in Honey steep'd, to charm the Guard.
Which, mix'd with powerful Drugs, she cast before
His greedy grinning Jaws, just op'd to roar:
With three enormous Mouths he gapes; and straight,
With Hunger press'd, devours the pleasing Bait.
Long draughts of Sleep his monstrous Limbs enslave;
He reels, and falling, fills the spacious Cave.
The Keeper charm'd, the Chief without Delay
Pass'd on, and took th' irremeable way.
Before the Gates, the Cries of Babes new born,
Whom Fate had from their tender Mothers torn,
Assault his Ears: then those, whom Form of Laws
Condemn'd to die, when Traitors judg'd their Cause.
Nor want they Lots, nor Judges to review
The wrongful Sentence, and award a new.
Minos, the strict Inquisitor, appears;
And Lives and Crimes, with his Assessors, hears.
Round, in his Urn, the blended Balls he rolls;
Absolves the Just, and dooms the Guilty Souls.
The next in Place, and Punishment, are they
Who prodigally throw their Souls away.
Fools, who repining at their wretched State,
And loathing anxious life, suborn'd their Fate.
With late Repentance, now they would retrieve
The Bodies they forsook, and wish to live.
Their Pains and Poverty desire to bear,
To view the Light of Heav'n, and breathe the vital Air:

560

570

580

590

162

But Fate forbids; the *Stygian* Floods oppose;
And, with nine circling Streams, the captive Souls enclose.
    Not far from thence, the mournful Fields appear;
So call'd, from Lovers that inhabit there.
The Souls, whom that unhappy Flame invades,
In secret Solitude, and Myrtle Shades,
600 Make endless Moans, and pining with Desire,
Lament too late, their unextinguish'd Fire.
Here *Procris, Eriphile* here, he found
Baring her Breast, yet bleeding with the Wound
Made by her Son. He saw *Pasiphae* there,
With *Phaedra*'s Ghost, a foul incestuous pair;
There *Laodamia*, with *Evadne*, moves:
Unhappy both; but loyal in their Loves.
Caeneus, a Woman once, and once a Man;
But ending in the Sex she first began.
610 Not far from these *Phoenician Dido* stood;
Fresh from her Wound, her Bosom Bath'd in Blood.
Whom, when the *Trojan* Hero hardly knew,
Obscure in Shades, and with a doubtful view,
(Doubtful as he who sees through dusky Night,
Or thinks he sees the Moon's uncertain Light:)
With Tears he first approach'd the sullen Shade;
And, as his Love inspir'd him, thus he said.
'Unhappy Queen! Then is the common breath
Of Rumour true, in your reported Death,
620 And I, alas, the Cause! By Heav'n, I vow,
And all the Powers that rule the Realms below,
Unwilling I forsook your friendly State:
Commanded by the Gods, and forc'd by Fate.
Those Gods, that Fate, whose unresisted Might }
Have sent me to these Regions, void of Light, }
Through the vast Empire of eternal Night. }
Nor dar'd I to presume, that, press'd with Grief,
My Flight should urge you to this dire Relief.
Stay, stay your Steps, and listen to my Vows:
630 'Tis the last Interview that Fate allows!'
In vain he thus attempts her Mind to move,

163

With Tears and Prayers, and late repenting Love.
Disdainfully she look'd; then turning round,
But fix'd her Eyes unmov'd upon the Ground.
And, what he says, and swears, regards no more
Than the deaf Rocks, when the loud Billows roar.
But whirl'd away, to shun his hateful sight,
Hid in the Forest, and the Shades of Night.
Then sought *Sichæus*, through the shady Grove,
640   Who answer'd all her Cares, and equall'd all her Love.
    Some pious Tears the pitying Hero paid;
And follow'd with his Eyes the flitting Shade.
Then took the forward Way, by Fate ordain'd,
And, with his Guide, the farther Fields attain'd;
Where, sever'd from the rest, the Warrior Souls remain'd.
Tideus he met, with *Meleager*'s Race;
The Pride of Armies, and the Soldier's Grace;
And pale *Adrastus* with his ghastly Face.
Of *Trojan* Chiefs he view'd a num'rous Train:
650   All much lamented, all in Battle slain.
Glaucus and *Medon*, high above the rest,
Antenor's Sons, and *Ceres*' sacred Priest:
And proud *Ideus*, *Priam*'s Charioteer;
Who shakes his empty Reins, and aims his Airy Spear.
The gladsome Ghosts, in circling Troops, attend,
And with unwearied Eyes behold their Friend.
Delight to hover near; and long to know
What business brought him to the Realms below.
    But *Argive* Chiefs, and *Agamemnon*'s Train,
660   When his refulgent Arms flash'd through the shady Plain,
Fled from his well known Face, with wonted Fear,
As when his thund'ring Sword, and pointed Spear,
Drove headlong to their Ships, and glean'd the routed Rear.
They rais'd a feeble Cry, with trembling Notes:
But the weak Voice deceiv'd their gasping Throats.
Here *Priam*'s Son, *Deiphobus*, he found:
Whose Face and Limbs were one continued Wound.
Dishonest, with lopp'd Arms, the Youth appears:
Spoil'd of his Nose, and shorten'd of his Ears.

He scarcely knew him, striving to disown
His blotted Form, and blushing to be known.
And therefore first began. ' O *Teucer*'s Race,
Who durst thy faultless Figure thus deface?
What heart could wish, what hand inflict this dire Disgrace?
'Twas fam'd, that in our last and fatal Night,
Your single Prowess long sustain'd the Fight:
Till tir'd, not forc'd, a glorious Fate you chose:
And fell upon a Heap of slaughter'd Foes.
But in remembrance of so brave a Deed;
A Tomb, and Fun'ral Honours I decreed:
Thrice call'd your *Manes*, on the *Trojan* Plains:
The place your Armour, and your Name retains.
Your Body too I sought; and had I found,
Design'd for Burial in your Native Ground.'
   The Ghost replied, 'Your Piety has paid
All needful Rites, to rest my wand'ring Shade:
But cruel Fate, and my more cruel Wife,
To *Grecian* Swords betray'd my sleeping Life.
These are the Monuments of *Helen*'s Love:
The Shame I bear below, the Marks I bore above.
You know in what deluding Joys we past
The Night, that was by Heav'n decreed our last.
For when the fatal Horse, descending down,
Pregnant with Arms, o'erwhelm'd th' unhappy Town;
She feign'd Nocturnal Orgies: left my Bed,
And, mix'd with *Trojan* Dames, the Dances led.
Then, waving high her Torch, the Signal made,
Which rous'd the *Grecians* from their Ambuscade.
With Watching overworn, with Cares oppress'd,
Unhappy I had laid me down to rest;
And heavy Sleep my weary Limbs possess'd.
Meantime my worthy Wife, our Arms mislaid;
And from beneath my head my Sword convey'd:
The Door unlatch'd; and with repeated calls,
Invites her former Lord within my walls.
Thus in her Crime her confidence she plac'd:
And with new Treasons would redeem the past.

670

680

690

700

What need I more? Into the Room they ran;
And meanly murder'd a defenceless Man.
710   *Ulysses*, basely born, first led the way:
Avenging Powers! With Justice if I pray,
That Fortune be their own another day.

    But answer you; and in your turn relate,
What brought you, living, to the *Stygian* State?
Driv'n by the Winds and Errors of the Sea,
Or did you Heav'n's Superior Doom obey?
Or tell what other Chance conducts your way?
To view, with Mortal Eyes, our dark Retreats,
Tumults and Torments of th' Infernal Seats?'
720   While thus, in talk, the flying Hours they pass,
The Sun had finish'd more than half his Race:
And they, perhaps, in Words and Tears had spent
The little time of stay, which Heav'n had lent.
But thus the Sibyl chides their long delay;
'Night rushes down, and headlong drives the Day:
'Tis here, in different Paths, the way divides:
The right, to *Pluto*'s Golden Palace guides:
The left to that unhappy Region tends,
Which to the depth of *Tartarus* descends;
730   The Seat of Night profound, and punish'd Fiends.'
Then thus *Deiphobus*: 'O Sacred Maid!
Forbear to chide; and be your Will Obey'd:
Lo to the secret Shadows I retire,
To pay my Penance till my Years expire.
Proceed Auspicious Prince, with Glory Crown'd,
And born to better Fates than I have found.'
He said; and while he said, his Steps he turn'd
To Secret Shadows; and in silence Mourn'd.
    The Hero, looking on the left, espied
740   A lofty Tower, and strong on every side
With treble Walls, which *Phlegethon* surrounds,
Whose fiery Flood the burning Empire bounds:
And press'd betwixt the Rocks, the bellowing noise
    resounds.
Wide is the fronting Gate, and rais'd on high

With Adamantine Columns, threats the Sky.
Vain is the force of Man, and Heav'n's as vain,
To crush the Pillars which the Pile sustain.
Sublime on these a Tower of Steel is rear'd;
And dire *Tisiphone* there keeps the Ward:
750   Girt in her sanguine Gown, by Night and Day,
Observant of the Souls that pass the downward way:
From hence are heard the Groans of Ghosts, the pains
Of sounding Lashes, and of dragging Chains.
The *Trojan* stood astonish'd at their Cries;
And ask'd his Guide, from whence those Yells arise?
And what the Crimes and what the Tortures were,
And loud Laments that rent the liquid Air?
   She thus replied: 'The chaste and holy Race,
Are all forbidden this polluted Place.
760   But *Hecate*, when she gave to rule the Woods,
Then led me trembling through these dire Abodes:
And taught the Tortures of th' avenging Gods.
These are the Realms of unrelenting Fate:
And awful *Rhadamanthus* rules the State.
He hears and judges each committed Crime;
Inquires into the Manner, Place, and Time.
The conscious Wretch must all his Acts reveal:
Loath to confess, unable to conceal;
From the first Moment of his vital Breath,
770   To his last Hour of unrepenting Death.
Straight, o'er the guilty Ghost, the Fury shakes
The sounding Whip, and brandishes her Snakes:
And the pale Sinner, with her Sisters, takes.
Then, of itself, unfolds th' Eternal Door:
With dreadful Sounds the brazen Hinges roar.
You see, before the Gate, what stalking Ghost
Commands the Guard, what Sentries keep the Post:
More formidable *Hydra* stands within;
Whose Jaws with Iron Teeth severely grin.
780   The gaping Gulf, low to the Centre lies;
And twice as deep as Earth is distant from the Skies.
The Rivals of the Gods, the *Titan* Race,

Here sing'd with Lightning, roll within th' unfathom'd
　　space.
Here lie th' *Aloean* Twins (I saw them both)
Enormous Bodies, of Gigantic Growth;
Who dar'd in Fight the Thund'rer to defy;
Affect his Heav'n, and force him from the Sky.
Salmoneus, suff'ring cruel Pains, I found,
For emulating Jove; the rattling Sound
790　Of Mimic Thunder, and the glitt'ring Blaze
Of pointed Lightnings, and their forky Rays.
Through *Elis*, and the *Grecian* Towns he flew:
Th' audacious Wretch four fiery Coursers drew:
He wav'd a Torch aloft, and, madly vain,
Sought Godlike Worship from a Servile Train.
Ambitious Fool, with horny Hooves to pass
O'er hollow Arches, of resounding Brass;
To rival Thunder, in its rapid Course:
And imitate inimitable Force.
800　But he, the King of Heav'n, obscure on high,
Bar'd his red Arm, and launching from the Sky
His writhen Bolt, not shaking empty Smoke,
Down to the deep Abyss the flaming Felon struck.
There *Tityus* was to see; who took his Birth
From Heav'n, his Nursing from the foodful Earth.
Here his Gigantic Limbs, with large Embrace,
Enfold nine Acres of Infernal Space.
A rav'nous Vulture in his open'd side,
Her crooked Beak and cruel Talons tried:
810　Still for the growing Liver digg'd his Breast;
The growing Liver still supplied the Feast.
Still are his Entrails fruitful to their Pains:
Th' immortal Hunger lasts, th' immortal Food remains.
Ixion and *Pirithous* I could name;
And more *Thessalian* Chiefs of mighty Fame.
High o'er their Heads a mould'ring Rock is plac'd,
That promises a fall; and shakes at every Blast.
They lie below, on Golden Beds display'd,
And genial Feasts, with Regal Pomp, are made.

The Queen of Furies by their sides is set;
And snatches from their Mouths th' untasted Meat.
Which, if they touch, her hissing Snakes she rears:
Tossing her Torch, and thund'ring in their Ears.
Then they, who Brothers' better Claim disown,
Expel their Parents, and usurp the Throne;
Defraud their Clients, and to Lucre sold,
Sit brooding on unprofitable Gold:
Who dare not give, and ev'n refuse to lend
To their poor Kindred, or a wanting Friend:
Vast is the Throng of these; nor less the Train
Of lustful Youths, for foul Adult'ry slain.
Hosts of Deserters, who their Honour sold,
And basely broke their Faith for Bribes of Gold:
All these within the Dungeon's depth remain:
Despairing Pardon, and expecting Pain.
Ask not what Pains; nor farther seek to know
Their Process, or the Forms of Law below.
Some roll a weighty Stone; some laid along,
And bound with burning Wires, on Spokes of Wheels
          are hung.
Unhappy *Theseus*, doom'd for ever there,
Is fix'd by Fate on his Eternal Chair:
And wretched *Phlegyas* warns the World with Cries; ⎫
(Could Warning make the World more just or wise,) ⎬
Learn Righteousness, and dread th' avenging Deities. ⎭
To Tyrants others have their Country sold,
Imposing Foreign Lords, for Foreign Gold:
Some have old Laws repeal'd, new Statutes made;
Not as the People pleas'd, but as they paid.
With Incest some their Daughters' Bed profan'd,
All dar'd the worst of Ills, and what they dar'd, attain'd.
Had I a hundred Mouths, a hundred Tongues,
And Throats of Brass, inspir'd with Iron Lungs,
I could not half those horrid Crimes repeat:
Nor half the Punishment those Crimes have met.
But let us haste our Voyage to pursue;
The Walls of *Pluto*'s Palace are in view.

The Gate, and Iron Arch above it, stands:
On Anvils labour'd by the *Cyclops'* Hands.
Before our farther way the Fates allow,
Here must we fix on high the Golden Bough.'
    She said, and through the gloomy Shades they pass'd,
And chose the middle Path. Arriv'd at last,
The Prince, with living Water, sprinkl'd o'er
His Limbs, and Body; then approach'd the Door.
Possess'd the Porch, and on the Front above
He fix'd the fatal Bough, requir'd by *Pluto*'s Love.
These Holy Rites perform'd, they took their Way,
Where long extended Plains of Pleasure lay.
The verdant Fields with those of Heav'n may vie;
With *Ether* vested, and a Purple Sky:
The blissful Seats of Happy Souls below:
Stars of their own, and their own Suns they know.
Their Airy Limbs in Sports they exercise,
And, on the Green, contend the Wrestler's Prize.
Some, in Heroic Verse, divinely sing;
Others in artful Measures lead the ring.
The *Thracian* Bard, surrounded by the rest,
There stands conspicuous in his flowing Vest.
His flying Fingers, and harmonious Quill,
Strike seven distinguish'd Notes, and seven at once they fill.
Here found they *Teucer*'s old Heroic Race;
Born better times and happier Years to grace.
Assaracus and *Ilus* here enjoy
Perpetual Fame, with him who founded *Troy*.
The Chief beheld their Chariots from afar;
Their shining Arms, and Coursers train'd to War:
Their Lances fix'd in Earth, their Steeds around,
Free from their Harness, graze the flow'ry Ground.
The love of Horses which they had, alive,
And care of Chariots, after Death survive.
Some cheerful Souls were feasting on the Plain;
Some did the Song, and some their Choir maintain:
Beneath a Laurel Shade, where mighty *Po*
Mounts up to Woods above, and hides his Head below.

Here Patriots live, who, for their Countries' good,
In fighting Fields, were prodigal of Blood:
Priests of unblemish'd Lives here make Abode;
And Poets worthy their inspiring God:
And searching Wits, of more Mechanic parts,
900 Who grac'd their Age with new invented Arts.
Those who, to worth, their Bounty did extend;
And those who knew that Bounty to commend.
The Heads of these with holy Fillets bound;
And all their Temples were with Garlands crown'd.
    To these the Sibyl thus her Speech address'd: ⎫
And first, to him surrounded by the rest;   ⎬
Tow'ring his Height, and ample was his Breast: ⎭
'Say happy Souls, Divine *Musaeus* say,
Where lives *Anchises*, and where lies our Way
910 To find the Hero, for whose only sake
We sought the dark Abodes, and cross'd the bitter Lake?'
To this the Sacred Poet thus replied;
'In no fix'd place the Happy Souls reside.
In Groves we live; and lie on mossy Beds
By Crystal Streams, that murmur through the Meads:
But pass yon easy Hill, and thence descend,
The Path conducts you to your Journey's end.'
This said, he led them up the Mountain's brow, ⎫
And shows them all the shining Fields below;   ⎬
920 They wind the Hill, and through the blissful Meadows go. ⎭
But old *Anchises*, in a flow'ry Vale,
Review'd his muster'd Race; and took the Tale:
Those Happy Spirits, which ordain'd by Fate,
For future Beings, and new Bodies wait.
With studious Thought observ'd th' illustrious Throng;
In Nature's Order as they pass'd along.
Their Names, their Fates, their Conduct, and their Care,
In peaceful Senates, and successful War.
He, when *Aeneas* on the Plain appears,
930 Meets him with open Arms, and falling Tears.

171

'Welcome,' he said, 'the Gods' undoubted Race,
O long expected, to my dear Embrace;
Once more 'tis giv'n me to behold your Face!
The Love, and Pious Duty which you pay,
Have pass'd the Perils of so hard a way.
'Tis true, computing times, I now believ'd
The happy Day approach'd; nor are my Hopes deceiv'd.
What length of Lands, what Oceans have you pass'd,
What Storms sustain'd, and on what Shores been cast?
How have I fear'd your Fate! But fear'd it most,
When Love assail'd you, on the *Libyan* Coast.'
To this, the Filial Duty thus replies;
'Your sacred Ghost, before my sleeping Eyes,
Appear'd; and often urg'd this painful Enterprise.
After long tossing on the *Tyrrhene* Sea,
My Navy rides at Anchor in the Bay.
But reach your Hand, O Parent Shade, nor shun
The dear Embraces of your longing Son!'
He said; and falling Tears his Face bedew:
Then thrice, around his Neck, his Arms he threw;
And thrice the flitting Shadow slipp'd away;
Like Winds, or empty Dreams that fly the Day.
   Now in a secret Vale, the *Trojan* sees
A sep'rate Grove, through which a gentle Breeze
Plays with a passing Breath, and whispers through the Trees.
And just before the Confines of the Wood,
The gliding *Lethe* leads her silent Flood.
About the Boughs an Airy Nation flew,
Thick as the humming Bees, that hunt the Golden Dew;
In Summer's heat, on tops of Lilies feed,
And creep within their Bells, to suck the balmy Seed.
The winged Army roams the Fields around;
The Rivers and the Rocks remurmur to the sound.
Aeneas wond'ring stood: then ask'd the Cause,
Which to the Stream the Crowding People draws.
Then thus the Sire. 'The Souls that throng the Flood
Are those, to whom, by Fate, are other Bodies ow'd:
In *Lethe*'s Lake they long Oblivion taste;

Of future Life secure, forgetful of the Past.
970 Long has my Soul desir'd this time, and place,
To set before your sight your glorious Race.
That this presaging Joy may fire your Mind,
To seek the Shores by Destiny design'd.'
'O Father, can it be, that Souls sublime,
Return to visit our Terrestrial Clime?
And that the Gen'rous Mind, releas'd by Death,
Can Covet lazy Limbs, and Mortal Breath?'
    Anchises then, in order, thus begun
To clear those Wonders to his Godlike Son.
980 'Know first, that Heav'n, and Earth's compacted Frame,
And flowing Waters, and the starry Flame,
And both the Radiant Lights, one Common Soul
Inspires, and feeds, and animates the whole.
This Active Mind infus'd through all the Space,
Unites and mingles with the mighty Mass.
Hence Men and Beasts the Breath of Life obtain;
And Birds of Air, and Monsters of the Main.
Th' Etherial Vigour is in all the same,
And every Soul is fill'd with equal Flame:
990 As much as Earthy Limbs, and gross allay ⎫
Of Mortal Members, subject to decay, ⎬
Blunt not the Beams of Heav'n and edge of Day. ⎭
From this coarse Mixture of Terrestrial parts,
Desire, and Fear, by turns possess their Hearts:
And Grief, and Joy. Nor can the grovelling Mind, ⎫
In the dark Dungeon of the Limbs confin'd, ⎬
Assert the Native Skies; or own its heav'nly Kind. ⎭
Nor Death itself can wholly wash their Stains;
But long contracted Filth, ev'n in the Soul remains.
1000 The Relics of inveterate Vice they wear;
And Spots of Sin obscene, in ev'ry Face appear.
For this are various Penances enjoin'd;
And some are hung to bleach, upon the Wind;
Some plung'd in Waters, others purg'd in Fires,
Till all the Dregs are drain'd; and all the Rust expires:

173

All have their *Manes*, and those *Manes* bear:
The few, so cleans'd to these Abodes repair:
And breathe, in ample Fields, the soft *Elysian* Air.
Then are they happy, when by length of time
1010   The Scurf is worn away, of each committed Crime.
No Speck is left, of their habitual Stains;
But the pure Ether of the Soul remains.
But, when a Thousand rolling Years are past,
(So long their Punishments and Penance last;)
Whole Droves of Minds are, by the driving God,
Compell'd to drink the deep Lethaean Flood:
In large forgetful draughts to steep the Cares
Of their past Labours, and their Irksome Years.
That unrememb'ring of its former Pain,
1020   The Soul may suffer mortal Flesh again.'
  Thus having said; the Father Spirit leads
The Priestess and his Son through Swarms of Shades,
And takes a rising Ground, from thence to see
The long Procession of his Progeny.
'Survey' (pursu'd the Sire) 'this airy Throng;
As, offer'd to thy view, they pass along.
These are th' *Italian* Names, which Fate will join
With ours, and graft upon the *Trojan* Line.
Observe the Youth who first appears in sight;
1030   And holds the nearest Station to the Light:
Already seems to sniff the vital Air;
And leans just forward, on a shining Spear;
Silvius is he: thy last begotten Race;
But first in order sent, to fill thy place,
An *Alban* Name; but mix'd with *Dardan* Blood;
Born in the Covert of a shady Wood:
Him fair *Lavinia*, thy surviving Wife,
Shall breed in Groves, to lead a solitary Life.
In *Alba* he shall fix his Royal Seat:
1040   And, born a King, a Race of Kings beget.
Then *Procas*, Honour of the *Trojan* Name,
Capys, and *Numitor*, of endless Fame.
A second *Silvius* after these appears;

Silvius Aeneas, for thy Name he bears.
For Arms and Justice equally renown'd;
Who, late restor'd, in *Alba* shall be crown'd.
How great they look, how vig'rously they wield
Their weighty Lances, and sustain the Shield!
But they, who crown'd with Oaken Wreaths appear,
1050   Shall *Gabian* Walls, and strong *Fidena* rear:
Nomentum, Bola, with *Pometia*, found;
And raise *Colatian* Tow'rs on Rocky Ground.
All these shall then be Towns of mighty Fame;
Though now they lie obscure; and Lands without a Name.
See *Romulus* the great, born to restore
The Crown that once his injur'd Grandsire wore.
This Prince, a Priestess of our Blood shall bear;
And like his Sire in Arms he shall appear.
Two rising Crests his Royal Head adorn;
1060   Born from a God, himself to Godhead born.
His Sire already signs him for the Skies,
And marks his Seat amidst the Deities.
Auspicious Chief! Thy Race in times to come
Shall spread the Conquests of Imperial *Rome*.
Rome whose ascending Tow'rs shall Heav'n invade;
Involving Earth and Ocean in her Shade.
High as the Mother of the Gods in place;
And proud, like her, of an Immortal Race.
Then when in Pomp she makes the *Phrygian* round;
1070   With Golden Turrets on her Temples crown'd:
A hundred Gods her sweeping Train supply;
Her Offspring all, and all command the Sky.
    'Now fix your Sight, and stand intent, to see
Your *Roman* Race, and *Julian* Progeny.
The mighty *Caesar* waits his vital Hour;
Impatient for the World, and grasps his promis'd Power.
But next behold the Youth of Form Divine,
Caesar himself, exalted in his Line;
Augustus, promis'd oft, and long foretold,
1080   Sent to the Realm that *Saturn* rul'd of old;
Born to restore a better Age of Gold.

175

Afric, and *India*, shall his Power obey,
He shall extend his propagated Sway,
Beyond the Solar Year; without the starry Way.
Where *Atlas* turns the rolling Heav'ns around;
And his broad Shoulders with their Lights are crown'd.
At his foreseen Approach, already quake
The *Caspian* Kingdoms, and *Maeotian* Lake.
Their Seers behold the Tempest from afar;
And threat'ning Oracles denounce the War.
Nile hears him knocking at his sevenfold Gates;
And seeks his hidden Spring, and fears his Nephews' Fates.
Nor *Hercules* more Lands or Labours knew,
Not though the brazen-footed Hind he slew;
Freed *Erymanthus* from the foaming Boar,
And dipp'd his Arrows in *Lernaean* Gore.
Nor *Bacchus*, turning from his *Indian* War,
By Tigers drawn triumphant in his Car,
From *Nysa*'s top descending on the Plains;
With curling Vines around his purple Reins.
And doubt we yet through Dangers to pursue
The Paths of Honour, and a Crown in view?
  'But what's the Man, who from afar appears,
His Head with Olive crown'd, his Hand a Censer bears?
His hoary Beard, and holy Vestments bring
His lost Idea back: I know the *Roman* King.
He shall to peaceful Rome new Laws ordain:
Call'd from his mean abode, a Sceptre to sustain.
Him, *Tullus* next in Dignity succeeds;
An active Prince, and prone to Martial Deeds.
He shall his Troops for fighting Fields prepare,
Disused to Toils, and Triumphs of the War.
By dint of Sword his Crown he shall increase;
And scour his Armour from the Rust of Peace.
Whom *Ancus* follows, with a fawning Air;
But vain within, and proudly popular.
Next view the *Tarquin* Kings: th' avenging Sword
Of *Brutus*, justly drawn, and *Rome* restor'd.
He first renews the Rods, and Axe severe;

1120 And gives the Consuls Royal Robes to wear.
His Sons, who seek the Tyrant to sustain,
And long for Arbitrary Lords again,
With Ignominy scourg'd, in open sight,
He dooms to Death deserv'd; asserting Public Right.
Unhappy Man, to break the Pious Laws
Of Nature, pleading in his Children's Cause!
Howe'er the doubtful Fact is understood, }
'Tis Love of Honour, and his Country's good: }
The Consul, not the Father, sheds the Blood. }

1130 Behold *Torquatus* the same Track pursue;
And next, the two devoted *Decii* view.
The *Drusian* Line, *Camillus* loaded home
With Standards well redeem'd, and foreign Foes o'ercome.
The Pair you see in equal Armour shine;
Now, Friends below, in close Embraces join:
But when they leave the shady Realms of Night,
And, cloth'd in Bodies, breathe your upper Light,
With mortal Hate each other shall pursue:
What Wars, what Wounds, what Slaughter shall ensue!

1140 From *Alpine* Heights the Father first descends; }
His Daughter's Husband in the Plain attends: }
His Daughter's Husband arms his Eastern Friends. }
Embrace again, my Sons, be Foes no more:
Nor stain your Country with her Children's Gore.
And thou, the first, lay down thy lawless claim;
Thou, of my Blood, who bear'st the *Julian* Name.
Another comes, who shall in Triumph ride;
And to the Capitol his Chariot guide;
From conquer'd *Corinth*, rich with *Grecian* Spoils.

1150 And yet another, fam'd for Warlike Toils,
On *Argos* shall impose the *Roman* Laws:
And, on the *Greeks*, revenge the *Trojan* Cause:
Shall drag in Chains their *Achillaean* Race; }
Shall vindicate his Ancestors' Disgrace: }
And *Pallas*, for her violated Place. }
Great *Cato* there, for Gravity renown'd,
And conqu'ring *Cossus* goes, with Laurels crown'd.

Who can omit the *Gracchi*, who declare
The *Scipios'* Worth, those Thunderbolts of War,
1160 The double Bane of *Carthage*? Who can see,
Without esteem for virtuous Poverty,
Severe *Fabricius*, or can cease t' admire
The Ploughman Consul in his Coarse Attire!
Tir'd as I am, my Praise the *Fabii* claim;
And thou great Hero, greatest of thy Name;
Ordain'd in War to save the sinking State,
And, by Delays, to put a stop to Fate!
Let others better mould the running Mass   )
Of Metals, and inform the breathing Brass;   }
1170 And soften into Flesh a Marble Face:)
Plead better at the Bar; describe the Skies,
And when the Stars descend, and when they rise.
But, *Rome*, 'tis thine alone, with awful sway,)
To rule Mankind; and make the World obey;   }
Disposing Peace, and War, thy own Majestic Way.)
To tame the Proud, the fetter'd Slave to free;
These are Imperial Arts, and worthy thee.'
      He paus'd: and while with wond'ring Eyes they view'd
The passing Spirits, thus his Speech renew'd.
1180 'See great *Marcellus*! How, untir'd in Toils,
He moves with Manly grace, how rich with Regal Spoils!
He, when his Country (threaten'd with Alarms,)
Requires his Courage, and his Conqu'ring Arms,
Shall more than once the *Punic* Bands affright:
Shall kill the *Gaulish* King in single Fight:
Then, to the Capitol in Triumph move,
And the third Spoils shall grace *Feretrian Jove*.'
Aeneas, here, beheld of Form Divine
A Godlike Youth, in glitt'ring Armour shine:
1190 With great *Marcellus* keeping equal pace;
But gloomy were his Eyes, dejected was his Face:
He saw, and, wond'ring, ask'd his airy Guide,
What, and of whence was he, who press'd the Hero's side?
His Son, or one of his Illustrious Name,
How like the former, and almost the same:

Observe the Crowds that compass him around;
All gaze, and all admire, and raise a shouting sound:
But hov'ring Mists around his Brows are spread,
And Night, with sable Shades, involves his Head.
1200 'Seek not to know' (the Ghost replied with Tears)
'The Sorrows of thy Sons, in future Years.
This Youth (the blissful Vision of a day)
Shall just be shown on Earth, and snatch'd away.
The Gods too high had rais'd the *Roman* State;
Were but their Gifts as permanent as great.
What groans of Men shall fill the *Martian* Field!
How fierce a Blaze his flaming Pile shall yield!
What Fun'ral Pomp shall floating *Tiber* see,
When, rising from his Bed, he views the sad Solemnity!
1210 No Youth shall equal hopes of Glory give:
No Youth afford so great a Cause to grieve.
The *Trojan* Honour, and the *Roman* Boast;
Admir'd when living, and Ador'd when lost!
Mirror of ancient Faith in early Youth!
Undaunted Worth, Inviolable Truth!
No Foe unpunish'd in the fighting Field,
Shall dare thee Foot to Foot, with Sword and Shield.
Much less, in Arms oppose thy matchless Force,
When thy sharp Spurs shall urge thy foaming Horse.
1220 Ah, couldst thou break through Fate's severe Decree,
A new *Marcellus* shall arise in thee!
Full Canisters of fragrant Lilies bring,
Mix'd with the Purple Roses of the Spring:
Let me with Fun'ral Flow'rs his Body strew;
This Gift which Parents to their Children owe,
This unavailing Gift, at least I may bestow!
    Thus having said, he led the Hero round
The confines of the blessed *Elysian* Ground.
Which, when *Anchises* to his Son had shown,
1230 And fir'd his Mind to mount the promis'd Throne,
He tells the future Wars, ordain'd by Fate;
The Strength and Customs of the *Latian* State:
The Prince, and People: and forearms his Care

With Rules, to push his Fortune, or to bear.
Two Gates the silent House of Sleep adorn;
Of polish'd Iv'ry this, that of transparent Horn:
True Visions through transparent Horn arise;
Through polish'd Iv'ry pass deluding Lies.
Of various things discoursing as he pass'd,
Anchises hither bends his Steps at last.
Then, through the Gate of Iv'ry, he dismiss'd
His valiant Offspring, and Divining Guest.
Straight to the Ships *Aeneas* took his way;
Embark'd his Men, and skimm'd along the Sea:
Still Coasting, till he gain'd *Caieta*'s Bay.
At length on Oozy ground his Galleys moor:
Their Heads are turn'd to Sea, their Sterns to Shore.

1240

Notes

ANNUS MIRABILIS: AN ACCOUNT OF THE ENSUING POEM. In this letter to his brother-in-law, the dramatist Sir Robert Howard (1626–98), Dryden describes his intention in writing *Annus Mirabilis*, and how this historical poem may have affinities with the epic.

5–6. Royal Admiral: James, Duke of York.

two incomparable Generals: Prince Rupert and the Duke of Albemarle.

9. Argument: subject-matter.

14–15. Commonalty: the common people.

23. wanted: lacked.

29. A single book of the *Iliad* or the longest book of the *Aeneid*.

32. Marcus Annaeus Lucanus (A.D. 39–65) was the author of the unfinished poem *Pharsalia*, describing the Civil War between Caesar and Pompey. The poem was generally regarded as the finest Roman epic after Virgil's *Aeneid*.

33. Silius Italicus (A.D. 25–101) was the author of the *Punica*, an epic poem on Hannibal's invasion of Italy during the second Punic War.

37. number: metre.

41. quantity: length.

42. A spondee is a metrical foot of two long syllables, a dactyl is a foot of one long and two short syllables.

57. Female Rhymes: rhymes of two syllables, the second being unstressed.

59–64. Dryden wrote *Annus Mirabilis* at Charlton in Wiltshire, the home of his father-in-law, the Earl of Berkshire.

76. Omnia sponte sue reddit justissima tellus:'The most righteous earth returns everything by its own free will.' The line is Dryden's own.

91. elocution: an oratorical style.

94. School distinction: the style of differentiating, as used in medieval scholastic philosophy.

104. In his essay *Of Heroic Plays* (1672), Dryden criticised Lucan for having 'too often offer'd at somewhat which had more of the Sting of an Epigram, than of the Dignity and State of an Heroic Poem'.

107. Paranomasia: pun.

108. sentence: maxim, moral sentiment.

ANNUS MIRABILIS: THE YEAR OF WONDERS, MDCLXVI. The poem was completed in November 1666 and published early in 1667. It has two subjects, first the naval war against the Dutch (and specifically the two battles of June and July 1666), and the fire of London, which broke out on 2 September 1666 and within five days destroyed much of the city. Commercial rivalry between England and Holland had already resulted in war in 1652–54, but in 1664 an English fleet under Sir Robert Holmes seized Dutch possessions in west Africa, though these were recaptured by de Ruyter. A second English fleet under James, Duke of York, brother of Charles II, and Prince Rupert, raided Dutch shipping in the English Channel. Charles tried to negotiate an alliance with France but the French chose to let England and Holland weaken one another, and also persuaded the Spanish to remain neutral. In December 1664 Sir Thomas Allin attacked the Dutch merchant fleet from Smyrna, as it was off Cadiz, but most of the ships evaded him.

War was officially declared in March 1665, the French joining the Dutch in January 1666 but taking no active part. In 1665 the Dutch fleet was heavily defeated off Lowestoft. They lost 2,000 men, including their commander, Opdam, and twenty-five ships. Dryden describes the two battles of 1666. The first and most important of these began off the sandbanks of the Dutch coast on 1 June and lasted for four days (lines *185–552*). This first battle was a partial defeat for the British under the Duke of Albemarle and Prince Rupert but after new building and repairs (lines *561–612*), the English ships put to sea again and defeated the Dutch off the North Foreland on 25 July (lines *665–812*). This gave the English sufficient command of the seas to enable them to raid the Dutch coast with little interference. However, the most remarkable raid was carried out by the Dutch in 1667, shortly after the publication of this poem, when they attacked Chatham harbour, burnt four English warships and towed away a fifth. A month later the war was ended by the treaty of Breda.

Dryden's second subject (lines *833–1208*) is the fire of London and the care of Charles II for his people. Thirteen thousand houses were destroyed, as well as churches and other buildings, and though there were comparatively few deaths, 100,000 people had died in the great plague of 1665–66, which had driven the Court to Salisbury, and Parliament to Oxford.

By objective standards, 1666 was not a year of wonders: the events of the poem amount, strictly speaking, to one naval defeat; one temporary naval victory, and one natural disaster. However, the purpose of heroic poetry is not objective reporting but, as Dryden says, 'to beget admiration'. So the Duke of Albemarle, or de Ruyter, may assume the stature of Achilles or Hector; the sirens and Tritons of mythology attend the fleets and, as in some huge allegorical painting, the angels draw back the curtain of the skies above the English Channel to look down on the scene. Finally, after the prayer of Charles II (lines *1045–80*), the conclusion of the action is brought about, as in the *Iliad* or the *Aeneid* by divine intervention.

Dryden himself provided some notes and subheadings for the poem. Where these are quoted, they are indicated thus: (*Dryden*).

1–56. The maritime rivalry of England and Holland is described. After resisting the pressure of public opinion for some time, Charles II resolves on naval action against the Dutch.

5–6. An image drawn from the circulation of the blood, discovered by William Harvey (1578–1657).

10. Precious Stones at first are Dew condens'd and harden'd by the warmth of the Sun, or Subterranean Fires (*Dryden*).

11. Idumea is a district of Palestine, also known as Edom. The balm is the juice of the balsam tree.

14. According to their opinion, who think that great heap of waters under the Line [Equator] is depressed into Tides by the Moon, towards the Poles (*Dryden*).

16. *Belgian*: Dutch. Belgium did not become an independent country finally until 1831. In 1666 part of it was ruled by Holland and part by Spain.

17–20. For an account of Carthage and the Punic Wars, see the *Historical Note* on the *Aeneid,* p. 216 England's first 'Punic War' with Holland was in 1652–54.

21. *pretend*: lay claim.

28. Only England can thwart French ambitions.

29–32. Louis XIV wished to annex the Spanish Netherlands on behalf of his Spanish-born wife, Maria Theresa. However, he feared this would unite Spain, Holland, and England against him. He persuaded Spain to let England and Holland fight each other unaided, but when Philip IV of Spain died in 1665 and was succeeded by his infant son, Charles II, Louis occupied part of the Spanish Netherlands.

35–6. Louis was content to let the Dutch win their naval war against England, knowing that he could always defeat them on land.

39–40. Charles II 'freed' England from Cromwellian republicanism.

49. *charge*: accusation.

51. *Limbecs*: alembecs, distillation flasks used in the seventeenth century.

53. At last he resolved to assert his sway over the world's oceans.

57–92. The opening of the war. The battle of 3 June 1665, off Lowestoft, is referred to. Admiral Sir John Lawson was killed on the British side, as was the Dutch commander, Opdam.

59. When *Proteus* blows, or 'Caeruleus Proteus immania ponti armenta, & magnas pascit sub gurgite Phocas'. *Virgil (Dryden)*. ('Under the waves, azure Proteus feeds his monstrous sea-herds and mighty seals') Virgil, *Georgics* iv, 387–9; 394–5. Dryden quotes only the general sense of the lines. Proteus is one of the sea gods.

64. Two comets, sighted in 1664 and 1665, were regarded by some observers as omens.

65–6. Comets were believed to consist of earth's vapours drawn up by the sun.

70. A bright constellation in the noon sky, a favourable omen, was recorded when Charles II was born on 29 May 1630.

73. James, Duke of York, commanded the fleet at the battle of Lowestoft.

79. Gage: pledge. *cast*: require.

80. Sir John Lawson had served in Cromwell's navy but had subsequently helped to restore Charles II.

82. The image of mythical sea creatures lamenting Lawson's death suggests another parallel between Dryden's heroic style and the manner of allegorical painting.

85–6. The death of Opdam is described in a tone which verges on the burlesque, rather than the heroic.

93–152. 'The attempt at Bergen' (*Dryden*). The poem describes the partially successful attempt by the English fleet, in August 1665, to blockade and capture the Dutch merchant fleet at Bergen in Norway, after its return from the East. The Bishop of Munster (line *145*) was offered English subsidies to attack Holland by land but when the French supported the Dutch, the Bishop prudently withdrew his troops. Despite Dryden's disdain, Pepys in his *Diary* (7 April 1666) records that the money for the Bishop's campaign had never been paid.

95. Southern Climates, Guinea (*Dryden*).

97. Castor was one of the Argonauts who brought back the Golden Fleece to Thessaly.

113–16. There is a black humour in the incongruous image of men killed by their own porcelain and spice. Like lines *85–86*, it seems closer to satire than to pure heroic verse.

121–4. Some of the merchantmen were captured by the English fleet after escaping from Bergen.

137. Such are, &c. from *Petronius*. 'Si bene calculum ponas ubique fit naufragium' (*Dryden*). ('If you work it out properly, you can be shipwrecked anywhere') *Satyricon*, 115.

146. The *German* faith. *Tacitus* saith of them, 'Nullos mortalium fide aut armis ante Germanos esse' (*Dryden*). ('No man could stand higher than the Germans in loyalty or in war') *Annals*, xiii, 54.

153–84. 'War declar'd by France' (*Dryden*). Louis XIV joins the Dutch at the beginning of 1666. King Charles prepares for renewed battle, secure in the affections of his people.

169–70. When war was declared, Charles II offered protection to all French and Dutch subjects in England who remained loyal to him. He also offered asylum to French Protestants.

181. A reference to the extra money (£1,250,000) voted by Parliament for the war in 1665.

185–212. 'Prince Rupert and Duke Albemarle sent to sea' (*Dryden*). The English fleet sailed to meet the Dutch, in April 1666, under these two commanders.

193. Rupert, Prince of Bavaria (1619–82) was a cousin of Charles II and had been the most brilliant Royalist general in the Civil War. He commanded that part of the fleet which had followed Charles II into exile. He was made a Privy Councillor in 1662, a member of the Royal Society in 1664, and Lord High Admiral in 1673.

195. The Amazons were a tribe of female warriors who invaded Attica but were defeated by Theseus, who captured their queen.

197. George Monck (1608–70) Duke of Albemarle, a Royalist commander in the Civil War who subsequently became one of Cromwell's generals and took part in naval battles against Holland in 1653. After Cromwell died, Monck worked for the Restoration of Charles II and was rewarded with a peerage.

For *Scipio* and *Carthage,* see the *Historical Note* on the *Aeneid,* p. 216

199. Fasces: rods.

204. Future People, 'Examina infantium futurusque populus'. *Pliny the Younger* (*Dryden*). ('Hosts of infants and a people unborn') *Panegyricus*, xxvi.

211–12. Dryden's use of contemporary scientific imagery offers a strong contrast to the traditional heroic similes from Virgil.

213–84. 'Duke of Albemarle's Battle, first day' (*Dryden*). Prince Rupert with twenty ships had sailed to meet the French. On 1 June 1666, Albemarle's force fought the Dutch alone. Sir William Berkeley became separated from the fleet but fought on till he was killed. The two fleets pause from combat during the night.

214. The Dutch commander, de Ruyter, had about ninety ships.

215. Narrow Seas: The Dutch fleet lay between Dunkirk and the North Foreland.

223. Th' *Elean*, &c. Where the Olympic Games were celebrated (*Dryden*).

225–40. The two navies sailed in parallel lines, bombarding each other broadside on. After each exchange, the lines of ships would turn back for a further engagement.

228. Lands unfix'd, from *Virgil*: 'Credas innare revulsas Cycladas, &c.' (*Dryden*). ('You would think that the Cyclades islands were uprooted and floating') *Aeneid*, viii, 691–2.

235. port: demeanour.

243. All bare: despite the flattering comparison of Albemarle to an immovable oak, the first two words seem to be a facetious reference to the official account of the battle in the *London Gazette*, which described how in one exchange of fire, Albemarle lost his breeches 'to his Skin'.

251–2. When the Gauls captured Rome in 390 B.C., they were amazed to find the city's leaders calmly continuing to carry out public business.

253. Patroclus, the friend of Achilles, was killed at the siege of Troy by Hector.

268. Creüsa, the first wife of Aeneas, was lost in the chaos and slaughter when the Greeks captured Troy.

285–408. 'Second Day's Battle' (*Dryden*). More Dutch ships arrive, and the Duke of Albemarle, even more heavily outnumbered, sails to attack them. Militarily, this action was extremely foolish but Dryden presents it as a gallant fight against overwhelming odds.

292. 'Spem vultu simulat premit alto corde dolorem.' *Virgil* (*Dryden*). ('He assumes a hopeful look, and suppresses the grief deep in his heart.') *Aeneid*, i, 209.

314–16. Like the swordfish swallowed by the whale, the English cut their way out of the closely packed Dutch fleet, giving the appearance of a single fleet at war with itself.

326. Chase guns were mounted in the bows or stern, for use in attacks other than broadsides.

327. Fire ships, often blazing rafts propelled towards the enemy, were commonly used in sea battles of the seventeenth and eighteenth centuries.

330. Cacus was the fire-breathing son of the god Vulcan, and was killed by Achilles.

342. stoops: swoops.

344. Turns aside for a smaller prey and flies downwind.

352. Suetonius, in his life of Julius Caesar, describes how when mortally wounded by assassins' knives, Caesar pulled the top of his gown over his face to hide his death agony and allowed the lower part to cover his legs.

367–8. Cf. Exodus 14: 19–20. 'And the angel of God, which went before the camp of Israel, removed and went behind them; and the pillar of the cloud went from before their face, and stood behind them. And it came between the camp of the Egyptians and the camp of Israel; and it was a cloud and darkness *to them*, but it gave light by night *to these*: so that the one came not near the other all the night.'

371–2. The Greek historian Xenophon accompanied the invasion of Persia in 401 B.C. After the defeat of the army and the deaths of its generals, Xenophon led the survivors back to safety. His achievement prompted Sparta to attack Persia.

374. Ark: wooden chest containing the tables of Jewish law. Cf. 1 Chronicles 13: 10. 'And the anger of the Lord was kindled against Uzza, and he smote him because he put his hand to the ark: and there he died before God.'

384. The simile is *Virgil's*. 'Vestigia retro improperata refert &c.'

(*Dryden*). ('He retraces his steps unhurriedly.') *Aeneid*, ix, 797–8.

391. Weary waves, from *Statius Sylvae*. 'Nec trucibus fluviis idem sonus: occidit horror aequoris, ac terris maria.acclinta quiescunt' (*Dryden*). ('Nor is the sound of the threatening floods the same, the heaving of the waters dies, and the recumbent seas are at rest') *Sylvae*, V, iv, 5–6.

396. The third of June, famous for two former victories (*Dryden*). English naval victories over the Dutch in 1653 and 1665 had both taken place on 3 June.

409–72. 'Third day' (*Dryden*). Prince Rupert's squadron, having failed to bring the French fleet to battle, sails to join the beleaguered Duke of Albemarle.

439. Martlet: swallow.

443. Ken: power or exercise of vision.

449–52. The Dutch ships were of shallower draught, which gave them an advantage near sandbanks, whereas some of Albemarle's ships struck the Galloper shoal, off the Thames estuary.

453–4. An image reminiscent of *Paradise Lost* and *Paradise Regained*. The fallen angels, princes of hell, dread the prophesied coming of Christ.

472. Cf. Joshua 10: 12–13. 'Then spake Joshua to the Lord in the day when the Lord delivered up the Amorites before the children of Israel, and he said in the sight of Israel, Sun stand thou still upon Gibeon; and thou, Moon, in the valley of Ajalon. And the sun stood still, and the moon stayed until the people had avenged themselves upon their enemies.'

473–564. 'Fourth day's Battle' (*Dryden*). The four days' battle is presented as a virtual English victory, thwarted by Dutch cowardice. It was, in fact, more nearly an English defeat.

476. Another reference to the thick smoke of battle.

479. breath'd: rested.

485. offends: attacks.

490. sullenly: grimly.

491. So glides &c. from *Virgil*. 'Quum medii nexus extremaeque agmina caudae solvuntur: tardosque trahit sinus ultimus orbes &c.' (*Dryden*). ('When the winding middle and the movements of the tail's end are impaired, and the last loop drags in slow curves') *Georgics*, iii, 423–4.

494–6. Dryden uses an image from dice, and as in throwing dice each man now wishes to influence the outcome.

502. Patrimonies: estates, inheritances. The shattered navy looks like a denuded wood or forest.

508. An allusion to falconry. The Prince is seen as flying so purposefully at his prey that they will not rise again.

514. shades below: ghosts in the underworld.

515. *Without*: outside.

520. *offends*: attacks.

526. *flix*: fur.

533. *Batavian*: Dutchman.

536. From *Horace*: 'Quos opimus fallere & effugere est triumphus' (*Dryden*). ('Those whom it is a great triumph to baffle and evade') *Odes*, IV, iv, 52.

565–600. 'His Majesty repairs the fleet' (*Dryden*). After 4 June, the fleet was speedily repaired, new ships completed, and the navy put to sea again to meet the Dutch on 19 July. In view of the damage sustained this was a considerable success. The section shows Dryden's almost technical interest in the details of ship repair.

570. To imp a bird's wing, usually a falcon's, is to graft on new feathers to make good those lost and to improve its flight.

573. 'Fervet opus': the same similitude in *Virgil* (*Dryden*). ('The work glows warm') *Georgics*, iv, 169.

582. *Oakum*: fibres of old rope which, mixed with pitch, were used for stopping up or caulking the seams of a ship.

586. *instops*: stops up.

587. *paid*: smeared with pitch.

588. *beak*: prow.

589. *gall'd*: frayed. *dauby Marling*: untwisted rope dipped in pitch.

590. *cere-cloth*: a verb. To cere-cloth a mast is to wrap it in waxed cloth.

595. *big-corn'd*: big grained.

600. *Road*: anchorage.

601–16. 'Loyal London describ'd' (*Dryden*). The first *London* had blown up in 1665, and in 1666 the city of London had a warship built for Charles II to replace her. This second *London* was destroyed by the Dutch in 1667.

602. The new *London* rose, like a phoenix, from the ashes of her predecessor.

606. *sanguine*: blood red.

610. *laves*: washes.

617–56. 'Digression concerning Shipping and Navigation' (*Dryden*). Dryden traces the history of seamanship and shows that English supremacy is the result of a spirit of science and invention, characteristic of the nation in the seventeenth century.

625. *Kern*: foot-soldier.

627. *stem*: make headway against.

629–33. According to Roman mythology, Saturn was overthrown by his son, Jupiter, and sailed to Rome to become one of its early kings.

639. 'Extra anni solisque vias'. *Virgil* (*Dryden*). ('Beyond the course of the years and the sun') *Aeneid*, vi, 796.

649. By a more exact measure of Longitude (*Dryden*).

653–6. Dryden reverts to the old-fashioned idea that there was an edge or 'verge' of the world, where earth and heavens met. He uses it as a poetic image, not as a scientific truth.

657–64. 'Apostrophe to the Royal Society' (*Dryden*). The Royal Society received its charter in 1662, and Dryden was admitted as a member on 26 November that year.

665–740. Dryden describes the British fleet and its commanders sailing to meet the Dutch on 19 July 1666.

677. stayed: delayed, waited.

681–4. The Plymouth Squadron, under Sir Jeremy Smyth had been protecting English merchant shipping in the Mediterranean, and had blockaded the French fleet in Toulon.

685. Sir Thomas Allin (1612–85) had never wavered in his support for the Royalist cause. He led the vanguard of the fleet in the coming battle.

687–92. Sir Robert Holmes (1622–92) had led the attack on Dutch possessions in west Africa at the beginning of hostilities. Much of the 'Gold Coast' had fallen to Britain in 1664.

689. Achates is the faithful companion of Aeneas in Virgil's *Aeneid*.

691–2. Cato had urged the Roman senate into a third Punic War against Carthage by showing them figs picked in Carthage only a few days earlier.

693–4. Sir Edward Spragge, who died in 1673, was knighted for his bravery in the battle of 3 June 1665 off Lowestoft.

695–6. Sir John Harman, who also died in 1673, had his ship the *Henry* twice set on fire by the Dutch in the earlier battle of 1666, but he and his crew brought her safely home.

697–700. Sir Frescheville Holles (1641–72), son of Gervase Holles, a Civil War soldier. There is no evidence that his mother earned the title of 'a *Muse*'. Holles had his left arm shot away in the earlier battle and was killed in a naval battle with the Dutch in 1672.

699. fatal: destructive.

700. succeeds: Holles made it take the place of the other.

701. darker: less well known.

713–16. Cf. lines *449–52* and note.

728. gross: the main body.

731. blind: concealed.

735. officious: dutiful.

736. 'Levat ipse Tridenti & vastas aperit Syrtes &c.' *Virgil* (*Dryden*). ('He lifts them himself with his trident and opens the huge quick-sands') *Aeneid*, i, 145–6.

739. They: the Dutch.

740. This refers to the drawing back of curtains round a bed.

741–812. 'Second Battle' (*Dryden*). This section describes the engagement of 25 July 1666, which resulted in the defeat and withdrawal of the Dutch fleet.

742. *Battles*: ships in battle order.

743. *Sleet*: metal flakes from the guns.

747. *describe*: survey.

750. Linstocks were flame-holders used in igniting gunpowder. *expires*: is blown out.

760. 'Possunt quia posse videntur.' *Virgil* (*Dryden*). ('They are able because they seem to be able') *Aeneid*, v, 231.

762. *Caesar*: Charles II.

773–6. The Dutch commander was Michael Adrianszoon de Ruyter, his country's greatest sailor at this time. Varro led the defeated Romans at the battle of Cannae in 216 B.C., and gathered the survivors together afterwards.

780. *dar'd*: terrified.   *Hobby's*: falcon's.

788. The day of the battle, 25 July, was the feast of St James, patron saint of Spain. Dryden describes the English policy of aiding the Dutch against Spain, since the time of Elizabeth, as mistaken. It had increased the power of Holland and France.

790. *Philip's Manes*: *Philip* the second of *Spain*, against whom the *Hollanders* rebelling, were aided by Queen *Elizabeth* (*Dryden*). *Manes*: spirit.

801–4. Henry IV of France would disown his grandson, Louis XIV, the '*Bourbon* Foe', for his hostility to England. The first Prince of Orange, William the Silent, would also deplore the use of a Dutch fleet against its former English allies.

813–32. 'Burning of the Fleet in the Vlie by Sir Robert Holmes' (*Dryden*). Dutch shipping is attacked and troops are landed to capture stores.

824. *Holland*: Holland linen.

825. *vex'd*: Dryden puns upon the word, which meant to twist, or weave, but also to torment.

827. *doom*: consign.

829. *rummage*: empty.

833–1044. 'Transitum to the fire of London' (*Dryden*). The third of the wonders of 1666 was how, when the fire of London seemed to be burning uncontrollably, the King's efforts and his intercession with God, caused its extinction. Dryden describes the outbreak of the fire and the devastation of London.

833. *unsincere*: mixed.

836. *post*: express.

838. *wanted*: lacked.

847. 'Quum mare quum tellus correptaque regia Coeli, ardeat, &c.' *Ovid* (*Dryden*). ('When the sea, when the land, and the royal palace of heaven will catch fire and burn') *Metamorphoses*, i, 257–8.

849–56. A possible reference to Oliver Cromwell.

857–60. The fire of London broke out at a bakery in Pudding Lane, during the night of 1–2 September 1666. A strong east wind drove it rapidly through the crowded wooden buildings of that area. It spread quickly during the next twenty-four hours and attempts to form a fire-break, by pulling down houses in its path, failed, since the flames soon spread across the debris. On the third night, the wind dropped. On the fifth day the fire was put out but a fresh fire began that evening. It was quickly dealt with by blowing up the buildings in its path.

857. prodigious: ominous.

868. big: pregnant. Dryden describes the fire's origin in terms of pregnancy and birth.

877. insulting: exulting.

880. repair: haunt.

881. 'Haec arte tractabat cupidum virum, ut illius animum inopia accenderet' (*Dryden*). ('She ruled the man's desire artfully, to inflame his passion by frustrating it') Terence, *Heauton Timorumenos*, II, iii, 125–6. Having described the fire in images of a murderer's progress, Dryden now depicts the winds in those of prostitutes, with whom the murderer consorts.

885. letted: held back from.

888. nods: inclines.

889–92. The heads of those executed in 1662 for their part in the death of Charles I were among those exhibited on London bridge. 'Fanatic' suggests that the ghosts were those of Puritan or republican traitors. The 'Sabbath Notes' are those of a witches' sabbath, though in this context there is also a hint of Puritan sabbatarianism.

914. The leather fire-buckets were kept in churches.

915. Water for fighting the fire was obtained by cutting through the wooden water pipes.

917. a Belgian wind: Even after the naval battles, Dryden still shows Holland as the agent of England's destruction.

922. 'Sigaea igni freta lata relucent.' *Virgil* (*Dryden*). ('The wide Sigaean straits reflect the fire') *Aeneid*, ii, 312.

929. in a broader gross: in a larger formation.

949. The concern of Charles II and his brother, the Duke of York, for the victims of the fire is confirmed by contemporary accounts. The *London Gazette* for 3–10 September 1666 remarked that the fire had raged 'notwithstanding His Majesty's own, and His Royal Highness's indefatigable and personal pains to apply all possible remedies to prevent it, calling upon and helping the people with their guards'. John Evelyn noted in his diary for 6 September: 'It is not indeed imaginable how extraordinary the vigilance and activity of the King and the Duke was, even labouring in person, and being present to command, order, reward, and encourage workmen.'

995. retire: withdraw, take away, as in French *retirer*.

1006. permitted: abandoned.

1008. Vulcan is the god of fire in classical mythology.

1014. the gen'ral doom: the Day of Judgment.

1022. require: seek for, as in Latin *requirere*.

1028. repeat: recall.

1029. The homeless fled to the open spaces of Moorfields, to the north of the city.

1030. obnoxious: susceptible to, exposed to.

1045–1148. 'King's Prayer' (*Dryden*). Charles II prays that God will put an end to the calamity with which London has been afflicted, and which has followed the scourge of the great plague in 1665–66. He asks that, if his own life has been at fault, he alone may be the recipient of God's wrath. A cherub, despatched from heaven, drives back the flames which threaten the magazines of gunpowder used by the navy. The frustrated flames attack St Paul's instead, which is no longer invulnerable as a holy place, since it was desecrated by Cromwell's soldiers. After the destruction of St. Paul's, however, God quenches the fire, and the King's prayer is answered. This is Dryden's answer to the Puritans and the anti-royalists who attacked Charles II and his government as the causes of God's anger with the nation.

1045–80. There is a resemblance between the prayer of Charles II and the circumstances of King David's prayer in 1 Chronicles 21: 11–17, especially in lines *1057–60* and *1077–80* of Dryden's poem.

1066. spotted deaths: the plague.

1076. doom: judgment.

1091. affect: aim to achieve.

1092. St Paul's and other medieval churches had been built before the time of Calvin and, of course, the Puritans who believed in salvation by faith, rather than by good works.

1093–96. A reference to the damage done to Christ's Hospital, though its orphans had, in fact, been evacuated from the building.

1099. A reference to Edmund Waller's poem 'Upon His Majesty's Repairing of Paul's.'

1100. Amphion played his harp so exquisitely that the sounds drew stones together to build the walls of Thebes.

1103. Cromwell's soldiers stabled their horses in St Paul's and sawed up the wood of the interior.

1116. damps: quietens.

1120. give on: attack.

1127. Genius: spirit of the place.

1128. Lares: household gods in Roman society.

1141–4. Two Royal proclamations of 5 September 1666 required other parts of England to requisition food for the homeless and to receive refugees from the fire.

1145–8. Cf. *London Gazette*, 3–10 September 1666. 'His Majesty and his Royal Brother, out of their care to stop and prevent the fire, frequently exposing their persons with very small attendance in all parts of the Town, sometimes even to be intermixed with those who laboured in the business, yet nevertheless there hath not been observed so much as a murmuring word to fall from any, but on the contrary, even those persons whose losses rendered their conditions most desperate, and to be fit objects of other prayers, beholding those frequent instances of His Majesty's care of his people, forgot their own misery, and filled the streets with their prayers for His Majesty, whose trouble they seemed to compassionate before their own.'

1149–1216. 'City's request to the King not to leave them' (*Dryden*). Dryden urges that the King should not leave his loyal citizens and, in the closing stanzas, predicts that a new city shall rise, which will be the envy of the rest of the mercantile world.

1150. Auspice: auspicious influence.

1151. hatch: produce something new from. A reference to the Phoenix.

1157–60. Cf. Ezra 1–6. Cyrus, King of Persia, issued an order for the building of a temple in Jerusalem, to which the Jewish people should return.

1165. A trine is the positioning of two planets 120 degrees apart, regarded as a favourable omen in astrology.

1166. The planet Jupiter is in the ascendant.

1168. succeed: cause to succeed.

1169. Chemic: alchemic.

1171. Mexico (*Dryden*).

1177. Augusta, the old name of *London* (*Dryden*). The name was used in the fourth century A.D.

1195. A reference to the alliance of France and Holland against England.

1204. vindicate: defend from interference.

1210. left behind: left unfinished.

ABSALOM AND ACHITOPHEL: A POEM. The historical background, the Popish Plot and Whig sedition, which prompted Dryden to write this poem have been dealt with in the general Introduction. The specific circumstances of publication are that it was published in November 1681, not later than 17 November, and that the trial of Shaftesbury for treason opened on 24 November. The King had dissolved the Oxford Parliament in March and for six months, with the aid of his supporters, had ruled by royal authority to quell the political disturbances of the previous two or three years. He appeared to have been largely successful. The Whigs, after their strong attacks on the King and the Tory party were now on the defensive and Shaftesbury, their leader, was about to be tried for his life. In such a situation it might seem that Dryden's poem was an attempt to ensure that Shaftesbury would be convicted, yet it is significant, particularly if he wrote it at the King's suggestion, that neither Absalom nor Achitophel is entirely condemned. As Dryden says in his introduction, he has omitted the conclusion of the biblical story in which Absalom is at length put to death, and would be happy to have concluded it with the reconciliation of Absalom and King David. This is a sentiment expressed by David himself in the speech at the end of the poem. In this sense, the poem may be an offer of peace to the King's enemies, but it is an offer made from a position of strength.

Not all the minor characters in the poem have been either positively or convincingly identified through the names borrowed from the biblical story in 2 Samuel 14–18, but the most important identifications of individuals, groups, and places are as follows.

David–Charles II; *Absalom*–Duke of Monmouth; *Achitophel*–Earl of Shaftesbury; *Zimri*–Duke of Buckingham; *Corah*–Titus Oates; *the Jews*–the English; *the Jebusites*–the Catholics; *the Levites*–the Dissenting clergy; *the Sanhedrin*–Parliament; *Israel*–England; *Sion* or *Jerusalem*–London; *Hebron*–Scotland; *Egypt*–France, and *the Jordan*–the English Channel.

The terms 'Whig' and 'Tory' would, of course, be anachronistic in the poem itself but Dryden uses them in his introduction. They both have their origins in the political crisis of 1679 and were, to begin with, forms of abuse. *Whigs* or *Whiggamores* were Scottish Presbyterian rebels, while *Tories* were Irish Catholic bandits.

TO THE READER. The Latin epigraph is from Horace, *De Arte Poetica*, 361–2: 'If you stand nearer, you will be all the more fascinated.'

6–7. *Treasury of Merits*: the accumulated holiness of Catholic saints, which they may use on behalf of others.

7. *Fanatic Church*: Puritans or Dissenters.

10–11. *Anti-Bromingham*: Tory. The Tories referred to their Whig enemies as '*Birmingham* Protestants', since Birmingham was notorious for its counterfeit coinage.

13. *Genius*: spirit.

33. *Commonwealth's-men*: Whigs who were accused of wanting a return to the sort of republican Commonwealth which Cromwell had created.

34. *Unconscionable*: unreasonable.

36–7. A jury chosen by a Whig Lord Mayor of London, or a sheriff, would be packed to acquit any Whig pamphleteer.

54. The conclusion of the story: 'And ten young men that bare Joab's armour compassed about and smote Absalom and slew him', 2 Samuel 18:15.

67. Origen (*c.* A.D. 185–*c.* 254) believed in the original and indestructible unity of God and all spiritual beings, which implied that no soul could be eternally damned.

76–7. Ense rescindendum: 'cutting with a sword', Ovid, *Metamorphoses*, I, 191.

79. Act of Oblivion: amnesty.

ABSALOM AND ACHITOPHEL

1–42. The narrative describes King David's 'Promiscuous use of Concubine and Bride', and summarises the character, appearance, and military prowess of his illegitimate son, Absalom.

11. Michal: Catherine of Braganza, whom Charles II married in 1662, and by whom he had no children.

23. Monmouth commanded an English army in Holland (1673) and in France (1678).

34. Annabel: Anne, Countess of Buccleugh, celebrated for her beauty and her wealth.

39. Amnon's Murder: Sir John Coventry was attacked, though unlike Amnon in 2 Samuel 13: 28–9, he was not killed. The attack was carried out by Monmouth's men in 1670 after a jibe of Coventry's against the mistresses of Charles II.

43–84. The lack of gratitude shown by the Jewish nation to King David for the political stability which his reign has brought them.

43. sincerely: completely.

44. proves: puts to the test.

51. Adam-wits: as unappreciative of their liberty as Adam before the Fall.

55–6. Envying the freedom of primitive life and not realising, as Hobbes taught, that such a life is the war of each man against every other.

57. Saul: Oliver Cromwell.

58. Ishbosheth: Richard, son of Oliver Cromwell.

59. Charles II was crowned King of Scotland in 1651, before going into exile. He was not crowned King of England until ten years later.

66. Golden Calf: An idol or false God worshipped by the Israelites; cf. Exodus 32: 4–8.   *a State*: a Cromwellian Commonwealth or republic.

72. dishonest: dishonourable.

75. qualified: judicious.

82. Good old Cause: Puritan republicanism.

85–133. The ungrateful people encourage rumours of a plot hatched by the Jebusites (Catholics), who are already impoverished by taxation and stripped of political powers.

92–7. Catholics were excluded from all civil or military office by the Test Act of 1673. In 1678 they were excluded from Parliament and no Catholic sat in either House until 1829.

104. Jewish Rabbins: Clergy of the Church of England.

108–9. that Plot: the Popish Plot, whose existence was falsely sworn to by Titus Oates before the Privy Council in September 1678, though denied by innocent men who were condemned and executed as traitors. See the general Introduction.

113. A reference, by way of a play on words, to the sacrament of the Mass.

114. dash'd and brew'd: diluted and blended.

118. Egyptian Rites: the rites of Catholic France. The pun suggests political rights, as well as rites of the Church.

119–21. A further reference to the eating of bread and drinking of wine in the Mass, being to Catholics the body and blood of Christ.

127. Stews: brothels. Dryden ironically brackets these with the Court.

129. Fleece: a reference to the income enjoyed by the Church of England.

130–1. William Ireland, Thomas Pickering, and John Grove were tried and executed, on the evidence of Titus Oates, for plotting the murder of Charles II by shooting him.

134–229. In consequence of the rumours, factions spring up which are hostile to the King as well as to the Jebusites. The leader of this subversion is the energetic, inconstant politician Achitophel. Had Achitophel been content to remain a judge and to curb his political ambition, he would have earned the gratitude of his country. Instead, he chose to unite the common people against their monarch, even suggesting that the King himself was a Jebusite.

138. Humour: Men were believed to have four bodily humours, hot, cold, moist, and dry. Their characters or moods were determined by the greater or smaller proportion of each humour within them.

150. Achitophel: Anthony Ashley Cooper, 1st Earl of Shaftesbury (1621–83) supported Charles I in the Civil War until 1644, and then changed sides. He supported Cromwell but after Cromwell's death in 1658, he returned to the Royalist side. He was made Chancellor of the Exchequer, as Baron Ashley, in 1661. After being a member of the 'Cabal', he was made Lord Chancellor, as Earl of Shaftesbury, in 1672. He was dismissed in 1673 and, having always been a staunch Protestant, soon became a leader of the anti-Catholic movement, and of the 'country party', later the Whigs, which opposed the 'court party'.

166. Shaftesbury was sixty years old when *Absalom and Achitophel* was published.

170. Plato was said to have described man as having two legs, like a bird, but, unlike a bird, no feathers.

171. Shaftesbury's son was born in 1652, shortly before Shaftesbury joined parliamentary administration.

175–7. *Triple Bond*: England's alliance with Holland and Sweden (1668) was broken by an alliance with France in 1670, though it was the King rather than Shaftesbury who was responsible for this. The triple bond might also be the constitutional one of King, Lords, and Commons.

180–91. These lines first appeared in the second edition of the poem, published a few weeks after its first edition.

184. *wink*: close their eyes to misdeeds.

187. *Judge*: a reference to Shaftesbury as Lord Chancellor.

188. *Abbethdin*: judge of the Jewish civil court.

193. *Gown*: the robes of a judge or counsel.

195. *Cockle*: a purple-flowered weed found among corn.

204. *manifest*: clearly guilty.

206. *Buckler*: shield.

216–19. A Prime is the first in a lunar cycle of 19 years. The Long Parliament of 1641; the Restoration of 1660, and the crisis of 1679 had occurred at nineteen-year intervals.

227. *Democracy*: Like the word 'patriot', 'democracy' did not have the modern tone of approval associated with it.

230–302. Achitophel's address to Absalom. He encourages Absalom to seize the opportunity of becoming the people's champion, since David's power and influence are declining and the time is ripe to replace him. In Achitophel's view, it is the will of the people, not the law of succession by birth, which gives a man the right to be king.

233. Cf. Exodus 13:21. 'And the Lord went before them by day in a pillar of a cloud, to lead them the way; and by night in a pillar of fire, to give them light; to go by day and night.'

235. Cf. Exodus 14:21. 'And Moses stretched out his hand over the sea; and the Lord caused the sea to go back by a strong east wind all that night, and made the sea dry land, and the waters were divided.'

238. *Diviners*: prophets, soothsayers.

251. *Or . . . or*: either . . . or.

257. *Bent*: course, direction.

264. *Gath*: Brussels. Cf. 1 Samuel 27:4. 'And it was told Saul that David was fled to Gath: and he sought no more again for him.'

270. *Jordan's Sand*: Dover beach; cf. 2 Samuel 19:15. 'So the king returned and came to Jordan'.

272. *Strand*: shore.

273–4. The fall of Lucifer from heaven after his rebellion against God. Milton uses the story in *Paradise Lost*, describing the rebellion in books v and vi.

281. Pharaoh: Louis XIV.

299–302. Monmouth's right to the throne would have been less clear than that of Charles II. This would have enabled Shaftesbury and others to control Monmouth's power as king more strictly.

303–72. Achitophel's flattery stimulates Absalom's ambition, but he still remains loyal to his father David. He points out that David has sole right to rule, and that he is wise and moderate. When David dies, the crown must pass, by strict order of succession, to his brother. Yet Absalom recognises his own longing for power.

310. A pun on 'mettle' and 'metal', as well as 'Angel' in both the sense of a gold coin and that of an angelic being.

320. Wonders: Cf. *Annus Mirabilis*.

334. Dog-star: Sirius, whose appearance was associated in Roman literature with a period of intense summer heat.

336. Popularly: as the common people or mob might do.

344. Prevents: anticipates.

353. For the campaign against the Duke of York, see the general Introduction.

373–476. Achitophel makes a final effort to sway Absalom in favour of rebellion. He points out Absalom's royal virtues, shown in his scrupulous conduct, and suggests how Parliament may deprive the King of revenue and so force him to make Absalom, his illegitimate son, his heir. Achitophel expounds the Whig view that the people have a right to determine who shall succeed to the throne. He warns Absalom of the personal danger he must face if David's brother becomes King, and hints that David is only restrained from legitimating Absalom by fear of this brother.

373. There is a Miltonic sound to this line, caused by the use of English words in Latin syntactical forms, as in 'Him Staggering', which is a prominent feature of the verse in *Paradise Lost*.

385. suppose: suggest.

390–2. Sanhedrin: Parliament. To the Jews, the Sanhedrin was a supreme court of justice and legislature. The attempts of Charles II to rule without Parliament were often frustrated by his dependence on Parliament for revenue.

401. The next Successor: James, Duke of York.

409–16. Shaftesbury, as Achitophel, expresses the Whig view of limits to be placed on the right of royal succession. In primitive societies, men entrusted kings with the power of government, but this did not necessarily include the power of handing on kingship, or 'resuming' it, for their descendants indefinitely.

414. In its own wrong: to its own detriment.

417. Before Cromwell became Lord Protector in 1653, the English republicans had tried to create a state which would acknowledge God alone as supreme ruler.

438. a Legacy of Barren Land: the Border estates of Monmouth's wife.

458. A maxim of Thomas Hobbes in *Leviathan* (1651).

461. Prevail: avail.

477–542. Ambition appears as Absalom's great weakness and Achitophel exploits this by uniting all the malcontents of Israel against David. Some wish to limit the monarchy, others to abolish it. Spurred on by hatred of the Jebusites, both the mob and the Levites unite behind Achitophel.

490. Popularly: cf. line *336* and note.   *prosecute*: carry forward.

499. Springs of Property: the political rights of those who owned land.

512. Hating not only Charles II but the whole institution of monarchy.

513. Solymaean Rout: the Jerusalem (i.e. London) rabble. Jerusalem was also known as Solyma.

517. Ethnic: gentile. The Jebusites were gentiles, and were regarded as alien to Jewish culture, as Catholics were to that of England.

519. Levites: Dissenting ministers who had been deprived of their benefices in 1662 by the Act of Uniformity. The Act deprived those who would not subscribe to the beliefs of the Church of England.

520. Ark: cf. *Annus Mirabilis*, line *374* and note.

521–4. cf. line *417* and note.

524. Inspiration: divine inspiration.

525. Aaron: The maker of the Golden Calf (i.e. republic); cf. Exodus 28–32.

526. If they could take political power by virtue of being in a state of divine grace.

530. Enthusiastic: fanatical.

539–40. A reference to salvation by faith and not by works.

541. Hydra: To kill the Hydra was one of the labours of Hercules. As soon as one head was cut off, two would replace it, but with the aid of Iolaus, Hercules cut off each head and seared the stump with a burning brand before new heads could grow.

543–681. The supporters of Absalom and Achitophel are described. They include the erratic Zimri; the miserly and spiteful Shimei; and Corah, the inventor of non-existent plots.

544. Zimri: George Villiers, Duke of Buckingham (1628–87). As a young man, Buckingham was a friend of Charles II and, on the fall of Clarendon in 1667, became the King's adviser. However, when Oates 'exposed' the Popish Plot in 1679, Buckingham joined the King's opponents.

550. Chemist: alchemist.

574. well hung: fluent and lecherous. The words, as used by Dryden, have a double meaning. *Balaam* is Theophilus Hastings, Earl of Huntingdon, a leader of the attacks on the Duke of York and an opponent of the King's attempt to rule without Parliament. In

1681, however, he deserted Shaftesbury and joined the King.
Caleb: Arthur Capel, Earl of Essex.

575-6. Canting Nadab: William, Lord Howard of Escrick, a former Dissenting preacher, indicted in 1681 for libelling Charles II. While in the Tower he is said to have shown his loyalty to Church and King by taking Communion, using 'Lamb's Wool' (hot ale and pulped apple) for wine.

581. Jonas: Sir William Jones, Attorney-General until November 1679 and responsible for prosecuting the first victims of the Popish Plot. He was a leader of the campaign to exclude the Duke of York from succession to the throne and is said to have drawn up the Exclusion Bill.

585. Shimei: Slingsby Bethel, sheriff of London, a Whig with republican sympathies.

595. Vare: staff of office.

598. Sons of Belial: sons of the devil. 'Belial' is probably a pun, since during the sitting of Parliament at Oxford in 1681, the Whigs had lodged at Balliol.

599. not prodigal of pelf: not easily parted from his money.

607. Until the Juries Act of 1731, it was relatively easy for London juries to be packed so that they returned the desired verdict in a political trial. Both political parties made use of this and Shaftesbury's trial in November 1681 is a clear example.

617. Rechabite: the sons of Rechab did not drink wine.

632. Corah: Titus Oates (1649–1705). For further details of the life of Oates, see the general Introduction.

633-5. At God's command, Moses made a serpent of brass, as an antidote to the lethal bites of fiery serpents. 'And Moses made a serpent of brass, and put it upon a pole, and it came to pass that if a serpent had bitten any man, when he beheld the serpent of brass, he lived', Numbers 21:9.

636-7. Cf. *Annus Mirabilis*, lines *65-6* and note.

639. The father of Titus Oates was a Norfolk weaver and Anabaptist preacher.

642-3. St Stephen was condemned to death on the evidence of 'false witnesses'; cf. Acts 6:9–15.

647. Dryden's description is, in fact, of a choleric and aggressive person.

649. A red face, which shone like the face of Moses coming down from Mount Sinai; cf. Exodus 34:29–30.

657-9. Oates received the degree of Doctor of Divinity from the University of Salamanca, according to his own account, but the University denied this.

672-3. Oates alleged that the Queen was guilty of treason.

676-7. Agag: There are two possible identifications.

(i) Sir Edmund Berry Godfrey, allegedly murdered by Catholics.
(ii) Lord Stafford, a Catholic, condemned and executed in 1680 on the evidence of Oates; cf. 1 Samuel 15: 27–35.

682–758. Deluded by this show of support, Absalom joins David's enemies, ingratiating himself with the crowd. He tells the people that he has suffered for their cause, that the Jebusites are plotting against them, and that the aged, lecherous David is indifferent to their plight. Absalom is acclaimed and makes a lavish tour among his supporters.

697. Hybla drops: honey drops. Hybla, in Sicily, was renowned for its honey.

700. a Banished man: Monmouth was banished from the country in September 1679 but returned two months later.

705. Egypt and Tyrus: France and Holland.

710. Bathsheba: Louise-Renée de Kéroualle, Duchess of Portsmouth, mistress of Charles II who tried to influence him in favour of a French alliance.

738. Issachar: Thomas Thynne (1648–82) of Longleat, Wiltshire, one of Monmouth's richest supporters.

750. According to Oates, both the Queen and the Duke of York were plotting against the King's life.

759–810. This section of the poem expresses Dryden's own political philosophy, as it relates to the crisis of 1679–81. It is an argument designed to show that, whatever the faults of the present system, any change will be for the worse, and is, overwhelmingly, an argument for maintaining the *status quo*. Lines *759–64* put the point that tyrannical rule is unacceptable. Men should not totally surrender their political rights and those of their descendants. Lines *765–80* concede the Whig claim that kings rule by a covenant with their people rather than by divine right, but Dryden insists that the people cannot take back power, entrusted to a king, at any moment they choose, since this would destroy the basis of government. In lines *781–94* he points out that democratic or parliamentary opinion is not infallible. The judgment of the majority may be bad, as well as good. Rule by popular opinion will end in a state of anarchy, in which each man fights for himself. (The influence of Thomas Hobbes, who held that a state of nature is a state in which men fight each other, is evident in these lines.) In lines *795–810*, Dryden concludes that though kings may only rule by the general consent of their people, no sensible man would choose to overthrow the king and government. However bad their rule, the consequences of revolution would be worse. The wise course, therefore, is to renew the fabric of government, where necessary, but not to change its foundations.

767. resuming: continuing.

777–8. If property is the basis of power, then power will ultimately pass to the crowd.

786. The higher the tide, the more rapid the fall.

794. Cf. Hobbes, *Leviathan*: 'It is manifest that during the time men live without a common power to keep them all in awe, they are in that condition which is called war. . . . And thus much for the ill condition, which man by mere Nature is actually placed in.'

804. *Ark*: Cf. *Annus Mirabilis*, line 374 and note.

811–932. David's supporters are listed, including the wealthy Barzillai who shared defeat and exile with his master; Zadok the Priest; Adriel, a man of letters who supported David ably in debate; Jotham, a capable orator, and Hushai, expert in the management of finances. They view with grief the efforts of Absalom, Achitophel and their followers.

817. *Barzillai*: James Butler, Duke of Ormonde (1610–88), Lord Lieutenant of Ireland under Charles I and Charles II. He supported the Royalists in the Civil War and went into exile with Charles II.

825. *practis'd*: a play on this word which has both its modern sense and that of the French *pratiquer*, to frequent.

831. *His Eldest Hope*: Thomas, Earl of Ossory (1634–80), a naval commander who achieved distinction in the wars against France and Holland in the reign of Charles II.

832–4. Cf. Virgil, *Aeneid* v, 49–50.

> iamque dies, nisi fallor, adest, quem semper acerbum,
> semper honoratum (sic di voluistis) habebo.

'And now, unless I'm mistaken, the day is at hand which I shall always hold poignant and sacred, as you, the gods, have decreed.'

834. *unequal*: unjust, inequitable.

844–5. Cf. Virgil, *Aeneid* vi, 878–80.

> heu pietas! heu prisca fides invictaque bello
> dextera! non illi se quisquam impune tulisset
> obvius armato.

'Alas for piety! Alas for ancient faith and the right hand unvanquished in war! No foe would have met him in battle with impunity.'

847. *Short is the date*: soon is the end.

864–5. *Zadok the Priest*: William Sancroft (1617–93), Archbishop of Canterbury.

866. *Sagan*: Deputy of the Jewish high priest. In this case, the Sagan of Jerusalem is the Bishop of London, Henry Compton (1632–1713).

868. *Him of the Western dome*: John Dolben (1625–86), Dean of Westminster and, later, Bishop of Rochester. 'Dome' is a house or foundation, from the Latin *domus*. The foundation in this case is Westminster School.

870. *The Prophets' Sons*: the boys of Westminster School.

877. *Sharp judging Adriel the Muses' friend*: John Sheffield, Earl of

Mulgrave (1648–1721), a patron of Dryden and author of *An Essay upon Satire* (1679) to which Dryden may have contributed. For further details of the *Essay*, see the general Introduction.

882. Jotham: George Savile, Marquis of Halifax (1633–95). He supported Shaftesbury until 1679 but then led the opposition to the Exclusion Bill in the House of Lords. He was known as the 'Trimmer' from his habit of changing sides.

888. Hushai: Laurence Hyde, Earl of Rochester (1642–1711), a Tory leader who negotiated the alliance with Holland in 1678.

899. Amiel: Edward Seymour (1633–1708), Speaker of the House of Commons.

910. unequal Ruler of the Day: Phaeton, who in Greek mythology was allowed by his father, Helios, to drive the horses of the sun for a day. He lost control of them and Jove killed him with a thunderbolt to save the earth from destruction. The story is told in Ovid, *Metamorphoses*, book ii.

920. plume: pluck.

933–1031. King David is at last provoked to speak. He announces that he has so far shown mercy and forgiveness to his enemies, and would willingly forgive Absalom. But he warns those factions who reject his authority and his clemency that he will let them fight each other over their invented 'plot' and then, when they are exhausted, he will destroy them. At his words, the rebellion dies away and royal authority is restored. The two sources for David's speech appear to be the speech of Charles II to the Oxford Parliament of 1681, and the pamphlet *His Majesty's Declaration to all his Loving Subjects*, which appeared in the same year.

944. The Commons and the sheriffs of London challenged the right of the King to grant pardons or commute sentences.

955. Samson: a reference to Monmouth as the Samson who would destroy the Temple; cf. Judges 16: 25–31.

957–60. These lines first appeared in the second edition of the poem.

967. Brave: cut-throat.

982. Jacob obtained the blessing of his blind father, Isaac, by wearing goatskin on his hands and thus impersonating his elder brother Esau. Isaac was deceived because 'the voice is Jacob's voice, but the hands are the hands of Esau,' Genesis 27: 22.

1006–9. Grace, or pardon, is one aspect of the law which the King's enemies may safely confront. But if they insist on confronting the judgment of the law, face to face, they shall suffer the consequence of their temerity.

1012–13. Some of those who had given 'evidence' of the Popish Plot were prepared to give evidence against the inventors of it by 1681.

1018. event: outcome.

PROLOGUE TO THE DUCHESS ON HER RETURN FROM SCOTLAND. At the time of the rumoured Popish Plot, James, Duke of York and his Duchess had left London and had spent some time abroad and, later, in Scotland. In March 1682, the Duke returned to London, and Dryden greeted him with a special prologue on his reappearance in the Duke's Theatre. In May 1682, the Duke went to Scotland to escort the Duchess back to London, and this prologue was written for her. As a panegyric poem, it shares the heroic tone and mythological cosmography of *Annus Mirabilis*, though in a smaller compass and more intimate voice. It is not a private poem, addressed from one person to another, but it is addressed to a limited audience.

14. Nereids: sea-nymphs.

16. Thetis: the goddess Thetis, mother of Achilles, was one of the Nereids in Greek mythology.

24. Joseph's dream: Pharaoh's dreams of plenty and famine, interpreted by Joseph in Genesis xli.

37. Cynthia: Diana, the moon goddess of Roman mythology.

MAC FLECKNOE: OR, A SATIRE UPON THE TRUE–BLUE PROTESTANT POET T.S. *Mac Flecknoe*, meaning 'son of Flecknoe' was probably written on the death of Richard Flecknoe in 1678. It was first published, apparently without Dryden's authority, in 1682, after Dryden had been attacked by his enemy Thomas Shadwell in *The Medal of John Bayes*.

Richard Flecknoe was an Irishman and a Catholic priest, whose name became synonymous with a writer of feeble verse. 'How natural is the connection of thought between a bad poet and Flecknoe' wrote Dryden in 1680, a view shared by most contemporary critics. Flecknoe wrote five plays, including *Love's Kingdom* (1664), though four of them remained unperformed. He published collections of epigrams and in one collection, *Epigrams of All Sorts*, actually praised Dryden. For some years he lived in Lisbon and was patronised by King John of Portugal. His lute playing was said to be as bad as his poetry. Andrew Marvell, in *Fleckno, an English Priest at Rome*, describes his poems as 'ill made' and even worse when read aloud by Flecknoe himself. He recalls the sounds of Flecknoe's lute mingling with those of its owner's stomach:

> So while he with his gouty Fingers crawls
> Over the Lute, his murmuring Belly calls,
> Whose hungry Guts to the same straitness twin'd
> In echo to the trembling Strings repin'd.

In *Mac Flecknoe*, Dryden imagines Flecknoe, at the end of his life, choosing a successor to carry on the tradition of dullness and stupidity. The choice falls on the poet and playwright Thomas Shadwell (*c.* 1642–92), once Dryden's collaborator, now his enemy. Of course, Shadwell had more talent than Dryden suggests, being the author of such plays as *The Sullen Lovers* and *The Virtuoso*, as well as operas like *Psyche*. He had a gift for broad bawdy humour, and succeeded Dryden as Poet Laureate after the Glorious Revolution of 1689. Lord Dorset, who appointed him, explained: 'I do not pretend to say how great a poet Shadwell may be, but I am sure he is an honest man.' The truth is, that Dryden and Shadwell had quarrelled over two things. They had taken different sides in politics, and in drama. Shadwell had Whig sympathies and a style of comedy that bordered on farce: Dryden's sympathies were with the King, and he favoured a more sophisticated style of stage comedy. Though Dryden wrote a Prologue for Shadwell's *The True Widow* in 1676, the disputes of the next six years found them on opposing sides. With Shadwell's open attack in *The Medal of John Bayes*, Dryden was provoked into replying, both in *Mac Flecknoe* and in the second part of *Absalom and Achitophel*.

Satire may ridicule a man by belittling him or by inflating him to a size absurdly larger than life, an easy task with Shadwell who was distinguished by corpulence. It is this second, mock-heroic, style which Dryden uses here, adopting the vocabulary and intonation of extravagant praise to make Shadwell appear ridiculous. As the notes indicate, Dryden introduces comic echoes of such heroic master-pieces as Virgil's *Aeneid*, Milton's *Paradise Lost*, and, particularly, of Cowley's *Davideis*, for which Dryden himself had a great admiration. Abraham Cowley (1618–67) planned an epic poem in twelve books, the same number as Virgil's *Aeneid*, on the biblical history of King David. He chose to write his epic in rhymed couplets, and the first four books were published in 1656. The rest of the poem remained unfinished. The first book, with its description of hell and the fall of the angels, anticipates the theme of *Paradise Lost*, and the story then proceeds to unfold the events of David's earlier life, including the fight with Goliath. Though Cowley's epic style, its couplet verse and wide range of imagery, might be expected to appeal to Dryden in the later seventeenth century, this unfinished epic soon fell from critical favour.

Throughout *Mac Flecknoe*, the language and imagery are those of kingship, prophecy, and messiahship, skilfully juxtaposed with those of sham theatricality, appropriate to Shadwell's profession. At the end of the poem, Flecknoe disappears through a stage trap-door to echoes of the Old Testament account of Elijah being carried up to heaven in a chariot of fire. Shadwell assumes the proportions of a mock-hero: he is not dull as ordinary men are, he is dull (as he is fat) on a regal and almost godlike scale. One cause of his quarrel with Dryden was that Shadwell saw himself as the disciple of Ben Jonson, whom Dryden thought a good enough playwright for the early seventeenth century but rejected as a model to be copied sixty years later. In lines *193–4* he suggests that the only real resemblance between Jonson and Shadwell is in the size of their bellies. The satire in *Mac Flecknoe* works by inflating Shadwell, like a balloon, and then puncturing him at the appropriate moment. The first thirty lines of the poem provide the initial instance of this, starting gently and working up to the first complete denunciation in line *30*, whose beats fall like measured blows, while the consonants that were so soft in the previous lines strike sharply and precisely in their attack.

1–12. The scene is set, Flecknoe prepares to abdicate and name his successor as prince of dullness.

3. Augustus: Nephew and heir of Julius Caesar, he entered politics as Octavian, at the age of nineteen, when Caesar was murdered in 44 B.C. He reigned, as the Emperor Augustus, from 27 B.C. to A.D. 14.

13–63. Flecknoe announces his successor and the narrator comments briefly.

15–24. The rhythm and intonation of this description of Shadwell echo Cowley's description of Abdon in his *Davideis* book iv.

25. goodly Fabric: a reference to Shadwell's size.

28. supinely: lethargically.

29. Heywood and Shirley: Thomas Heywood (*c.* 1574–1641) and James Shirley (1596–1666), two dramatists not much admired by Dryden.   *Types*: prophetic symbols.

30. Tautology: useless repetition.

32. An echo of the words of St John the Baptist in Matthew 3: 3, 'Prepare ye the way of the Lord'. Shadwell is the messiah of dullness and Flecknoe is his prophet.

33. Norwich Drugget: coarse woollen cloth, worn by impecunious authors. Shadwell was born in Norfolk.

35. whilom: once.

43. Arion: a mythical Greek poet, saved from drowning by being carried ashore on a dolphin's back.

47. Pissing-Alley: an alley between Holywell Street and the Strand. Holywell Street became notorious as the market for obscene literature.

48. Aston Hall: Aston seems to be the name of a man, not of a place.

> for who would preach
> Morals to Armstrong, or dull Aston teach?
> Earl of Mulgrave, *Essay upon Satire* (1679), 29–30.

50. Toast: a beautiful woman, greatly admired.

53. St André: a French choreographer who assisted in the production of Shadwell's opera *Psyche* (1675).

57. Singleton: John Singleton was one of the King's musicians.

59. *Villerius*: a character in *The Siege of Rhodes* (1656), an opera by Sir William Davenant.

64–93. A description of the unsavoury but appropriate site chosen for Shadwell's throne.

64. *Augusta*: London.

66. *inform*: inspire.

67. *hight*: was called.

72–3. Cf. Cowley, *Davideis*, i, 79–80.

> Where their vast *Court* the *Mother-waters* keep,
> And, undisturb'd by *Moons*, in silence sleep.

74. *a Nursery*: a theatre where young actors were trained.

76–7. Cf. Cowley, *Davideis*, i, 75–6.

> Beneath the dens where *unfledg'd Tempests* lie,
> And infant *Winds* their tender *Voices* try.

78. *Maximins*: Maximin is a bombastic tyrant in Dryden's *Tyrannic Love* (1670).

79–80. John Fletcher (1579–1625) and Ben Jonson (1572–1637). The second of these two dramatists was much admired by Shadwell. *Buskin*: tragedy; *Sock*: comedy, from the footwear worn by Greek actors for the two styles; cf. Milton, *L'Allegro*, 131–2:

> Then to the well-trod stage anon,
> If *Jonson's* learned Sock be on.

81. *Simkin*: a simpleton, the name traditionally given to the character of a cobbler in a dramatic interlude or sketch.

82. Cf. Davenant, *Gondibert* (1651), ii, v, 36.

> This to a structure led, long known to Fame,
> And call'd The Monument of vanish'd Minds.

83. *Clinches*: puns.

84. *Panton*: said to have been a well-known punster but this may, in fact, be the name of a character in a comedy.

87. *ancient Dekker prophesied*: *Satiromastix: or, The Untrussing of the Humorous Poet* by Thomas Dekker (1570–1641).

90–3. References to Shadwell's own plays: *The Humorists* (1670); *The Miser* (1672); *Psyche* (1675). No play by Shadwell called *The Hypocrite* is known to survive. Raymond and Bruce are characters in *The Humorists* and *The Virtuoso*, respectively.

94–138. An account of the preliminaries to Shadwell's coronation.

94. Cf. Virgil, *Aeneid*, iv, 173–4.

> extemplo Libyae magnas it Fama per urbes,
> Fama, malum qua non aliud velocius ullum.

'Rumour at once ran through the great towns of Libya, rumour the swiftest of all evils.'

102. *Ogilby*: John Ogilby (1600–76), translator of Homer, Virgil, and Aesop.

105. *Herringman*: Henry Herringman, publisher of both Dryden and Shadwell.

107. Cf. Milton, *Paradise Lost*, ii, 1–2.

> High on a Throne of Royal State, which far
> Outshone the wealth of *Ormus* and of *Ind* . . .

108. *Ascanius*: the son of Aeneas, described as Rome's other hope in *Aeneid*, xii, 168, 'magnae spes altera Romae'.

112–13. Hamilcar Barca made his son Hannibal swear an oath of enmity towards Rome.

120. *sinister*: left. The monarch holds the sceptre in his right hand and the orb in his left.

122. *Love's Kingdom*: the title of a 'pastoral tragi-comedy' by Flecknoe (1664).

129–31. Romulus won his argument with Remus about the site to be chosen for Rome, since he saw twelve vultures in flight, whereas Remus saw only six.

134–6. Cf. the anointing of David by Samuel in Cowley's *Davideis*, book i, and the anointing of Saul by Samuel in book iv.

137. *the raging God*: the god of dullness speaking through his prophet Flecknoe; cf. Virgil's account of Apollo speaking through the Sibyl in *Aeneid*, vi, 45–101 (lines *68–154* in Dryden's translation in the present selection).

139–210. Flecknoe's abdication speech.

149. In his prologue to *The Virtuoso*, Shadwell attacks those prolific authors who 'scribble twice a year', and suggests that worthwhile literature must be written more slowly.

151. *gentle George*: Sir George Etherege (*c.* 1634–*c.* 1691). Dorimant, Sir Fopling Flutter, and Mrs Loveit are characters in his play *The Man of Mode* (1676), Cully in *The Comical Revenge* (1664), and Cockwood in *She would if she could* (1668).

163–4. Sir Charles Sedley wrote a prologue for Shadwell's *Epsom Wells* (1673) but Shadwell denied rumours that Sedley had also written part of the play itself.

168. *Sir Formal*: Sir Formal Trifle is a character in Shadwell's *Virtuoso*. It is said of him that 'he never speaks without Flowers of Rhetoric'.

170. *Northern Dedications*: Shadwell dedicated five plays to the Duke or Duchess of Newcastle.

171–86. A reference to Shadwell's admiration for Ben Jonson.

176. For Dryden's views on nature and art, see the general Intro-

duction. The point here is that there is no place for Flecknoe or Shadwell either in literature which is true to the laws of nature or in literature which is deliberately artificial, since they fall below the level of both; cf. lines 207–8 and note.

179. *Prince Nicander*: Psyche's lover in Shadwell's opera.

181. *sold Bargains*: went too far.　　*Whip-stitch, kiss my Arse*: Sir Samuel Hearty in *The Virtuoso* exclaims on several occasions, 'Whipstitch, your nose in my breech'.

183–4. Jonson did not steal from Fletcher, as Shadwell is alleged to have stolen material from the plays of Etherege.

188. *New Humours*: Shadwell tried to imitate Jonson in basing comedy on the belief that men's characters are determined by humours: hot, cold, moist, and dry.

189–92. Cf. Shadwell, Epilogue to *The Humorists*, 15–18.

> A Humour is the Bias of the Mind,
> By which with violence 'tis one way inclin'd:
> It makes our Actions lean on one side still,
> And in all Changes that way bends the will.

194. *Tympany*: a flatulent swelling caused by an obstruction.

195. *Tun*: a large cask for beer or wine, holding 252 gallons.

196. *Kilderkin*: a quarter of a tun.

202. *Irish*: Shadwell remarked, 'Sure he goes a little too far in calling me the *dullest* and has no more reason for that than for giving me the Irish name of *Mack*, when he knows I never saw Ireland till I was three-and-twenty years old, and was there but four months.'

203–4. Cf. John Cleveland, *The Rebel Scot* (c. 1643), 27–8.

> Come keen Iambics with your badger's feet,
> And badger-like bite till your teeth do meet.

204. *Anagram*: the transposition of the letters of a word or phrase to form a new word or phrase.

206. *Acrostic*: a poem with lines whose initial letters spell out a word.

207. *Wings . . . Altars*: poems shaped like wings or altars; cf. George Herbert, 'Easter Wings' and 'The Altar' in *The Temple* (1633). Such artificiality was condemned as contrary to nature, whose rules the poet must follow, by Dryden and his contemporaries in the later seventeenth century. True art was the natural use of language, metre, and imagery, not the distortion of them. In 1650, in his *Answer to D'Avenant's Preface to Gondibert*, Thomas Hobbes derided those who 'seek glory from a needless difficulty, as he that contrived Verses into the forms of an Organ, a Hatchet, an Egg, an Altar, and a pair of Wings'.

208. A reference to ingenious punning.

212. Bruce and Longvil are characters in Shadwell's *Virtuoso*, in which Sir Formal Trifle is made to fall through a trap-door in the middle of a speech.

214–17. The theme of messianic succession which runs through the poem is echoed finally in the biblical image with which it ends. The mantle of Flecknoe falls on Shadwell, as that of Elijah fell on Elisha; cf. 2 Kings 2: 11–13, 'And Elijah went up by a whirlwind into heaven. And Elisha saw it . . . He took up also the mantle of Elijah that fell from him.'

THE SECOND PART OF ABSALOM AND ACHITOPHEL: A POEM. The second part of *Absalom and Achitophel* was published in November 1682. Dryden had been urged to write a sequel to the extremely successful first part and to bring the story of the political crisis up to date, but he declined to do this. However, at Dryden's suggestion, a second part was undertaken by the dramatist Nahum Tate (1652–1715), author of a new version of *King Lear* which ended happily with the marriage of Cordelia and Edgar; librettist for Purcell's opera *Dido and Aeneas*, and author, with Nicholas Brady, of a metrical version of the Psalms. Tate's satire fell far short of Dryden's, but Dryden revised the second part of *Absalom and Achitophel*, as well as contributing a number of passages of his own. According to the publisher, Jacob Tonson, the whole of the extract reprinted in this selection (lines *310–509*) was Dryden's work. Dryden uses the passage principally as an attack on Shadwell (Og), and another rival dramatist, Elkanah Settle (Doeg).

313. A reference to former sequestrations of property by the Cromwellians.

320. Hebronite: Scotsman.

321. Judas: Robert Ferguson, who held a living in Kent under Cromwell, but was expelled at the Act of Uniformity in 1662 and became a Dissenting preacher. He organised the financing and administration of the Whig press.

324–7. Ferguson was responsible for a Dissenting Academy at Islington.

330. Phaleg: James Forbes, also a Scotsman, tutor to the Duke of Ormonde's family.

333. Omer: the amount of manna which God ordered each Israelite to gather; cf. Exodus 16: 15–27.

335. alter'd: altered ownership of.

338. 'And he said unto me, Son of man, can these bones live?' Ezekiel 37: 3. Dryden refers to Forbes's thinness. There is no evidence to support the accusation in the following lines that Forbes seduced any member of Ormonde's family.

344–9. Forbes travelled as tutor to the Earl of Derby, husband of

Ormonde's grand-daughter, but was so ill-used that he returned home.

353. Ben-Jochanan: Samuel Johnson (1649–1703), chaplain to Lord Russell, who was executed after the Rye House Plot of 1683, which aimed to prevent the progress of Catholicism in England by assassinating Charles II. Three years later, Johnson himself was flogged from Newgate to Tyburn for publishing his *Address to all the English Protestants in the English Army*, urging them not to fight for James II.

358–9. An ephod was a vestment of Jewish priests, but this one is mere linen, in which Ben-Jochanan makes a living by conducting funeral services.

360. Charge: charges, expenses.

370. The devil rewards his servants with gifts of shame.

371. Johnson's *Julian the Apostate* (1682) was a biography of the Roman Emperor Julian, but he used it to oppose the succession of James II, and was imprisoned.

382. Leading-Card: incentive.

384–5. Cf. Genesis 9: 20–7. When Noah was drunk, his son Ham saw him and told his two brothers, Shem and Japheth, who covered Noah without looking at him. Noah blessed them and cursed Ham.

386–7. According to Johnson, rebelliousness was a characteristic of the primitive Church.

390–5. The saint, Johnson's 'hot *Father*', is St Gregory Nazianzus, whose attacks on the Emperor Julian are quoted by Johnson. But the saint's descendants, in Dryden's view, are a fanatical sect and not the true Church. Johnson's version of history, according to Dryden, is the result of an invalid diet of asses' milk, and too much writing.

396–9. Balack: Gilbert Burnet (1643–1715), Bishop of Salisbury (1689) and author of the great Whig history of the period, the *History of His Own Times*, published posthumously in 1724–34. Charles II regarded him as a sworn enemy.

400. Levi: Johnson.

401. Gown: ecclesiastical dress.

403. A reference to the metrical translation of the Psalms by Sternhold and Hopkins (1548–62).

405. Mephibosheth: Samuel Pordage (1633–91), son of a clergyman who was deprived of his living for conversing with evil spirits. After the first part of *Absalom and Achitophel* appeared, Pordage attacked Dryden in *Azariah and Hushai*, and, later, in *The Medal Reversed*.

407. Uzza: unidentified.

408. Og: Shadwell.   *Doeg*: Elkanah Settle (1648–1724), a rival dramatist and author of *The Empress of Morocco* (1673). He had joined the Whigs as a supporter of Shaftesbury at the time of the Popish Plot, and attacked Dryden in *Absalom Senior: or, Achitophel*

Transpros'd, an answer to the first part of Dryden's poem.

418. Picking work: fastidious work.

419. Faggoted: gathered in bundles like loose firewood.

429. Almonds were given to parrots as a reward in training them to talk.

430. In Settle's *Absalom Senior*, Absalom is the Duke of York.

437. Buggery: bestiality, in this context.

444–6. Absalom Senior opened with a parody of *Absalom and Achitophel*:

> In gloomy times, when Priestcraft bore the sway,
> And made Heaven's Gate a Lock to their own Key . . .

Dryden, in turn, now parodies Settle's parody.

452. Serpents: fireworks.

458. tun: cf. *MacFlecknoe*, line *195* and note.

481. strong Nativity: favourable horoscope.

502. unlick'd: unpolished.   *unpointed*: unpunctuated.

TO MY INGENIOUS FRIEND, MR HENRY HIGDEN, ESQ; ON HIS TRANSLATION OF THE TENTH SATIRE OF JUVENAL. Henry Higden, a member of the Middle Temple, published his *Essay on the Tenth Satire of Juvenal* in 1687. In what is really a verse letter, Dryden writes in a more intimate, relaxed and prosaic style. He discusses the origin and purpose of satire. By describing Higden as 'ingenious' he means 'skilful' rather than 'artful'.

2. Pasquins: authors of lampoons.

7. Drolls: wags.

16. Yours: Juvenal.

22. your Author's principle: In Satire x, 346–66, Juvenal offers his recipe for a contented life. He recommends trust in the gods, who alone know what is best for men, and adds that only such gifts as health, wisdom, courage, and endurance are worth praying for. Wise men do not worship fortune.

40. Your Tribe: lawyers.

43. Clients would fail: The supply of clients would fail.

TO SIR GEORGE ETHEREGE. Sir George Etherege, the dramatist, was sent as envoy of James II to Ratisbon, in Bavaria, in 1685. He sent home two verse letters on the charms and shortcomings of German women. Dryden replies to these in a tone of good-humoured badinage, and in a much freer verse form than in his public poetry. He reduced the length of the line from ten to eight syllables to give the verse a more lively movement, in keeping with personal correspondence.

1–4. Etherege moved two degrees south from London's latitude to

Ratisbon's, but he does little to improve the cold of Bavaria by coming from the north. Ratisbon lies at 49, not 53 degrees.

14. To infidels' territory. Etherege has been sent like a missionary to a heathen land.

20. Pinto: Ferñao Mendes Pinto (1510–83), the Portuguese explorer and adventurer who wrote an account of his travels in Asia, *Peregrinaçam*, posthumously published in 1614.

25. Chopp'd: chapped.

30. Triptolemus, according to the nine Muses, was sent by Demeter in a chariot drawn by dragons to teach the art of agriculture by sowing corn.

33. Almaine: German.

45. Rhenish Rummers: Rhineland drinking cups.

47. The Archbishops of Mainz, Trèves, and Cologne were three of the Electors of the Holy Roman Empire.

59. tope: drink.

65. defied: renounced.

73. Duke St. Aignan: François de Beauvilliers, one of Louis XIV's courtiers wrote the drama *Bradamante*.

75–7. A reference to Buckingham's *Rehearsal*, in which Dryden was satirised.

A DISCOURSE CONCERNING THE ORIGINAL AND PROGRESS OF SATIRE. This discourse forms the dedication of Dryden's translation of the satires of Juvenal and Persius to his patron, Lord Dorset. The translation, undertaken by Dryden and others, was published in 1693. In these extracts from the discourse Dryden discusses: (i) The irresponsible satire of lampoons; (ii) his own former ambition to write a British epic poem; (iii) the origin of satire; (iv) the dangers of personal satire, and the circumstances under which it is justified; (v) the use of 'fineness of Raillery' in satire.

6. vindictive: able to take revenge.

8. at Rovers: at random.

10–18. In his play *The Rehearsal* (1672) the Duke of Buckingham satirised Dryden in the character of Mr Bayes. William Smith and Johnson were both actors.

65. Machines: supernatural agencies, introduced in the epic poetry of Greece and Rome, as well as in Milton's *Paradise Lost* and in Dryden's own *Annus Mirabilis*, which he regarded as heroic in tone, though not epic in form.

69. The 'little Salary' of £200, raised to £300 in 1679, was paid to Dryden as Poet Laureate and Historiographer.

72–3. A reference to Dryden's fall from favour, as a Catholic, after the Revolution of 1689.

116. Interest: partiality.

131. Brand: stigma.

152. neglect of: neglect by.

178. Jack Ketch was public executioner during the years 1663–86 and, until the Victorian period, the name was traditionally given to any public executioner or hangman.

190. obnoxious: liable.

190–1. The frolic was begun by Buckingham, who satirised Dryden in *The Rehearsal* but was then satirised himself, far more effectively, as 'Zimri' in *Absalom and Achitophel*.

THE DEDICATION OF THE AENEIS. Dryden dedicated his translation of the *Aeneid* to the Earl of Mulgrave, author of the *Essay upon Satire* (1679) in which Dryden was suspected of having collaborated. He appears as 'sharp judging *Adriel*' in *Absalom and Achitophel* (lines 877–81).

17–18. Ludovico Ariosto (1474–1533) was the author of *Orlando Furioso* (1532), a Renaissance epic poem. Though the poem's theme is the wars of the Christians and Saracens, it has a number of sub-plots and digressions. These are the 'novels' to which Dryden refers and which interrupt the main action. In the seventeenth century, 'novel', from the Italian *novella*, was still used to describe a short story or tale, often of a romantic or improbable kind. It was not used in the modern sense until the middle of the eighteenth century.

24–6. Dryden chooses an apt image of Romance to describe the type of meandering, romantic tale which destroys epic unity.

31–8. The subject of Homer's *Iliad* is the anger of Achilles after his quarrel with Agamemnon, leader of the Greek expedition against Troy. Achilles sulked in his tent until his friend Patroclus was killed by the Trojan prince Hector in battle. Maddened by grief, Achilles then joined in the fighting, killed Hector, and obliged King Priam to ransom the body, which he otherwise threatened to throw to the dogs.

57. Numbers: metre.

68. Segrais: Jean Regnauld de Segrais translated the *Aeneid* into French and published it with a critical preface in 1668.

76. Martial: Marcus Valerius Martial (A.D. 40–104), wrote twelve books of *Epigrams*. Many of these are open or thinly-veiled attacks on the political, social and sexual morals of his contemporaries. Some of the epigrams were so obscene that English translations omitted them.

77–81. In this analogy with parliamentary government, Dryden compares the lowest class of readers to French and Dutch migrants, who are foreign to England. The lowest class of readers are foreign to Parnassus, the Greek mountain sacred to Apollo and the Muses.

They do not even own enough land there to entitle them to vote.
97. Fustian: bombast.   *Sentences*: maxims.
98–9. Owen's Epigrams: John Owen (1560–1622) produced eleven
books of epigrams between 1606 and 1613.
99–100. Statius, or Lucan: Publius Papinius Statius (A.D. 40–96) wrote
two epics, the *Thebaid*, and the *Achilleid*. For Lucan, see *Annus
Mirabilis: An Account of the Ensuing Poem*, line 32 and note.
100. Paste: mixture.
112–13. A reference to a remark of the Earl of Rochester, recorded
in Dryden's Preface to *Fables Ancient and Modern*: 'For, as my Lord
Rochester said, though somewhat profanely, *Not being of God, he
could not stand.*'

THE SIXTH BOOK OF THE AENEIS. *The Works of Virgil: Containing his
Pastorals, Georgics, and Aeneis* was published in 1697. In it, according
to Samuel Johnson, Dryden 'appears to have satisfied his friends,
and, for the most part, to have silenced his enemies'. Some, like
Luke Milbourne, attacked Dryden for having embellished or
distorted the sense of the original: but Alexander Pope, himself the
translator of Homer, regarded it as 'the most noble and spirited
translation I know in any language'. All translations are, to some
extent, a compromise between a literal translation of the original,
which may make it sound as dull as a railway timetable, and a
version which reads as a work of imagination in its new language,
though it may not be literally accurate in every detail. It is in this
second style that Dryden is supreme, as Johnson remarked. 'It is not
by comparing line with line that the merit of great works is to be
estimated, but by their general effects and ultimate result. . . . Works
of imagination excel by their allurement and delight; by their power
of attracting and detaining the attention. That book is good in
vain which the reader throws away.'

Of the twelve books of Virgil's *Aeneid*, composed in the years
30–19 B.C., book vi is the most remarkable. It deals with the age-old
human preoccupation with life after death, and narrates the descent
of Aeneas to Hades, the kingdom of the dead and the unborn.
(Homer, in book xi of the *Odyssey*, described the visit of Odysseus
to the underworld on his journey home to Greece after the Trojan
War. In the fourteenth century, the first book of Dante's *Divine
Comedy* describes the poet's tour of hell with Virgil as his guide.)
In Virgil's account, Aeneas in search of his dead father, Anchises,
encounters the monsters, the burning lake, the tortures of the
damned, the pleasures of the 'Happy Souls', and sees the men, yet
unborn, who were to be the leaders of the Roman Empire in Virgil's
own lifetime.

The *Aeneid* was, in part, an attempt to show that though Roman civilisation was later than that of Greece, its origins were no less ancient and venerable. The poem shows the Romans as descendants of the Trojans, and Aeneas and his followers as survivors of the destruction of Troy by the Greeks. Aeneas was no ordinary mortal, since his mother was the goddess Venus, and his destiny was to found a kingdom in Latium from which the Roman state would grow.

Book i of the *Aeneid* describes Aeneas and his fleet scattered near Sicily by a storm, raised by the goddess Juno who foresees the defeat of her favourite city of Carthage by Rome in the Punic Wars of the third century B.C. The fleet reaches Carthage and Aeneas is received by the widowed Queen Dido.

Books ii and iii are Aeneas's account, given to Dido, of the fall of Troy, his escape, and the instructions given him by the ghost of his dead wife that he is destined to find a new homeland for the Trojan race.

Book iv describes the tragic love of Dido and Aeneas. They are parted by Jupiter, who reminds Aeneas of the destiny and duties which call him. The Trojan fleet sails from Carthage and Dido, deserted by Aeneas, kills herself.

Book v describes the Trojans' return to Sicily, and the voyage from Sicily to Italy, during which Palinurus, the helmsman, falls asleep and is dragged overboard as the rudder parts from the ship.

Book vi opens with the arrival of the Trojans at Cumae, in southern Italy.

Historical note

Dryden's translation of book vi of the *Aeneid*, particularly lines *1021–1187*, is best understood against a general background of Roman history. The following brief sketch may be helpful. According to Virgil's version of the legend, the Italian kingdom of Alba Longa was founded by the son of Aeneas, Silvius (line *1033*), though the usual tradition was that Ascanius was the son and Silvius the grandson of Aeneas. The kingdom of Alba Longa lasted until the eighth century B.C. (lines *1039–48*). The last rightful king, Numitor (line *1042*), was overthrown by Amulius, who made Numitor's daughter, Rhea Silvia, a Vestal Virgin, so that she should have no children. When Rhea Silvia had two children, the twins Romulus and Remus, by Mars the god of war, Amulius threw both mother and children into the Tiber.

The twins were washed ashore and suckled by a she-wolf at the spot where Romulus founded the city of Rome in 753 B.C. and, according to legend, killed his brother Remus for jumping over the wall of it in derision. After Romulus (lines *1055–62*), six more kings

216

ruled Rome (*1103–18*). They included Numa Pompilius, the lawgiver; Tullus Hostilius, a warrior; Ancus Marcius; Tarquinius Priscus; Servius Tullius, and Tarquinius Superbus. The last of these, Tarquin the Proud, was driven out by Brutus in 510 B.C. and the Roman Republic was born.

In place of the king, two Consuls were elected annually, and there were, subsequently, elections for Tribunes of the people. The Roman Republic was involved in wars in the Italian peninsula until, by about 270 B.C., it controlled all Italian territory. Its first conquest had been Veii, twelve miles from Rome, taken by Camillus (line *1132*) c. 396 B.C. Yet in 390 B.C. the invading Gauls captured and sacked Rome itself.

During the third century B.C., Rome extended its power beyond Italy and became involved in two wars, the Punic Wars, against the north African state of Carthage. The first Punic War, 264–241 B.C. involved military disasters for the Romans in north Africa but secured their conquest of Sicily. The second Punic War, 218–202 B.C., was chiefly remarkable for the Carthaginian expedition led by Hannibal, which marched from Spain, crossed the Alps complete with elephants, and attacked Rome from the north. For fifteen years Hannibal's army remained in Italy while Quintus Fabius Maximus (lines *1164–7*) harassed him by guerrilla warfare but avoided a pitched battle. The elder Scipio (lines *1159–60*) defeated Hannibal's brother, Hasdrubal, in 207 B.C., forcing Hannibal's withdrawal to Carthage, where Scipio finally defeated him as well in 202 B.C.

There was a third Punic War in the following century, during which the younger Scipio (lines *1159–60*) captured and destroyed Carthage in 146 B.C. In the same year, Macedonia was annexed and the rival trading city of Corinth destroyed by Mummius (line *1149*). By this time, Roman rule had spread to many parts of the Mediterranean.

The final period of the Roman Republic was characterised by a struggle for a more democratic form of government. The brothers Gracchi (line *1158*) were prominent in this. After their deaths, power struggles and civil wars destroyed the republican system. Caesar, Crassus, and Pompey created the first Triumvirate in 60 B.C. and ruled as guardians of democracy. However, after the death of Crassus, Caesar returned from Gaul with his legions and fought a civil war against Pompey's forces from 49 B.C. to 45 B.C. (line *1134–44*). A year after his final victory, Caesar was assassinated and was succeeded by his nephew, Augustus, to whom Virgil read the *Aeneid*. The old republic had become a new empire.

1–17. Aeneas lands in Italy and goes to the Temple of Apollo at Cumae to consult the Sibyl, or prophetess.

1. *He said*: a reference to Aeneas's lament for Palinurus, with which book v of the *Aeneid* ends.

2. *Cumaean Shore*: Cumae, some ten miles west of modern Naples, was a Greek colony of the eighth century B.C. It was the site of the grotto of the Cumaean Sibyl.

6. *fiery Seed*: flame.

11. *Pious Prince*: Aeneas.

12. *Phoebus*: Phoebus Apollo, the sun god, who spoke through the Sibyl and to whom a temple had been built at Cumae.

15. *Fate*: knowledge of fate or destiny.

16. *Trivia's Grove*: Trivia is identified with Diana, goddess of woods and wild nature, and with Hecate. CF, line *352* and note.

18–50. An account of the Temple of Apollo and the carvings of Daedalus on its gates.

18. Daedalus was a legendary craftsman of great skill. He built the Labyrinth for Minos, King of Crete, but Daedalus and his son Icarus were imprisoned in it by the King. Daedalus made wings for them both, from feathers and wax, but Icarus flew too near the sun, so that the wax melted and he fell into the sea, and was drowned.

24. *steerage of his Wings*: his wings which had steered him.

26. Androgeos, son of Minos and Pasiphae, was treacherously killed by rivals whom he had defeated in the Panathenaic games Another version of the legend attributes his death to King Aegeus of Athens, who sent him to his death in a fight against the Marathonian bull. After his son's death, Minos besieged Athens and exacted the annual sacrifice of seven Athenian youths and seven maidens to the Minotaur.

33–41. From the love of Pasiphae for a bull was born the Minotaur, half bull, half man. It was kept in the Labyrinth designed by Daedalus.

42–6. Theseus ended the yearly sacrifices to the Minotaur by finding his way into the Labyrinth, killing the monster, and escaping again. Daedalus devised the scheme and Ariadne, daughter of Minos, being in love with Theseus, gave him a length of thread. By following this back he could find his way out from the centre of the maze.

51–146. The Sibyl summons Aeneas and Achates. Aeneas prays to Apollo for knowledge of the future. As Apollo's mouthpiece, the Sibyl foretells that the Trojans will have more battles to fight before they build a new state in Italy.

53. Achates is the friend and lieutenant of Aeneas, usually referred to as *fidus*, i.e. faithful.

90. *Dardan*: Trojan.

91. A reference to the heel of Achilles. As a child, he was dipped in the River Styx by his mother, Thetis, to make him invulnerable, but the water did not cover the heel by which she held him.

93. *ambient*: surrounding.

94. *Ausonian*: Italian.

103. *Latian*: Latin.

104. *wand'ring Gods*: the gods of the household of Aeneas and the city of Troy.

107. *twin Gods*: Phoebus Apollo and Diana.

131. *Event*: outcome.

135. Simois and Xanthus were two rivers of the Trojan plain, where the long war against the Greeks was fought. The Sibyl foresees equally bitter warfare for the Trojans in the future.

136. *A new Achilles*: Turnus, King of the Rutuli, rival of Aeneas for the hand of Lavinia, daughter of Latinus, King of Latium. Much of books vii–xii of the *Aeneid* is an account of Turnus's war to prevent the Trojans settling in Italy. In book xii, Aeneas kills him in single combat.

137. *Goddess-born*: The mother of Turnus was the goddess Venilia. *Juno's Hate*: the goddess Juno favoured Carthage, as opposed to the new Roman state.

141. *Ilium*: Troy.

142. Helen, wife of Menelaus, welcomed Paris; as Lavinia, daughter of Latinus, welcomed Aeneas.

146. *a Grecian Town*: A Greek colony, founded by Evander, came to the aid of Aeneas against Turnus.

147–89. Aeneas accepts his fate but asks that he may first be allowed to pass through the nearby entrance of Avernus to visit his dead father, Anchises, in the underworld.

150. *ambiguous God*: Apollo is described in the Latin text as mingling truth with obscurity.

154. *the God*: the presence of the God.

155. *the Chief*: Aeneas. He is also referred to as 'the Hero', or 'the Prince'.

161. Acheron is one of the rivers of Hades. Lake Avernus, near Cumae, was said to be one of its outlets.

164–72. In book ii of the *Aeneid* Virgil describes how Aeneas rescued Anchises from the sack of Troy. Anchises died after the voyage to Sicily (book iii).

176. *Proserpine*: Queen of the underworld in Roman mythology, as Persephone was in that of the Greeks.

178–80. After the death of his wife, Eurydice, Orpheus persuaded the Queen of the underworld to release her. This was agreed, on condition that Orpheus led her from Hades without once looking back at her. At the last moment, Orpheus forgot this condition and, as he looked back, Eurydice vanished from his sight.

181–3. After the death of Castor, his brother, Pollux persuaded Zeus to allow him to spend alternate days in Hades, during which Castor returned to life.

184–5. Theseus assisted Pirithous in an unsuccessful attempt to carry off the Queen of the underworld. For this he was imprisoned in hell until Hercules released him.

190–233. The Sibyl instructs Aeneas to find the golden bough, his passport to the underworld. But he must first find and inter the body of a dead comrade.

201. Cocytus was one of the rivers of Hades.

207. Stygian Jove: Pluto, King of the underworld. His Queen is Proserpine. 'Stygian' is the adjectival derivation from 'Styx', the river which the dead must cross to reach hell's kingdom.

234–70. Aeneas and Achates discover the body of Misenus. Preparations are made for his funeral.

242. Misenus was the Trojan trumpeter who appeared in battle next to Hector, the son of King Priam of Troy.

243. the God of Winds: Aeolus. ·

249. Pelides: Achilles, son of Peleus.

253. Triton: a merman, shaped like a fish from the waist down.

264. Pitch-Trees: pitch-pines.

271–305. Two doves, birds sacred to Venus, mother of Aeneas, lead him to the golden bough.

294. slow Lake: Avernus.

298. sacred Oak: sacred to Jove.

306–35. The funeral and memorial of Misenus.

322. Victims: animals sacrificed at the altar.

327. Choryneus: a follower of Aeneas, not otherwise identified.

333. Falchion: curved sword.

335. lofty Cape: Punta di Miseno, near Naples.

336–73. Aeneas offers sacrifices to the deities of the underworld at the descent to Hades.

348. sable: black.

352. Hecate: a goddess associated with the underworld, protectress of enchanters and witches.

360. Holocausts: whole burnt-offerings.

374–409. Virgil invokes the gods of Hades and describes the monsters who guard the threshold of the underworld.

378. Obscure: in darkness.   *Shades*: shadows.   *dreary*: gloomy.

383. Crescent: crescent moon.

389. Sentry: vigil.

392. Furies: Allecto, Magaera, and Tisiphone. They were the legendary avengers of crimes, particularly crimes committed within families.

396. The God of Sleep: Morpheus.

399. Centaurs: horses with the heads and necks of men.

400. Hydra: Cf. *Absalom and Achitophel*, line *541* and note.

401. Briareus: a giant with 100 hands, son of Uranus.

402. Gorgons: The Gorgon's gaze turned its victims to stone. Medusa, one of the three gorgons, was killed by Perseus, who used a mirror to avoid looking directly at her. *Geryon*: a monster with three bodies, killed by Hercules.

403. Chimaera: a monster combining the head of a lion, the body of a goat, and the tail of a dragon.

410–52. Aeneas and the Sibyl reach the River Styx, where the souls of the dead are ferried across to Hades. The unburied dead, however, are condemned to wander for 100 years on the bank before they are taken across.

417. obscene: unclean in the physical rather than the moral sense.

419. Bottom: hull.

420. in Years: advanced in years.

437. rude: rough.

453–520. Aeneas looks at the crowd and sees among them some of his drowned comrades, including Palinurus, the helmsman, whose death Virgil describes in book v. Palinurus gives an account of his death and asks aid from Aeneas in crossing the Styx. The Sibyl warns him that the laws of hell forbid him to cross but prophesies that his body shall be entombed and his memory revered.

457. Leucaspis: a follower of Aeneas, not otherwise identified.

458. Lycian: the Lycians were allies of Troy against Greece.

459. Tyrrhene Seas: the sea between south-west Italy and Sicily.

490. dropping: dripping.

499. Velin: Italian.

511. Attend the term: await the end.

512. dooming: judging.

521–61. Charon challenges Aeneas but, on seeing the golden bough, ferries him over the Styx.

531. Theseus: Cf. line *184* and note.

533. Alcides: Hercules, the last of whose twelve labours was to go to the underworld and bring back Cerberus, the watch-dog of King Pluto.

535–6. The labour of Hercules.

537. The attempted abduction of Proserpine by Theseus and Pirithous.

552. his Queen: Proserpine.

562–95. At the entrance to Hades, the Sibyl throws a drugged sop to Cerberus, who guards the gate. She and Aeneas then pass into the region of souls who have died an untimely death.

574. charm'd: bewitched.

582. Because of the justice of his life, Minos became one of the three judges of the dead. Rhadamanthus and Aeacus were his colleagues.

584. The names of those to be judged were engraved on tablets and shaken in an urn until one jumped out.

589. suborn'd: corrupted.

596–640. The Mournful Fields, where love's victims wander. Aeneas encounters Dido, Queen of Carthage, who had killed herself when he deserted her. He tries, unsuccessfully, to justify himself to her.

602. Procris, suspecting her husband Cephalus of infidelity, hid in a bush to watch him while he was hunting. Cephalus, thinking an animal was in the bush, threw his spear and killed her. Eriphile was bribed by Polynices to send her husband, Amphiarus, on the expedition of the seven against Thebes. Amphiarus was killed but, on his orders, his son Alcmaeon returned to kill Eriphile as an act of vengeance.

604. Pasiphae: Cf. lines *33–41* and note.

605. Phaedra, daughter of Minos and wife of Theseus, fell in love with her stepson Hippolytus, who rejected her advances. She wrote a letter denouncing him as her seducer and then hanged herself. Theseus prayed to Poseidon to punish Hippolytus, which the god did by terrifying the horses of the young man's chariot, so that he was thrown from it and dragged to death.

606. Laodamia's husband, Protesilaus, a Greek prince, was killed in the Trojan war. The gods allowed him to return to her for three hours, after which she killed herself. Evadne was the wife of Capaneus, one of the seven champions who attacked Thebes. After he fell in battle, she threw herself on his funeral pyre.

608. Caeneus: a girl who was changed by the god Poseidon into a young man.

610. Phoenician Dido: Cf. summary of *Aeneid* book iv.

613. Shades: shadows.

616. sullen Shade: gloomy ghost. It is possible that Dryden also implies the Latinate meaning of sullen, i.e. 'lonely'.

639. Sicheus was Dido's husband, who had died before the arrival of Aeneas in Carthage.

641–719. Aeneas sees those who died in battle. He is welcomed by the Trojans but the Greeks draw back from him in fear. He finds the mutilated Deiphobus, who describes how he was betrayed by his wife, Helen, and killed.

646. Tideus and Parthenopaeus were two of the seven champions who fought against Thebes.

648. Adrastus, King of Argos, who led the seven champions in their battle against Thebes.   *ghastly*: ghostly.

651. Glaucus and Medon are Trojan warriors in Homer, *Iliad*, xvii, 216. Virgil adds Thersilochus, whom Dryden omits.

652. Antenor's sons, Polybus, Agenor, and Acamas, fought for Troy. Cf. *Iliad*, xi, 59–60. Ceres's sacred priest is named as Polyphetes by Virgil. Ceres was the goddess of corn.

659. Argive: Greek. Agamemnon, son of Atreus and brother of Menelaus, commanded the victorious Greek army at Troy but on his return to Greece was murdered by his wife Clytemnestra and her lover Aegisthus.

660. refulgent: splendidly bright.

662-3. Homer tells in the *Iliad*, book xv, how the Trojans almost defeated the Greeks and burnt their invasion fleet.

666-712. After the death of Paris, Deiphobus married his widow, Helen, whose abduction by Paris from her Greek husband, Menelaus, had caused the war between Greece and Troy. Helen betrayed Deiphobus to the Greeks and Menelaus killed him.

668. Dishonest: shamefully wounded.

681. call'd your Manes: Part of the funeral ceremony was a last greeting to the dead. The call was either *'Vale, vale, vale'*, 'Farewell, farewell, farewell', or, more probably, *'Ave atque vale'*, 'Hail and farewell'.

693-4. The Greeks built a huge wooden horse, which the Trojans were persuaded was a peace offering. They drew it into Troy and discovered, too late, that its belly was full of Greek soldiers.

698. Ambuscade: ambush.

705. her former Lord: Menelaus.

710. Ulysses, King of Ithaca was known in Greek mythology as 'Odysseus' and is the hero of the *Odyssey*.

716. Doom: judgment.

720-860. The Sibyl rebukes Aeneas for his long delay. She guides him past Tartarus, from which come sounds of eternal punishments inflicted on the damned. The place is forbidden to all others, but the Sibyl has been permitted to visit it once and she describes the torments of condemned spirits.

741. Phlegethon is a fiery river of Hades.

745. Adamantine: impenetrably hard. This echoes Milton's description of hell in *Paradise Lost*, i, 48, with its reference to 'adamantine chains and penal fire'.

749. Tisiphone: one of the three furies; cf. line *392* and note. *Ward*: watch.

750. sanguine: blood red.

760. Hecate: cf. line *352* and note.

764. Rhadamanthus: one of the judges of the dead; cf. line *582* and note.

778. Hydra: Cf. *Absalom and Achitophel*, line *541* and note.

782-3. The twelve Titans were children of the primeval Uranus and Ge. They fought against the gods and lost.

784. Aloean Twins: Otus and Ephialtes, sons of Aloeus. By piling Ossa and Pelion on top of Mount Olympus, these two giants tried to reach heaven and defeat the gods. They imprisoned the god of war in a bronze jar for thirteen months before Hermes rescued him.

788–99. Salmoneus, son of Aeolus, tried to imitate Jove's thunder by driving in a bronze chariot, and threw firebrands in imitation of Jove's thunderbolts.

802. writhen: whirling.

804. Tityus: Son of Ge. He was killed by Apollo and Artemis for threatening their mother, Leto.

814. Ixion, King of the Lapithae, murdered his father-in-law and tried to win the love of Juno. He was the father of the centaurs. Cf. line *399* and note. *Pirithous*: cf. line *184* and note. Ixion was tied to a wheel which turned eternally.

815. Thessalian Chiefs: So Dryden translates Virgil's *Lapithas*. The Lapithae and the centaurs both lived in Thessaly. When the centaurs tried to carry off Hippodamia, wife of Pirithous, and other Lapithan women, the two races fought and the Lapithae were victorious.

835. Despairing: despairing of.

842. Phlegyas, father of Ixion, set fire to the Temple of Apollo at Delphi.

858. The three Cyclops were single-eyed giants who made thunderbolts for Jove.

861–928. The Sibyl leads Aeneas to the Elysian Fields, the region of 'Happy Souls'. She asks Musaeus where Anchises is to be found, and he leads them there.

870. Ether: upper air.

877. The Thracian Bard: Orpheus; cf. lines *178–80* and note.

878. Vest: vestments.

879. Quill: plectrum.

880. Strikes seven distinct notes on the seven strings of his lyre.

881. Teucer: an early King of Troy.

883. Assaracus was the great-grandfather of Aeneas. Ilus, the brother of Assaracus, founded the city of Troy.

884. him who founded Troy: Dardanus, son of Zeus (Jupiter), founder of the Trojan race but not of the city of Troy, which was founded by his great-grandson, Ilus.

893. Po: Virgil uses the Latin name 'Eridanus', but Dryden gives the river its modern Italian name.

898. Apollo was the god who inspired poets, as well as prophets.

899. Wits: intellects.   *Mechanic parts*: practical abilities.

903. Fillets: head-bands.

908. The legendary Greek poet Musaeus was said to have been a pupil of Orpheus.

915. Meads: meadows.

922. took the Tale: counted the number.

929–952. The reunion of Aeneas and his father Anchises.

941. A reference to Dido and Aeneas.

953–1020. Some of the souls crowd the banks of Lethe, the river of oblivion. Aeneas is told that these spirits, after drinking from the river, will forget their previous lives and be born again in new bodies. Anchises explains how souls are purified before their reincarnation.

966. the Sire: Anchises.

979. To clear: to clarify.

982. both the Radiant Lights: the sun and moon. Virgil refers only to the moon but Dryden adds the sun.

990. allay: alloy.

997. Assert the Native Skies: acknowledge the heavens, where the mind or soul is born.

1006. their Manes: their character as formed in life. As on other occasions, Dryden leaves the Latin word untranslated.

1021–1187. Among the crowd of souls destined to inhabit new bodies, Anchises points out those who will be heroes of the Roman state and will help to make Roman power supreme throughout the world. For background information on this section of the poem, see the *Historical note* on page 216.

1031. vital Air: the air of the living.

1033. Silvius was either the son or grandson of Aeneas; cf. *Historical note*.

1041–4. A list of the Alban Kings.

1050–2. Gabii; Fidenae; Nomentum; Pometii, and Collatia were old Latin towns in the vicinity of Rome. Bola is unknown.

1056. Numitor, deposed King of Alba Longa, was father of Rhea Silvia and grandfather of Romulus.

1057. Rhea Silvia had been a Vestal Virgin.

1059. The double crest was the emblem of Mars.

1066. Involving: covering.

1069–70. The walls of Rome shall be like the golden circle of the crown worn by the Phrygian goddess Cybele. Virgil mentions her more specifically than Dryden's version suggests.

1074. Julian Progeny: Descendants of Iulus (Ascanius), son of Aeneas. Julius Caesar claimed descent from Aeneas.

1079. Julius Caesar was succeeded as Emperor by his nephew and adopted son, Augustus. Virgil is careful to praise Augustus, who was still ruling Rome, in the following lines:

1080. Saturn: cf. *Annus Mirabilis*, lines *629–32* and note.

1084. without: beyond.

1085. Atlas, one of the Titans, was punished for his revolt against the gods by being made to support the heavens on his head and hands.

1088. A reference to the Crimea.

1093–6. Hercules hunted the hind of Ceryneia for a year before he caught it; he ran the boar to exhaustion in the snows of Mount

Erymanthus, and trapped it with a net; he killed the Hydra at Lerna. These were three of his twelve labours.

1097–1100. Bacchus, god of wine, was born on Mount Nysa, in India. He was believed to have conquered much of Asia.

1103–29. Cf. *Historical note.* Tarquin the Proud was driven out of Rome by Brutus after the rape of Lucretia by his son. Brutus became one of the first Consuls of the Roman Republic and ordered the execution of his own two sons for attempting to restore the monarchy.

1130. When the Gauls attacked Rome in 361 B.C., Manlius Torquatus defeated one of their champions in single combat.

1131. Decii: two consuls, father and son, who dedicated themselves to die in battle for their country's cause in 340 and 295 B.C.

1132. Drusus, a Consul who defeated Hannibal's brother, Hasdrubal, in the second Punic War, 207 B.C. Camillus recaptured Rome from the Gauls in 390 B.C.

1134–44. A reference to the Civil War between Caesar and Pompey's forces 49–45 B.C. Caesar's daughter, Julia, married Pompey but died in 54 B.C. Pompey was defeated and died in 48 B.C. but his supporters fought on for another three years. Caesar had crossed the Alps from Gaul into Italy with his army.

1149. A reference to the destruction of Corinth by Mummius in 146 B.C.

1150–5. L. Aemilius Paullus defeated Perseus of Macedonia, who claimed descent from Achilles, at Pydna in 168 B.C. Pallas Athene was identified by the Romans with Minerva, goddess of war.

1156. Cato, 'the censor' 234–149 B.C., was Consul in 195 B.C., and became censor in 184 B.C., when he tried to reform public morals.

1157. Cornelius Cossus was a Roman general of the fifth century B.C.

1158. the Gracchi: Two brothers, both Tribunes of the people and political reformers. They died violent deaths, Tiberius Sempronius Gracchus in 133 B.C.; Caius Gracchus in 121 B.C. An earlier Tiberius Sempronius Gracchus was twice Consul, in 215 and 212 B.C.

1159–60. Scipios: see *Historical note.*

1160–3. Fabricius was a Consul (282 and 278 B.C.) who lived a life of stern simplicity. The 'Ploughman Consul' was Serranus, elected in 257 B.C.

1164–7. The greatest of the Fabii was Quintus Fabius Maximus, Cunctator or 'Delayer'. When Hannibal invaded Italy (see *Historical note*) and defeated the Romans at Lake Trasimene in 217 B.C., it was Fabius Maximus who wore down the invaders by delaying tactics and by avoiding a pitched battle.

1180–7. great Marcellus: Marcus Claudius Marcellus was five times Consul. In 222 B.C. he killed Britomartus, King of the Gauls, and won the *spolia optima*. These were the spoils taken when the Roman general himself killed the opposing general. They were won only three times in Roman history, once by Romulus himself.

1187. Feretrian Jove: Jupiter as god of trophies.

1188–1247. Aeneas notices a young man of godlike appearance. He asks his identity and is told that this is the young Marcellus, nephew and son-in-law of the Emperor Augustus, adopted by the Emperor as his son and heir. But the hopes for his future were to be cruelly disappointed. Anchises then takes leave of Aeneas, who returns to the world and to his fleet through the gate of ivory, one of the two gates of sleep.

1200–26. The young Marcellus died of fever in 23 B.C., when he was only nineteen years old. When Virgil read his *Aeneid* to Augustus and the Imperial Court, the death of Marcellus would still have been poignantly recent. According to tradition, Octavia, sister of Augustus and mother of Marcellus, collapsed with renewed grief when these lines were read by the poet.

1242. Divining Guest: the Sibyl. She and Aeneas return from the underworld as though they were waking from a dream.

1245. Caieta's Bay: The Bay of Gaeta lies immediately north of the Bay of Naples with the modern town of Gaeta at its northern end.

Further Reading

The authoritative edition of Dryden's poetry is *The Poems of John Dryden*, ed. James Kinsley (Oxford University Press, 4 vols, 1963) while the most complete modern collection of poetry and prose together will be that appearing under the general editorship of H. T. Swedenberg, Jr. from the University of California Press. Four volumes have so far appeared.

The best general histories of the end of the seventeenth century are those by DAVID OGG (*England in the Reign of Charles II* (1956) and *England in the Reigns of James II and William III* (1955), both published by Oxford University Press), while a briefer account appears in G. N. CLARK, *The Later Stuarts: 1660–1715* in the Oxford History of England (1934).

SAMUEL JOHNSON'S account of Dryden in his *Lives of the English Poets* is indispensable, while the most recent modern biography is that by C. E. WARD (Oxford University Press, 1961). Other valuable recent studies include the following:

BREDVOLD, L. L. *The Intellectual Milieu of John Dryden* (University of Michigan Press, 1934)

DOBRÉE, BONAMY, *John Dryden* (Longman, for the British Council, rev. ed. 1961)

DOREN, MARK VAN, *John Dryden: A Study of his Poetry* (Holt, Rinehart, 1946)

ELIOT, T. S., *John Dryden: the poet, the dramatist, the critic* (Holliday, 1932)

HOFFMAN, ARTHUR W., *John Dryden's Imagery* (University of Florida Press, 1962)

MINER, EARL, *Dryden's Poetry* (University of Indiana Press, 1967)

ROPER, ALAN, *Dryden's Poetic Kingdoms* (Routledge, 1965)

SCHILLING, BERNARD N., *Dryden and the Conservative Myth: A Reading of Absalom and Achitophel* (Yale University Press, 1961)

WILLEY, BASIL, *The Seventeenth Century Background* (Chatto & Windus, 1934)

WILLEY, BASIL, *The Eighteenth Century Background* (Chatto & Windus, 1940). The first chapter of this book includes a valuable discussion of the term, Nature.

Two collections of articles, most of them originally available only in academic journals, may also be noted:

SCHILLING, BERNARD N., ed. *Dryden: A Collection of Critical Essays* (Prentice-Hall, 1963)

SWEDENBERG, H. T., ed. *Essential Articles for the Study of John Dryden* (Cass, 1966)